T0281375

Mastering Zoho Creator

Build Cloud-Based Business Applications from the Ground Up

Ali Shabdar

Apress®

Mastering Zoho Creator: Build Cloud-Based Business Applications from the Ground Up

Ali Shabdar
Vancouver, British Columbia, Canada

ISBN-13 (pbk): 978-1-4842-2906-4 ISBN-13 (electronic): 978-1-4842-2907-1
DOI 10.1007/978-1-4842-2907-1

Library of Congress Control Number: 2017954494

Cover image designed by Freepik

Managing Director: Welmoed Spahr
Editorial Director: Todd Green
Acquisitions Editor: Louise Corrigan
Development Editor: James Markham
Technical Reviewer: Massimo Nardone
Coordinating Editor: Nancy Chen
Copy Editor: Kezia Endsley
Compositor: SPi Global
Indexer: SPi Global
Artist: SPi Global

Distributed to the book trade worldwide by Springer Science+Business Media New York, 233 Spring Street, 6th Floor, New York, NY 10013. Phone 1-800-SPRINGER, fax (201) 348-4505, e-mail `orders-ny@springer-sbm.com`, or visit `www.springeronline.com`. Apress Media, LLC is a California LLC and the sole member (owner) is Springer Science + Business Media Finance Inc (SSBM Finance Inc). SSBM Finance Inc is a **Delaware** corporation.

For information on translations, please e-mail `rights@apress.com`, or visit `http://www.apress.com/rights-permissions`.

Apress titles may be purchased in bulk for academic, corporate, or promotional use. eBook versions and licenses are also available for most titles. For more information, reference our Print and eBook Bulk Sales web page at `http://www.apress.com/bulk-sales`.

Any source code or other supplementary material referenced by the author in this book is available to readers on GitHub via the book's product page, located at `www.apress.com/9781484229064`. For more detailed information, please visit `http://www.apress.com/source-code`.

Printed on acid-free paper

To my wife Maryam, who patiently supported me while I burned the midnight oil writing this book (and another one), and gave me nothing but smiles when I shamelessly sacrificed most of our weekends working.

Contents at a Glance

Contents

About the Author

Ali Shabdar is a Marketing and Technology Advisor helping a number of SMEs and non-profit organizations internationally to improve the efficiency and effectiveness of their tactical and strategic efforts.

Ali studied Electrical Engineering, IT, Sustainability, and Marketing and has more than 15 years of experience in various industries.

He spent his teenage years building software, a passion that later turned into a career and helped him keep his edge in diverse business environments.

Working with the Zoho suite since early 2008, Ali has helped many SMEs improve productivity, improve and manage processes, run effective marketing programs, increase sales, and serve clients better by utilizing Zoho offerings.

When designing cloud-based systems, Ali utilizes his applied knowledge in business process management, user experience and usability design, databases, and computer programming, which result in well-crafted solutions for real-life problems.

He loves reading about science, business, and history, watching movies, traveling, and savoring good food (anything but Hawaiian pizza).

Connect with Ali on Twitter (`@shabdar`), LinkedIn (`https://www.linkedin.com/in/shabdar/`), and Instagram (`ali.n.shabdar`).

About the Technical Reviewer

Massimo Nardone has more than 23 years of experience in security, web/mobile development, and cloud and IT architecture. His true IT passions are security and anything Android.

He has been programming and teaching people how to program with the Android, Perl, PHP, Java, VB, Python, C/C++, and MySQL for more than 20 years.

He holds a Master of Science degree in Computing Science from the University of Salerno, Italy. He has worked as a Project manager, software engineer, research engineer, chief security architect, information security manager, PCI/SCADA auditor, and senior lead IT security/Cloud/SCADA architect for many years.

His technical skills include security, Android, Cloud, Java, MySQL, Drupal, Cobol, Perl, web and mobile development, MongoDB, D3, Joomla, Couchbase, C/C++, WebGL, Python, Pro Rails, Django CMS, Jekyll, Scratch, and more.

He worked as visiting lecturer and supervisor for exercises at the Networking Laboratory of the Helsinki University of Technology (Aalto University). He holds four international patents (in the PKI, SIP, SAML, and Proxy areas).

He currently works as Chief Information Security Office (CISO) for Cargotec Oyj and he is a member of the ISACA Finland Chapter Board.

Massimo has reviewed more than 40 IT books for different publishing companies and is the coauthor of *Pro Android Games* (Apress, 2015).

Introduction

Before I started working on this book, I took a look at the first book I wrote on Zoho—*Foundation Zoho: Work and Create Online*—and I was amazed by how far we have come since 2009.

Technology has advanced so much in less than a decade that 2009 feels like ages ago. Smartphones, big data, Blockchain, 3D printing, civilian drones, artificial intelligence, and the Internet of Things (IoT) have all graduated from lab life and entered our daily lives.

However, none of these technologies (yet) has had as great an impact on our civilization as cloud computing. This may sound like a very bold claim, but bear with me for a moment.

Many of us nowadays keep our collection of documents on Dropbox or Google Drive, kill time (or do something more productive) on Instagram and Facebook, rely on CRM (Customer Relationship Management) systems to manage our sales processes, take notes on Wunderlist, and manage projects on Trello.

Back in 2009, cloud computing was a relatively new phenomenon, and many companies—small and large—were too hesitant to even give it a try. High-speed Internet was not as ubiquitous as it is now and mobile computing was in its infancy. Heck, the Blackberry was the king of the smartphones.

All these are courtesy of some SaaS (software as a service) on a public cloud platform. Remove cloud computing from the equation and you can't even play Pokémon Go on your smartphone.

Eight years later, Internet connectivity has doubled (`http://www.internetlivestats.com/internet-users/`) and almost half of the population of the planet is connected. Today, it is practically impossible to go through a full day (sometimes a full hour) without using the amazing apps and services that run on the cloud. But what is cloud computing anyway?

Cloud Computing

The Internet, also referred to as "the cloud" in IT jargon, powers today's civilization.

Why on earth do we use the word "cloud" as a metaphor for the Internet, you ask? Since the old days, it was common when someone wanted to refer to a big collection of servers (i.e., a server farm) in an IT diagram, that they would simply draw a cloud to hide the complexity and just connect other machines to it (see Figure 1).

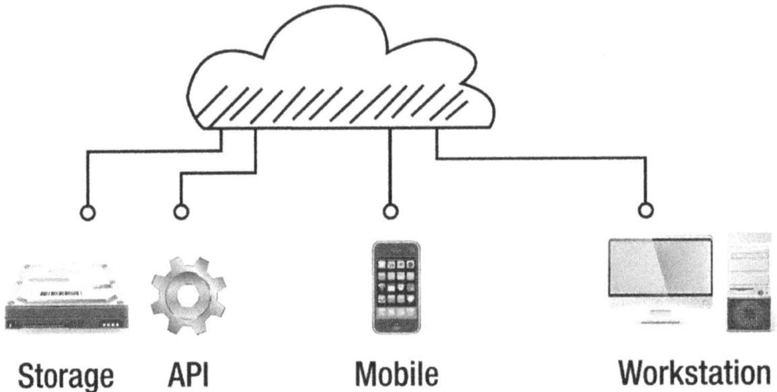

Figure 1. *The original cloud*

Cloud computing, to put it simply, uses the computing power of the cloud in combination, or instead of, the power of the computer on your desk or the one in your pocket. As trivial as this definition may sound, cloud computing offers unique features, such as:

- Availability—All you need is an Internet connection to connect to any cloud anywhere.
- Performance—The immense power of thousands of servers is at your disposal.
- Elasticity—You can only use and pay for the computing power and storage you need for the task in hand, scale up when you need more resources, and scale back down when you don't.
- Multi-tenancy—Multiple tenants (apps, services, users, etc.) can use the power of a cloud allowing for resources to be used efficiently and costs to be divided between such tenants.
- Security—Clouds can be way more secure than your local computer, or local server, since cloud providers have many more resources to allocate safeguarding their infrastructure, which in turn keeps the tenants more secure.
- Reliability—Your data is backed up and is available across multiple physical locations, thus minimizing the risk of data loss to almost zero.
- Maintenance—Cloud users (tenants) need not worry about upgrading servers, power outages, or software updates, all of which are done for them by the cloud provider.
- Cost—All these conditions contribute to a major benefit of cloud computing, which is lowering the cost across the board.

In general, there are three types of clouds:

- Public—As the name suggests, these are publicly available for everyone to utilize, such as Amazon AWS.
- Private—Only accessible to the organization or organizations owning that cloud.
- Hybrid—Obviously, a combination of public and private clouds.

Note I stay shallow with these definitions as this book is not about the science of cloud computing. The main audience of this book is businesspeople, who I can bet are least interested in the voodoo behind the technology and merely want to utilize tools that can make their lives easier.

The Importance and Scale of Cloud Computing

As mentioned, it is safe to say that anything digital nowadays runs on some sort of cloud infrastructure. Our civilization depends on the cloud, an industry that is poised to grow to $270 billion by the year 2020 (`http://247wallst.com/technology-3/2015/03/07/the-270-billon-cloud-computing-market/`).

In their 2009 report, "Cloud Computing Forecasting Change" (`http://public.deloitte.no/dokumenter/2_Cloud_Computing%5B1%5D.pdf`), Deloitte called cloud computing the "next technological disruption to transform enterprise IT delivery and services". It is a brilliant piece, and it counts cloud computing along with social networks, mobile, and the Internet of Things (IoT) among the major disruptors and contributors to the maturity of the Internet.

Deloitte's prediction about cloud computing was impressively accurate. What Deloitte and many other experts did not quite predict, however, was the great impact on and massive adoption of cloud computing by small to medium size businesses (SMBs).

In January 2016, RightScale surveyed 1,060 technical professionals (627 from SMBs) about their adoption of cloud computing. (`http://assets.rightscale.com/uploads/pdfs/RightScale-2016-State-of-the-Cloud-Report.pdf`). The results are a testament to how successful cloud computing has been in the recent years:

- 77% of the SMBs are using cloud computing in some capacity in their organizations
- Only 9% said they have no plans for cloud adoption
- Cloud security is no longer the top challenge, dethroned now by lack of resources and expertise
- Cloud users leverage six clouds on average
- Amazon AWS leads the pack while Microsoft Azure is growing market as a major cloud infrastructure provider

At its core, cloud computing allows organizations (and individuals) to harness the virtually unlimited computing and storage power of hundreds of thousands of servers located in a myriad of datacenters across the world.

With the immense power of cloud at their fingertips, even the smallest companies can analyze terabytes of data at will, fast, and cheap, which helps them create massively useful applications and stay ahead of the competition.

Companies such as Uber, Airbnb, Waze, Instagram, Snapchat, and hundreds of others whose apps you use on daily basis all started small by writing their apps on top of cloud platforms. The startup revolution in the past decade owes its success heavily to the availability, affordability, and scalability of cloud platforms such as Amazon AWS, Google AppEngine, and Microsoft Azure.

Now with the next wave of computing—mainstream AI (Artificial Intelligence)—upon us, companies such as Amazon are working to make it possible for the software developers and cloud users to have access to sophisticated AI capabilities on the cheap. (`http://www.allthingsdistributed.com/2016/11/amazon-ai-and-alexa-for-all-aws-apps.html`).

The Service Economy

Cloud computing allows various services and applications to be implemented on it. This allows a "service" model in which virtually everything can be offered as a service that is implemented and distributed on some sort of a cloud. This concept is called Everything as a Service or X as a Service (XaaS).

Platform as a Service (PaaS) and Infrastructure as a Service (IaaS) are two examples of what can be offered as a service in the cloud. But the most evident and most relevant to of all these to the end users (including you, dear reader) is Software as a Service (SaaS).

Let's start with a real-life example.

A few years ago, if I needed Microsoft Office, I had to pay full price for and buy and own the software before I could use it. A few hundred dollars wouldn't break the bank maybe, but now imagine if I wanted to have Office on all 15 workstations at work and had to commit a few thousand dollars in basic software expenses. Plus, I needed to have IT take care of updates and patches (more expense) and then pay again for every major version released.

Today, with Office 365, not only will I always have access to the latest version of the Office software on my laptop, tablet, and phone with the same license, but software updates run automatically, so I get to use 1TB (yes, that is 1000 gigabytes) of free space on OneCloud (Microsoft's cloud storage service). Plus I have access to all my documents with editing capability in the browser.

That means I can leave my laptop at home and go on a vacation and edit my documents wherever there is a computer connected to the Internet. The best part? I pay a fraction of the cost on a monthly basis and I can cancel my contract anytime I want.

The same applies for my company. I pay for new monthly license when someone joins the team and I cancel their contract when someone leaves.

This is the power of Software as a Service, or SaaS.

Unlike Microsoft Office, the majority of SaaS apps do not even need to install on your local computer. You can access them on a modern Internet browser on a desktop, laptop, tablet, or a mobile device.

The main advantage here is that SaaS doesn't rely much on local computer power, so you don't need a high-performance machine to run your massive CRM used by 2000 employees across three continents. A $200 Chromebook (`https://www.google.com/chromebook/about/`) will do the job too.

This book is about one of these SaaS applications—Zoho Creator. By the end of this book, you will know how you can create world-class customized cloud-based applications. These applications will help you avoid cookie-cutter expensive solutions and use internal resources to automate and improve your business processes and manage your organizational information effectively.

The big news is that you will be able to do all this with little to no programming skills.

All About Zoho

Zoho, the company behind Zoho Creator and an impressive suite of 34 other SaaS apps, has been in business since 1996. Launched back in November 2007, Zoho Creator is one of Zoho's main offerings with unique features and little competition.

Note You can read more about history of Zoho and the brains behind it on the web site at `https://www.zoho.com/aboutus.html`.

I have been an avid user of the Zoho suite, especially Zoho Creator and Zoho CRM, since 2008. In fact, Zoho Creator was my first encounter with a full-fledged SaaS application.

I have recommended Zoho to many friends, colleagues, and clients, all of whom have ended up becoming happy users. Powerful and easy to use software, cost-effectiveness, and good support are some of the main factors that keep me and thousands of other organizations and individuals as loyal customers.

I hope this book helps you decide whether Zoho Creator is the right choice for you, and if it is, how to best utilize it in your day-to-day business.

Who This Book Is For

This book is for everyone who needs to avoid the cookie-cutter expensive information solutions and wants. With Zoho Creator, you can create an application tailor-made to your specific business requirements without paying an arm and a leg for it.

This book is for you if you:

- Want to create business applications and information solutions to solve your day-to-day problems without prior programming knowledge or the help of software developers and expensive external consultants
- Have little time and budget and still need a fully customized business application that doesn't break the bank

- Want to make a living creating cloud-based applications and offer consultancy for your clients
- Are already a Zoho Creator user, administrator, developer, or solution provider and want to learn more about its unique features

Zoho Creator is not and doesn't claim to be a replacement for advanced programming languages (e.g., Java), frameworks (e.g., Django), or enterprise platforms (e.g., SAP).

Creator is unlike anything you have seen before and you need to experience it to truly appreciate the vision of its makers and learn how you can leverage it in your business environment. From a single-person operation to a large enterprise, there is a place for Creator to come in handy and save the day.

What You Will Learn

In this book, you learn to:

- Basics of building good software
- Build Zoho Creator applications quickly and properly from the ground up
- Learn the inner workings of Creator and business application development best-practices
- Learn the Deluge scripting language, Zoho's modern and data-oriented language
- Create and launch a real-world business applications, a real estate management system, from idea to rollout
- Integrate your apps with third-party tools and services
- Extend the capabilities of other Zoho apps such as CRM

How the Book Is Structured

The aim of this book is to provide you with a practical guide to get up and running fast, but correctly, with Zoho Creator. Depending on your interest and requirements, you can delve deeper in each topic while having this book as a guide on your side.

Tip Throughout the book there are frequent references to the official documentation as well as other external sources. It wouldn't make sense to cover every single feature or capability of Zoho Creator in a single volume. Also, Zoho Creator, like any other cloud-based app, adds new features frequently. It is a good habit to check the documentation often and leverage the latest features and capabilities in your applications.

This book starts with a quick review of the Zoho suite of cloud-based apps in Chapter 1. This chapter gives you a brief idea of what other Zoho apps you could be using in your business.

In Chapter 2, you get a bird's eye view of the important concepts and methodologies you need to consider while designing any kind of software, including Zoho Creator. This chapter is a door opener to concepts that each could take multiple books to cover. However, merely giving you an idea about the importance of each topic will encourage you to employ them in your practice and learn more about them if you need to.

In Chapter 3, you create your very first app using Creator's ready-made templates to get a sense about what a Creator app looks like.

Chapter 4 teaches you how to create a simple inquiry form app from scratch and get more familiar with the inner workings of a Creator app.

In Chapter 5, you create a more advanced app to let visitors apply for job vacancies in your organization. You are introduced to Deluge, Zoho's scripting language, and make your app responsive to user behavior. You also learn about Creator's automation, notification, and scheduling features.

Chapter 6 is a tour of the Deluge scripting language. It is a robust, easy to learn, and easy to use language and is required for more advanced apps.

In Chapter 7, you combine your knowledge and build an advanced real estate management system. You learn more about Creator and software development best-practices in the process.

Finally, in Chapter 8, I give you quick tour on how to extend Creator's capabilities by integrating it into other Zoho apps as well as third-party software and services. The true power of cloud-based applications is when they join forces and accomplish more with minimal effort from the developers' side. There is no need to reinvent the wheel if you know how to reuse it for different vehicles.

How to Best Read This Book

If you are new to Zoho Creator or the subject of business application development in general, I recommend you start from the beginning and follow the order of the chapters.

If you have signed up for Creator, watched a couple of video tutorials, and built some basic apps, you can skip to Chapter 4 or 5, where things get interesting with code and automation. Then you can continue with the rest of the book.

For more experienced Creator developers, I suggest skimming through Chapters 4 to 6, and then reading Chapters 7 and 8.

For developers coming from other languages, regardless of experience level, I recommend having a quick read of Chapters 3 and 4, then spending more time on the rest of the chapters. I can guarantee that you will be amazed by how much you can accomplish with little to no coding. Then make sure you read Chapter 8 and review the REST API documentation online.

CHAPTER 1

Zoho Suite from 10,000 Feet

The Zoho Corporation has come a long way since they released their first SaaS apps, Writer and CRM (Customer Relationship Management), in 2005. Writer became an inseparable part of the productivity apps and CRM has grown to be one of the core Zoho products, serving millions of people around the world, yours truly included.

From the app diversity and completeness of offerings perspective, Zoho still holds a unique and strong position in the market while other companies have focused on one or a few products around a core objective.

There are many fantastic SaaS apps out there; however, none I used or read about offer the selection that Zoho does. This allows users to use a wide range of apps with single sign-on, familiar look and feel, and interoperability (i.e., the ability to exchange and use information between apps) out of the box.

Zoho apps are divided into six categories:

- Sales and Marketing
- E-mail and Collaboration
- Business Process
- Finance
- IT and Help Desk
- Human Resources

Now let's take a very quick look at each one of these categories and their respective apps before we dive into Zoho CRM.

Note This chapter merely scratches the surface and only provides a quick introduction of all members of the Zoho suite. The aim is to simply let you know what each app can do and leave further investigation to you to see whether one or more of these apps could help your business in any way.

A. Shabdar, *Mastering Zoho Creator*, DOI 10.1007/978-1-4842-2907-1_1

Sales and Marketing Apps

The beating heart of any business, be it a home-based solo operation or a multinational conglomerate, is sales. Marketing, on the other hand, provides insights of the market and helps the business stay competitive while promoting its products and services to the world. The duo of Marketing and Sales is inseparable.

At the core of Zoho suite, there are a number of apps that help you manage almost all your marketing and sales operations, all connected in the cloud.

CRM

Zoho CRM is arguably the star of the show with the highest number of users among Zoho apps. First released in 2005, CRM has grown from a small solution for beginners to a full-fledged suite of applications competing with the industry leaders in many fronts.

The landscape of cloud-based CRM systems for small and medium-sized businesses is quite competitive and there are formidable contenders in the market for every requirement and budget. The spectrum of SaaS CRM systems seems endless with open source and free offerings inside of the spectrum to full-fledged industry specific solutions on the other hand. Bitrix24, Highrise, Hubspot, Infusionsoft, Insightly, Microsoft Dynamics, Pipedrive, Salesforce, and Sugar CRM are just a few that come to mind.

A CRM is one of the most important, if not the most important, tools for your business. So, choosing the right one early on is crucial. No matter if you are about to start your business in a month, are currently bootstrapping, or have been in business for the past 15 years managing a team of 100 sales people across the globe, Zoho CRM can play a key role in managing and streamlining your marketing, sales, and client servicing efforts.

Zoho CRM offers five different editions, each of which packs a host of features suitable for different tastes and needs:

- **Free edition**—This edition offers the core modules such as Leads, Accounts, Contacts, Feeds, Documents, and mobile apps for up to 10 users, completely free of charge. This is a great way to start using Zoho CRM and then you can upgrade to one of the paid editions as your business needs grow.
- **Standard edition**—In addition to the features available in the Free edition, you have access to sales forecasting, reports and dashboards, document library, roles and profiles, mass e-mail, call center connectors, and the ability to store up to 100,000 records of information.
- **Professional edition**—Offers all the features available in Free and Standard editions, plus e-mail integration, social features, Google AdWords integration, workflow automation, inventory management, macros, and the ability to store unlimited records.
- **Enterprise edition**—This edition offers territory management, custom applications, custom buttons, workflow approval processes, page layouts, custom modules, and multiple currencies on top of the features available to Professional edition.

- **Ultimate edition**—Last, but not least, the Ultimate edition adds even more features to make it the choice for larger organizations by throwing in a sandbox, dedicated database cluster, priority support, advanced customization, advanced CRM analytics, and enhanced storage.
- **CRM Plus**—A recent addition to the CRM family, CRM Plus provides a more holistic approach to the traditional CRM system by combining the Enterprise edition with Zoho Campaigns, Desk, SalesIQ, Social, Projects, Survey, and Reports. This package allows users to centralize all their marketing, sales, and client servicing processes in one place without the need to jump between different platforms, while saving considerably in direct and indirect costs.

One of the areas that Zoho CRM excels compared to its rivals is the lower barrier to entry. Zoho CRM allows organizations of up to 10 employees to use it free of charge for sales management and then later upgrade to a suitable paid edition as they need more features.

■ **Note** If you want to learn more about Zoho CRM and how you can leverage its power to succeed in your business, feel free to pick up my other book, *Mastering Zoho CRM*, by Apress. This book is a practical, no-nonsense guide for managing the three pillars of your business—marketing, sales, and client servicing—using one of the best CRM suites available in the market.

SalesInbox

A new addition to the Zoho suite, SalesInbox claims to be the first mailbox specifically designed for salespeople. According to Zoho, SalesInbox automatically organizes and prioritizes sales activities based one sales pipeline and the stage of each deal. Using Zoho CRM criteria and rules features, SalesInbox could become the sales team's best friend and put an end to the manual work between e-mail and CRM.

■ **Reference** To learn more about SalesInbox, check out: `https://www.zoho.com/salesinbox/?src=zoho-snm`.

SalesIQ

Zoho SalesIQ is a live chat solution that you can install and enable on your web site to understand how visitors are interacting with your web site in real time. It provides the visitors of your web site with a familiar chat box placed on a corner of a web page, so they can ask the sales or support team for help right away, or leave a message without leaving the page.

You can use SalesIQ in conjunction with Zoho CRM and streamline the conversion of site visitors to prospects and ultimately buying customers. You should consider using SalesIQ if you are serious about capturing web site visitors and turning them into customers or providing them with an interactive support channel.

The Free edition provides a decent set of features for you to get up and running with SalesIQ and later upgrade to one of the paid editions as your requirements grow.

■ **Reference** To learn more about SalesIQ, check out: `https://www.zoho.com/salesiq/help/`.

Survey

Zoho Survey is a versatile tool to create online surveys and collect information from leads, prospects, or existing clients through a number of questions. You can dispatch surveys on your web site, via mobile or e-mail, and store the collected information from these channels in the backend of the survey for later analysis.

Apart from standard survey building and distributing features, Zoho Survey automatically translates your surveys to 30 languages (`https://www.zoho.com/survey/translate-survey.html`) and integrates well with e-mail campaign apps such as Zoho Campaigns and MailChimp.

■ **Reference** To learn more about Zoho Survey, check out: `https://www.zoho.com/survey/help/`.

Campaigns

Another powerful app in Zoho's arsenal is Campaigns, which offers all the tools you need to run successful e-mail campaigns. It integrates well with other core Zoho apps, especially CRM, removing the need for third-party solutions in most cases.

Any modern organization needs to include e-mail marketing in some shape or form in their business practice. Staying in touch with customers as well prospects is crucial and Campaigns allows you to do just that. Despite social media being a major channel for connecting with your audience, e-mail still remains the most effective way of communication and making sales happen.

Moreover, Campaigns offers e-mail templates to get you up and running in minutes, plus e-mail automation features to save you time and help your campaigns be more effective. It also provides you with detailed campaign reporting tools for monitoring and fine-tuning your efforts.

There is a free edition that allows storing up to 2,000 contacts and sending up to 12,000 e-mails every month, so you have little excuse not to start sending that monthly newsletter you have been delaying.

■ **Reference** To learn more about Zoho Campaigns, check out: `https://www.zoho.com/campaigns/help/`.

Sites

Unless you are visiting us from a planet where web sites are passé, you most probably have a web site for your business and chances are that setting it up was not particularly a pleasant experience.

There was a time, not so long ago, that if you needed a visually bearable and decently functional web site you either needed to know some graphic design and coding in HTML, CSS, and JavaScript (three of the main technologies behind every web site), or you were at the mercy of web design companies and freelancers.

Times have changed for the better. Now everyone can build a usable web site that looks modern, has most of the functionalities of a business web site, and works on mobile phones as well. Services such as Weebly and Wix allow you to simply drag and drop building blocks on web page skeletons and create a web site ready for prime time. Zoho also has their own web site creation wizard: Zoho Sites.

Zoho Sites provides you with a platform to easily and quickly create professional looking web sites with all the modern features you need, such as blogs, social, multimedia, e-commerce, and forms.

What is great is that you can do all of these without writing a single line of code or knowing what the difference between HTTP and HTML is.

Similar to other Zoho apps, you can start with a free plan, which offers enough features to get your web site up and running, and opt for the paid, more feature-rich edition down the road.

■ **Reference** To learn more about Zoho Sites, check out: `https://zohosites.wiki.zoho.com/`.

Social Media

Social media management has become a part of business routine of every forward-thinking business. The immense power of social media allows you to delight prospects and clients by conveying a more personal and conversational message across multiple channels.

With the multitude of available social channels, however, it is hard to stay on top of publishing, monitoring, and responding to communications while staying productive and keeping your sanity in the process.

Fortunately, there are tools that help you manage social media, including Zoho Social, a capable social management tool. As of this writing, it allows you to centrally manage your Twitter, Facebook, LinkedIn, Google+, and Instagram accounts.

You, and your team collaboratively, can publish on selected channels in one go, schedule messages, and monitor the performance of your messages. You can also listen to the social channel for what people are saying about your business or personal brand.

Another useful feature of Social is that it connects to Zoho CRM effortlessly and improves your productivity by providing you with contextual information about your social connections on the CRM as well.

As usual, you can start with Zoho Social free of charge and upgrade to a paid plan when you need more features.

■ **Reference** To learn more about Zoho Social, check out: `https://www.zoho.com/social/help/`.

Contact Manager

Having a standalone app for managing your contacts may seem totally unnecessary, but don't mistake Zoho Contact Manager for your average contact on your laptop or smartphone.

Contact Manager is actually a mini CRM that allows you to store and manage your contact database more effectively. You can share contacts within your team, define and assign tasks and follow-ups around contacts, manage deals related to contacts, and integrate your contact database with third-party services such as Google Apps or MailChimp.

If you believe you don't need a full-fledged CRM solution, Contact Manager is a great way to start introducing order to your sales processes and centralizing valuable client information.

■ **Reference** To learn more about Zoho Contact Manger, check out: `https://www.zoho.com/contactmanager/help.html`.

Forms

Sometimes you need to collect information (online) from staff members, local community, clients, or your web site visitors. To do so, you usually place some sort of a form on a web page and encourage people to fill it in and submit it back to you.

However, not all forms are created equally. A form could be a simple *Contact Us* form, a long survey, or a complex form with automation workflows embedded for approval collection.

Traditionally, you or someone you hire would need web programming knowledge to create a form with such capabilities. With Zoho Forms, all you need to do is drag and drop form fields to a form, do some configuration, and then publish your modern looking form online for people to populate.

Zoho Forms allows you to quickly create functional forms, collect data, analyze the performance of your forms, and integrate them with Zoho apps, such as CRM, or third-party apps, such as MailChimp, to automate tedious data entry tasks.

Again, you can start using Zoho Forms for free and upgrade to paid editions as your requirements grow.

■ **Reference** To learn more about Forms, check out: `https://www.zoho.com/forms/help/getting-started.html`.

Motivator

Another newcomer to the Zoho suite, Motivator, is a sales activity management tool. It allows you to set sales targets and KPIs (Key Performance Indicators) for your team, then it automatically analyzes sale information extracted from Zoho CRM to generate team member performance, so top sales people are identified, acknowledged, and rewarded for their achievements.

Motivator has a feature called TV Channels, which allows you to show a leaderboard of your team performance on big screen TVs to motivate the team and encourage employees to compete in a healthy and rewarding environment.

■ **Reference** To learn more about Zoho Motivator, check out: `https://www.zoho.com/motivator/help/`.

E-Mail and Collaboration Apps

To complement the core apps, Zoho offers essential apps that help you manage your e-mails, projects, and documents, all improved for the Internet age and built from the ground up to house modern features, such as social and collaboration features.

A number of other apps help you stay connected with your team and perform a number of essential tasks, such as safely storing your passwords in a centralized location.

Mail

Zoho Mail is Zoho's answer to popular services such as Gmail or Outlook.com. Although it may be much less popular compered other old timers, it is arguably one of the easiest to use and most feature-rich mail services in the market. Plus, it is ad-free. No more pesky ads in the sanctity of your inbox, ever.

In addition to the default web interface, Mail offers native smartphone apps for iOS and Android. You can also configure your favorite desktop or mobile e-mail client (Spark, Outlook, Apple Mail, etc.) to check your Zoho account e-mails.

For business users, Zoho Mail integrates well with other Zoho services such as CRM. You can enjoy single sign-on feature (one user account to use multiple services) and host one domain (i.e., `yourwebsite.com`), plus up to 25 users, all free of charge.

■ **Reference** To learn more about Zoho Mail, check out: `https://www.zoho.com/mail/help/`.

Notebook

Note-taking apps are everywhere. Many of them are average at best, and some of them are amazing. Good note-taking apps, such as Evernote and Microsoft OneNote, can massively contribute to your productivity and help you minimize clutter.

Zoho offers its own version of a note-taking app, called Zoho Notebook. It helps you organize your notes in a variety of formats: text, image, audio, checklists, and sketches. Notes offers a smartphone app for iOS and Android and a web clipper to capture content snippets while web surfing.

As of this writing, Zoho is yet to release a desktop versions for Notebook, similar to what Evernote and Microsoft OneNote offer. As an avid Evernote user since 2009, I can see that Zoho Notebook shows promise, especially since it sports a pleasant and easy-to-use interface and is 100% free.

■ **Reference** To learn more about Zoho Notebook, check out: `https://www.zoho.com/notebook/`.

Docs

Zoho Docs is a cloud-based storage space on steroids. You can store up to 5GB of files on free edition of Docs, sync your files between devices, and use Zoho productivity suite (Writer, Sheet, and Show) to edit your documents in the browser or via their native mobile apps.

You can download Zoho Docs desktop synchronization tool and share your documents between a local folder and the Docs folder seamlessly.

If you are already a Google Drive or Dropbox user, you will feel right at home with Zoho Docs. The free edition of Docs offers features almost identical to the free edition of Google Drive; however, the paid edition gives more bang for your buck compared to the paid edition of the Google Drive.

■ **Reference** To learn more about Zoho Docs, check out: `https://www.zoho.com/docs/resources.html`.

Projects

With hundreds of free and paid options available in the market, finding the right project management tool that covers all the bases and doesn't break the bank seems like a daunting job.

Luckily, Zoho has a powerful project management tool called Zoho Project. It offers a decent combination of ease of use, features, and cost-effectiveness, making it a formidable choice in the crowded market of cloud-based project management tools.

With Zoho Projects you can run multiple projects across multiple teams, share information with clients and outsourced teams easily, create time sheets for your projects, create Gantt charts and other complex reports, collaborate seamlessly with all the stakeholders, and mange project documents and in a central environment.

You have access to your projects via browser and native mobile apps. You can also connect Projects to other apps such as Zoho Books and Zoho Invoice as well as third-party services such as Google Apps and Dropbox to maximize your productivity and efficiency.

Zoho Projects comes free of charge if you are planning to manage one project at a time. You can always upgrade to paid editions if you need more from your project management tool.

■ **Reference** To learn more about Zoho Projects, check out: `https://www.zoho.com/projects/help/`.

Connect

Zoho Connect allows you to create a private social network for your organizations. It provides you with all the basic tools and features to set up a social network for your team to connect and collaborate in real time.

By allowing you to create custom apps and integrate other services such as Zoho Projects, Zoho Docs, Google Drive, and Calendar services, Connect helps you streamline internal communications processes and keep employees engaged while boosting their productivity.

Similar to other Zoho apps, Connect offers a free edition for you to start building your organizational social network and later upgrade to paid plans if you need more features.

■ **Reference** To learn more about Zoho Connect, check out: `https://www.zoho.com/connect/resources.html`.

BugTracker

If you are into software engineering, you know that during the software lifecycle, proper bug tracking is very important and using a powerful bug tracking service will make the lives of everyone involved in the project easier.

Zoho BugTracker offers all the essential features a robust bug tracking service should provide, plus bug automation features with workflows, out-of-the-box integration with GitHub and BitBucket, file sharing, collaborative dashboard environment, and SLA (Service Level Automation) automation.

■ **Reference** To learn more about Zoho BugTracker, check out: `https://www.zoho.com/bugtracker/help/`.

Meeting

Zoho Meeting is an easy-to-use and powerful web conferencing and live collaboration tool that takes your remote meetings to the next level. You can schedule and run unlimited meetings with up to 20 hosts (paid edition) and 100 guests (paid edition) to join your web meetings.

Zoho Meeting allows you to remotely control a participant's computer, making it a great tool for remote demoing or troubleshooting. Although there is a handy desktop plugin, Meeting doesn't need you to install an app to run or join meetings and is completely browser-based.

It also integrates well with other services such as Zoho CRM, Zoho Chat, Zoho Calendar, Google Calendar, and Google Apps.

As with most Zoho apps, you can start for free and set up one-on-one meetings right away.

■ **Reference** To learn more about Zoho Meeting, check out: `https://www.zoho.com/meeting/resources.html`.

Vault

We all use a myriad of apps and services every day, each requiring an account, which as prehistoric as it may be, requires a username and a password to log in. Until technology comes up with a better way of authenticating users, there is no escape from memorizing or storing account information somewhere in a secure place.

Fortunately, there are several apps and services such as 1Password, or Keychain Access in MacOS that store our passwords for us, so we can spend our precious brain power on Candy Crush, or something less disappointing.

For teams and businesses, Zoho Vault promises to alleviate this very challenge and make password management easy. Vault manages all your passwords securely and centrally, logs you into sites and services without the need for manual password entry, allows you to share managed passwords with select team members, monitor usage of each password, and grant or deny password access accordingly.

■ **Reference** To learn more about Zoho Vault, check out: `https://www.zoho.com/vault/getting-started.html`.

Showtime

If you teach or train people for a living, or just give occasional presentations to a large audience, you know how important it is to keep the audience engaged and turn them into active participants during a session.

Zoho Showtime builds on this simple but crucial fact and allows you to run a smooth show while keeping your audience fully engaged during and after a session. You can motivate the audience to express their opinion, run polls, ask questions, and later when the session is over, send feedback from and monitor how people engaged with your content.

Showtime is a promising and possibly game-changing service for forward-thinking trainers. The great news is that it is available for everybody to use, free of charge.

■ **Reference** To learn more about Zoho Showtime, check out: `https://www.zoho.com/showtime/help/`.

Chat

Zoho Chat provides a powerful communication platform for your team, free of charge, where you can create channels, share documents, and do more in a modern environment available on your computer and your mobile phone.

Zoho Chat is very easy to use and get up and running in your organization in a few minutes. You will feel quite at home if you have used other tools such as Yammer or Slack.

■ **Reference** To learn more about Zoho Chat, check out: `https://www.zoho.com/chat/help/`.

Business Process Apps

Another powerful set of apps that distinguishes the Zoho suite from the competition are the business process apps. Using these apps, you can build complex database applications to run your entire business, or complement other Zoho apps, such as CRM. You can also generate sophisticated business and scientific reports based on standalone databases or tie them back to other Zoho apps.

Creator

Zoho Creator is a powerful platform for creating fully customized cloud-based applications. If you have a specific set of business requirements that you can't find in any existing tool, or the available solutions are too expensive, too trivial, or too advanced, you can quickly create your very own solution with Creator.

One of the things that makes Creator great is that in many cases you don't need to do a single line of coding to make functional apps. Creator offers many tools to program and automate your business processes, but for simpler apps, you don't need to know any coding.

Simply drag and drop data fields (text boxes, lists, buttons, etc.) to create forms and Zoho Creator will do a lot of magic in the background to turn those forms into a full-fledged application.

This book is exclusively about Zoho Creator, so continue to Chapter 2 to start learning everything about it.

AppCreator

Another recent addition to the Zoho family, AppCreator allows you to quickly and with minimal or no coding create native mobile apps for iOS, Android, and Windows phones and tablets.

With AppCreator, you can publish your apps internally within your organization, or publicly through one of the app stores.

As of this writing, AppCreator is quite new and available via invitation only.

■ **Reference** To learn more about Zoho Creator, check out: `https://www.zoho.com/appcreator/help/overview.html`.

Reports

If you are into data crunching and analysis and spreadsheets don't meet your requirements anymore, Zoho Reports is a great option to consider. We live in the age of big data and data science is talk of the town. A plethora of powerful tools such as R, Python, and Tableau are available; however, not everyone needs the data scientist's toolbox.

Zoho Reports is one of the lesser known gems that provides you with a powerful toolset for collecting data from multiple sources, performing calculations and analysis, collaborating, data visualization, and more.

Using Zoho Reports you can manage millions of records and create business intelligence to contribute to the success of your business. You can also integrate it with Zoho Creator and other apps and services.

Zoho Reports offers a free edition for you to crunch up to 100,000 records of data, plus a number of paid editions for heavier use. If you still rely on spreadsheets for data analysis and visualization, I strongly suggest you give Reports a try.

■ **Reference** To learn more about Zoho Reports, check out: `https://www.zoho.com/reports/help/index.html`.

Site24x7

Site24x7 is for organizations, IT professionals, and developers who want to monitor the performance and availability of web sites, servers, and web applications. With a host of features to let you monitor how your business platforms are doing and make sure everything stays in check, Site24x7 could be a great help to your business.

■ **Reference** To learn more about Zoho Site24x7, check out: `https://www.site24x7.com/contact-support.html`.

Finance Apps

No business can afford to mismanage its finances. As you might have guessed, Zoho has you covered. A number of finance-related apps will help you keep track of your expenses, manage complex accounting operations, issue invoices, and streamline how you get paid by clients. There is even an app for managing your inventory, albeit, it may not quite fit under "finance" category.

Books

Zoho Books is powerful, yet affordable, accounting software in the cloud. With Books, you get all the features you (or your accountants) expect from an accounting and bookkeeping software, plus a host of other useful features.

You can issue customized invoices and accept online payments via service such as PayPal, connect to your bank accounts for automated cash flow and account monitoring, create powerful reports that management and clients can understand, track your inventory, and let clients see what concerns them during a project.

You can also connect Zoho Books to other apps such as Zoho CRM, Projects, and Reports and make them all operate as a big connected system to manage your entire business.

To make your life easier, Books offers mobile and smartwatch apps, so you are always up to speed with what is happening in your business financially.

■ **Reference** To learn more about Zoho Books, check out: `https://www.zoho.com/books/support/`.

Invoice

If you are happy with your current accounting software or don't need a complete accounting software, Zoho Books may not seem so appealing. Sometimes all you need as a solopreneur or freelancer is to be able to issue an invoice now and then. In this case, Zoho Invoice may just be the answer.

With Invoice, you can define your products and services, add clients, and quickly issue estimates and invoices. You can also customize your invoices to your liking and include the option to get paid online from within the invoice you send to clients.

Moreover, you can track expenses, set up reminders for your customers to pay you on time, and track time for your projects, so you can get paid accurately for the amount of work you put in.

The good news is that you can start using Zoho Invoice for free for up to 25 clients with all the features available to you.

Reference To learn more about Zoho Invoice, check out: `https://www.zoho.com/invoice/support/`.

Subscriptions

If you have recurring billing in your business, for example, you accept monthly payments for the subscription site you run, Zoho Subscriptions can take care of the entire backend of the payment system for you.

With Subscriptions, you can create your pricing model, automate billing and payment management, monitor your payments, and make strategic decisions accordingly.

Zoho Subscriptions connects to most of the common payment gateways such as PayPal and Stripe, and of course Zoho apps such as CRM and Books, to make your life easier.

Reference To learn more about Zoho Subscriptions, check out: `https://www.zoho.com/subscriptions/support/`.

Expense

Zoho Expense is an affordable and effective way to get your team expense management in order.

You can upload receipts for your daily business expenses on the go via a native mobile app, which is quite handy for business travelers. Employees can create expense reports by entering receipts and importing card transactions, and then submitting the expense reports for approval and reimbursement. Accounts will love this way of receiving clear and structured information.

You can connect Zoho Expense to Zoho Books, Invoice, and CRM, as well as QuickBooks and Slack (for notifications).

■ **Reference** To learn more about Zoho Expense, check out: `https://www.zoho.com/expense/support/`.

Inventory

Zoho Inventory offers an easy-to-use and cost effective inventory and order management solution in the cloud. Using Inventory, you can create and manage sales and purchase orders, keep track of available stock, and get real-time reports on your logistics operation. All of these are possible while you work from your office or on the go via the Inventory mobile app.

Zoho Inventory offers integration with shipping services, such as FedEx, UPS, and DHL, online stores such as Amazon, eBay, Etsy, and Shopify, as well as other Zoho apps such as Books and CRM.

If you manage a small inventory and shipping operation out of a single warehouse, you can give Zoho Inventory a try for free. As your business grows, you can opt for a suitable paid edition and manage tens of thousands of orders per month in multiple warehouses.

■ **Reference** To learn more about Zoho Inventory, check out: `https://www.zoho.com/inventory/support/`.

IT and Help Desk Apps

Zoho's IT apps will help organizations that need IT support tools to streamline their processes and stay productive. Four apps (as of Spring 2017) will help your IT team provide online and remote support and manage IT issues and mobile devices.

Desk

Per Zoho, Desk is the "industry's first context-aware help desk software."

Customer-centricity must be at the core of every business, and not degraded to merely a fluffy statement in marketing campaigns. Customer experience actually starts before customers buy your products or services and continues as long as the customers use them.

Zoho Desk tries to improve the often underwhelming (or worse) experience of dealing with help desks. Apart from standard issue tracking and ticket management tools, Desk offers a centralized, focused, and contextual interface to support teams to stay on top of the tasks in hand and manage incoming inquiries from various channels, such as phone and e-mail, efficiently.

Zoho Desk also allows you to create a customer service portal and knowledgebase for your customers, from which they can find solutions to common problems, or file and manage their tickets to new issues.

Detailed reporting, a mobile app for customer service on the go, and integration with other Zoho apps such as CRM and Projects, is also available out of the box.

Even if you are a tiny operation, customer service should still be a key aspect of your business culture. That's how you get loyal customers, repeat business, and referrals.

■ **Reference** To learn more about Zoho Desk, check out: `https://www.zoho.com/desk/help/`.

Assist

Zoho Assist provides an easy way to remotely access computers inside and outside your organization for tech-support and troubleshooting.

Zoho Assist is a great tool if you need to show a customer how to do a certain task, or better yet, do it for them remotely while they are watching (and hopefully learning). You can save time and money and most possibly reduce your carbon footprint by minimizing site visits for trivial troubleshooting tasks.

With Zoho Assist, you can also remotely access unattended computers (needs a software installed), so you don't need someone on the other side to give you access. You can transfer files, reboot devices remotely, and access multiple monitors on the host machines.

You can start using Zoho Assist for free for basic tasks, so nothing stands between you and helping your clients, colleagues, or your mom remotely with troubleshooting tasks. Now you can help her bring back that document that magically disappeared from her desktop.

■ **Reference** To learn more about Zoho Assist, check out: `https://www.zoho.com/assist/resources.html`.

ServiceDesk Plus

For serious IT support, Zoho offers ServiceDesk Plus On-Demand from ManageEngine (IT management division of Zoho). It allows you to track and manage IT tickets, resolve issues, and maximize end-user satisfaction.

With ServiceDesk Plus, you have various automation options at your disposal, self-service portal, out of the box ITIL (Information Technology Infrastructure Library) workflows, SLA (service level agreement) creation, and a host of other features to ensure successful service desk operation for your business.

■ **Reference** To learn more about Zoho ServiceDesk Plus, check out: `https://ondemand.manageengine.com/service-desk/support.html`.

Mobile Device Management

If you need enterprise-level mobile device management for your organization, then Mobile Device Manager Plus could be for you. Offered by ManageEngine, the IT division of Zoho, Mobile Device Manager Plus lets you set up, supervise, and secure your enterprise mobile devices and apps.

■ **Reference** To learn more about Zoho Mobile Device Management, check out: `https://www.manageengine.com/mobile-device-management/support.html`.

Human Resources Apps

It is argued that people are a company's greatest asset. Whether you agree with this statement or not, it is important to ensure human resource operations are managed properly at all time.

Zoho offers two powerful apps for small to medium businesses (SMBs) to manage recruiting fresh blood and smoothly manage the existing workforce.

Recruit

Zoho Recruit is a cloud-based recruitment solution for recruiting agencies and corporate HR (Human Resources) departments. You can create and manage job postings, publish them on company web site and job boards such as Monster and Indeed, parse resumes, manage candidates and communications, and automate tedious HR tasks with workflows.

There is a mobile app for HR ninjas and a free edition for you to give applicant tracking and interview scheduling features a try.

■ **Reference** To learn more about Zoho Recruit, check out: `https://www.zoho.com/recruit/resources.html`.

People

As you grow, your team grows too. Usually the moment you pass five employees, HR requirements, if not handled properly, start to impact productivity and other business processes. So, considering an HR solution early on may be a prudent way to go forward.

On the other hand, for companies larger than 5-10 employees, in-house or outsourced HR management will become a necessarily.

Zoho People is a cloud-based HR management service that helps you manage all HR-related tasks without losing your mind to needy employees. You can manage employee information securely, provide self-service features for managers and staff, perform time tracking and attendance, and create performance reviews and other important reports about your people.

You can start for free to manage up to five employees with Zoho People. Then as you hire more people, possibly through Zoho Recruit, you can upgrade to paid plans and utilize all the features that People provides in your HR processes.

■ **Reference** To learn more about Zoho People, check out: `https://www.zoho.com/people/help/home.html`.

Where to Start

As you saw in this chapter, Zoho offers a dizzying list of apps. Most of these apps work beautifully together and help you streamline your business and stay more productive.

Some of these apps have overlapping features and it may be confusing to choose one if you are just starting with Zoho or are new to SaaS. Therefore, I give a number of recommendations that I believe are applicable to many small businesses:

- No matter whether you are a solopreneur, a freelancer, or an organization of 1,000 employees, start with Zoho CRM. Make CRM a part of your day-to-day business process as well as long-term growth plans. The free edition is a great place to get started. In this book, I cover in detail how to best utilize CRM and make it work for your business.
- Become more productive by moving your e-mails to Zoho Mail for better integration with CRM. Although CRM offers integration with Google Apps and Microsoft Outlook, nothing beats native compatibility between Zoho apps. One big bonus here is that you can host up to 25 users on Mail for free, and that is with your own custom domain.
- Incorporate Zoho Campaigns as soon as you can. Almost no business, no matter how small, can ignore digital marketing. A big part of digital marketing is e-mail and social marketing and Zoho Campaign will help you win big here.
- Get serious about accounting and use either of Zoho Expense, Zoho Invoice, or Zoho Books depending on the size of your operation.
- Zoho Projects should be another key part of your cloud suite. With great integration with CRM and Books, you can easily stay on top of your projects and manage the operation of your team more effectively.
- When your team grows and requirements become more complex, use Zoho Creator and Zoho Reports for more advanced business processes and adapt Zoho Recruit and People to manage human resources.

Once you have these apps utilized, you will see how streamlined your processes will become and how much time and money you will be saving. Your team and your customers will be happier, which means you will be happier too.

Summary

In this chapter, you got a bird's eye view of the Zoho suite. I hope you see how interconnected the Zoho suite apps are and how using as many Zoho apps as possible in your business will improve your productivity and save you time and money.

In the next chapter, you will start your journey with Zoho Creator by making a simple app and learning some design concepts and best practices in the process.

CHAPTER 2

Fundamentals of Building Software

If you love blueberry pie as much as I do, especially when it is served warm accompanied by a scoop of French vanilla ice cream, you would care as much about the ingredients, the recipe, and the whole experience of enjoying every bite.

Fresh and natural ingredients, an old recipe tested and perfected for decades, an experienced baker, and of course the ice cream all decorated on a plate that makes the whole desert stand out. Who can resist this?

Good software is like good pie, but much harder to bake. There is not one element (ingredients, recipe, or the baker) that can guarantee an outcome that makes users drool.

To make drool-worthy software, everything—from the ingredients (code) and the recipe (methodologies and best-practices) to the baker (you, the programmer) and the plate (UX)—must be in perfect harmony to make users enjoy using your software, while solving their problems.

Note According to Nielsen Norman Group, user experience (UX) encompasses all aspects of the end-user's interaction with the company, its services, and its products. Read more on their web site for the full definition of UX and also how it differs from usability. Read more at: `https://www.nngroup.com/articles/definition-user-experience/`.

This all sounds nice and delicious, but making good software is hard. I remember back in the mid 90s when I was introduced to programming, that you needed to write at least a few hundred lines of code for anything mildly interesting to happen. But times have changed, mostly for the better.

Throughout time, the complexity of problems computers are expected to solve has grown exponentially, but so has the power of computers. There are also a plethora of tools and platforms developed to let businesses and individuals solve complex problems quicker and automate the few remaining mundane jobs of the 21st Century better.

Today, with platforms such as Zoho Creator, you can practically drag and drop building blocks of an application to a form, and Zoho Creator will "magically" create a working piece of software to, for example, help you manage your sales transactions.

A. Shabdar, *Mastering Zoho Creator*, DOI 10.1007/978-1-4842-2907-1_2

With Creator, there is no need to write a web application from scratch. Even with advanced frameworks, such as Django or Ruby on Rails, an app this simple could take hundreds of lines of code and a few days of development and testing.

A Little Bit of History

The magical ability of Creator to make software in a matter of hours was how I was introduced to the Zoho suite almost a decade ago.

Back in 2008 when I was in charge of the marketing department of an international real estate brand, we had a clunky CRM (Customer Relationship Management) system, which everyone loathed and no one used properly.

The CRM quickly became a bottleneck in our day-to-day operations and the company started losing valuable sales information. I needed the sales information for strategic and tactical marketing activities, so I decided to create software for the sales team. The idea was to help them to easily and quickly enter information on the go and then the admin team would clean up and transfer the data semi-automatically to the main CRM.

I envisioned a system that was easily available to our 20 salespeople and the admin team at all times with centralized data storage. As a former web developer, my natural choice was to create a fully web-based software for the job.

However, a quick estimate shattered my dreams. It would have taken me at least a month of full-time work to create something usable from concept to launch, but I had a department to run and my boss was quite skeptical about the whole idea.

By sheer luck and some help from Google search, I found Zoho Creator, a tool with a simple promise that would let me create fully functional web applications with no to little coding.

Creator reminded me of Microsoft Access, the legendary database software for Windows. Only Zoho Creator was designed for the Internet age.

Four days later, I finished creating a mini CRM for the sales team from scratch using only Zoho Creator. The app was multiuser, secure, always available, and provided a user-friendly way for the sales team to enter key information on the go.

The app even generated listing data to send to the local media for advertisement, all at a click of a button. The team loved the app and used it for a couple of years even after I left that company.

Zoho Creator has since grown to be a powerful platform for creating cloud-based business applications that can serve thousands of users with almost no IT maintenance needed.

Obviously, Creator is not an answer for all problems. There are many scenarios that need less or more complex solutions, but having created many complex Creator-based apps, I always keep it as an option when I look for tools to meet the requirements of the job at hand.

Getting Started

I can imagine that you are all excited to get to work and create your very first application in Zoho Creator. But before you do that, let's take a step back and remember the pie metaphor. You have found the right ingredients (Zoho Creator), and there are reliable recipes in this book and online, but how good are you at baking?

If you are a seasoned software engineer or a web developer, you already know about data modeling and design, flow charts, UI/UX, and prototyping. But if you just picked up this book as your first or second computer book to create software, I highly recommend you read this chapter and the additional resources online.

The rest of this chapter is a quick tour of some of the fundamental concepts of creating successful software. The aim is to get a taste of these concepts so you can make it a habit of using them to ensure a great outcome. You can find a multitude of books and online material on each topic, which are a mere Google search away.

It's All About Data

We live in the information age. It is only natural that some of the biggest problems computers help us solve has to do with data. But what is data and how does it concern us in our day-to-day business?

The Merriam-Webster dictionary defines data as "factual information (such as measurements or statistics) used as a basis for reasoning, discussion, or calculation" (`https://www.merriam-webster.com/dictionary/data`).

According to some estimates,[1] there are 2.7 Zettabytes of digital data (and growing) in the world. That is 2.7 billion terabytes. Welcome to the age of big data.

Aside from all the fancy statistics and the jargon, every small business and every individual needs to retain and manage a limited set of structured data. Your lists of to do items, contacts, inventory, sales orders, and any sort of information you can keep in a tabular form of rows and columns is structured data.

Spreadsheet software, such as Microsoft Excel, Google Sheets, or Zoho Sheet, are examples of applications that can store tabular collections of data and allow users to perform complex tasks on the data, such formulas, and charting.

■ **Note** The focus of this book is structured data. In contrast, unstructured data is also hot and relatively recent topic. You can read more about it at: `https://en.wikipedia.org/wiki/Unstructured_data`.

Table 2-1 shows a simple list of the titles in a small bookshop. Each row contains information about a specific book, structured in a particular order, according to the columns. This way of structuring information can make it easier to store, manage, and use information.

You can easily store hundreds of thousands of titles in one single data table and search for books based on each column—for example, to find books that are:

- Written by a specific author
- Published in a certain year
- Categorized under a subject

[1] `https://www.waterfordtechnologies.com/big-data-interesting-facts/`.

***Table 2-1.** Sample of Science Books in a Bookstore*

Title	Year	Author	ISBN-10	Publisher	Price
Astrophysics for People in a Hurry	2017	Neil deGrasse Tyson	393609391	W. W. Norton & Company	$18.95
Sapiens: A Brief History of Humankind	2015	Yuval Noah Harari	0062316095	Harper	$35
Homo Deus: A Brief History of Tomorrow	2017	Yuval Noah Harari	0062464310	Harper	$35
The Selfish Gene	2016	Richard Dawkins	0198788606	Oxford University Press	$15.95
Free Will	2012	Sam Harris	1451683405	Free Press	$10.99

These structured sets of data are called, not surprisingly, *datasets*. Software that houses and manages collections of datasets are often called *databases*. Databases come in all flavors and sizes. The simple contacts manager on your phone is actually a database. It allows you to store, retrieve, and alter data—i.e. your contacts. Your favorite spreadsheet software is a database.

However, in a broader sense, a database can be quite complex and with sophisticated features to manage thousands upon thousands of rows of information. A big chunk of those Zettabytes of information in the cyberspace is stored in a multitude of databases in thousands of data centers scattered around the world.

From the users' perspective, database software is just an interface through which they interact with data and solve their problems, e.g., find information, run calculations, and generate reports.

However, there is much more boring but important stuff happening behind the scenes and it has a lot to do with how the data is structured.

Data Modeling and Database Design

To solve information-related problems and to create software solutions that effectively and efficiently manage information, it is crucial to create a properly designed database first.

This starts with designing the structure of the data that will be housed in the database. This design is actually a conceptual (often visual) representation of how data tables will look in a database.

Modeling data prior to creating a database is a must no matter how small the project is. This will help you understand how data is stored, what the relationships between different pieces are, and how it flows to deliver the expected outcome. It also helps you find gaps early on, design optimum structure, and also review and sign off with the business (non-technical people who commissioned your work and will eventually use your database) to ensure you are on the right track.

Figure 2-1 shows a simplified data model depicting data entities (and their relationships) in a small real estate management system, which you will be building from the ground up in Chapter 7.

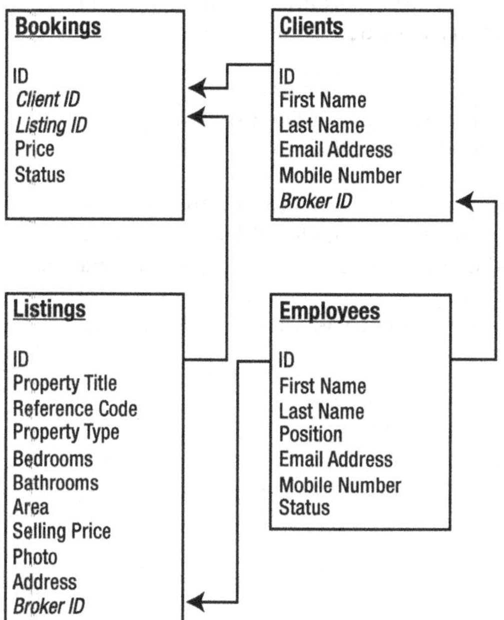

Figure 2-1. *A simple data model*

■ **Reference** Delve deeper into data modeling by reading articles on `LearnDataModeling.com`. (See `http://learndatamodeling.com/blog/data-modeling-concepts-what-is-data-modeling-data-modeling-overview/`).

Data modeling and design is one of the complex topics of computer science. You can read many books on the topic and read many articles on methods, tools, and best practices. However, for the purpose of this book, the minimum you should be doing for each app is think of all the information your app will manage and design accordingly.

For instance, in the simple list of the book titles in Table 2-1, the visual representation of the table is the first step to determine the key data that needs to be stored—Title, Edition, Year, Author, ISBN-10, ISBN-13, Publisher, and Price.

If say, three months down the road, you realize that you missed including the number of pages for each book, it will be a difficult job to go back, redesign the table, populate missing data for each book, modify the look and feel of the application, change reports, etc. It is always better to think ahead and design for the future.

Data Types

The next step is to decide what data type is most suitable for each column. Without getting into too much detail, you can store data in computers as two main types—string and number. *String* type (or *text*) is suitable for storing arbitrary strings of text and literal information. So, it is easy to guess that a book title or author name should be stored as a *string*.

On the other hand, the *number* type allows numeric computation on the values stored. For instance, price should be stored as a number so that you can run financial computations, such as the total value of the existing books in the bookshop.

It is possible to store numbers as strings, especially when you are 100% sure you won't be doing any numeric operations on them. For example, ISBN10 can be stored as a string of digits, not a real number, simply because you won't need to do any summation or other numeric operations on it.

Based on this information, the bookstore database has only one table with the columns, as indicated in Table 2-2.

Table 2-2. *Table Columns and Types*

Column Name	Type
Title	String
Edition	String
Year	Number
Author	String
ISBN-10	String
Publisher	String
Price	Number

There is more to data design than creating mere tables. Concepts, such as relationships and normalization, are beyond the scope of this book; however, they are essential if you are designing full-fledged databases.

Algorithms and Flowcharts

Arguably everything in the world happens within a process. Something as simple as making a peanut butter and jelly sandwich is actually a multi-step process.

Processes are more evident in manufacturing and corporate environments where efficiency, productivity, and automation are high priorities and need to be modeled and improved consistently. The importance of process-thinking expands to the computer world where the main goal of most software is to support the business.

Suppose in a simple sales transaction process, all the steps, the people involved, and the outputs and inputs of that process need to be identified, so it can be accurately and efficiently modeled in a computer program. Forget one step in the process, e.g., sending a notification to the accounts, and your software is useless.

In computer science jargon, step-by-step processes or a sequence of actions to perform a task, such as calculation, data processing, or performing transactions, are called *algorithms* while their visual representations are called *flowcharts* and *process maps*.

Figure 2-2 depicts a simple flowchart showing the steps that generate a report based on the year a book is published.

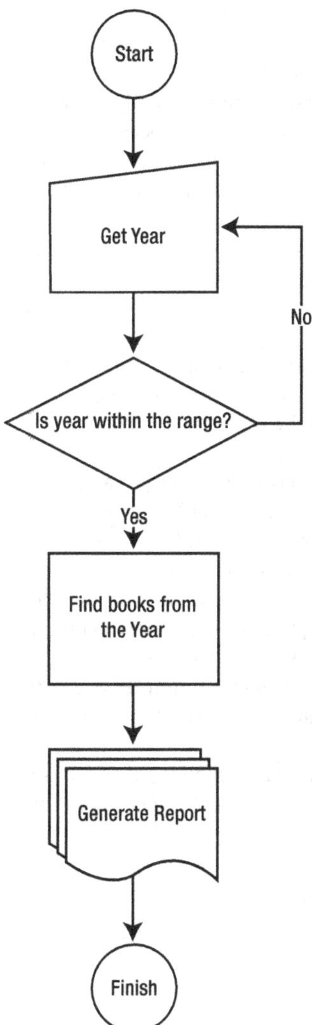

Figure 2-2. *A simple flowchart*

Each one of these steps in the flowchart could have processes and sub-processes underneath it. For example, the step before *Finish, Generate Report,* could have multiple steps describing how the report will be generated.

■ **Reference** I used Lucidchart (`https://www.lucidchart.com/`) to draw the flowchart in Figure 2-1. It is a powerful cloud-based diagraming tool that you can use for drawing virtually many kinds of diagrams.

It is evident that creating visual representations of how a software performs certain tasks is useful, as it allows all the steps to be taken into account and enables the project team and other stakeholders to review and sign off on each process.

For the purpose of this book, you can rely on simple drawings that logically explain various business processes. I still encourage you to learn about business process modeling, which helps you tackle more complex scenarios. I briefly talk about business process modeling in my other book, *Mastering Zoho CRM.* You can also read more about the topic online to gain basic knowledge.

Users at the Center of It All

Even if you design the best and the most robust database on the planet and create solid logic that makes your software tick like an atomic clock, you cannot afford to forget the part that has become more important than the others in the recent years: the user interface and the user experience.

In a world where there are more than five million apps in two of the largest app stores combined (`https://www.statista.com/statistics/276623/number-of-apps-available-in-leading-app-stores/`), the competition is fierce. The look and feel of your software and how easy and intuitive it is to use could make or break its success.

Designing engaging software has never been more relevant and the very first step to achieve stellar user interface (UI) and user experience is to go back to the drawing board and sketch how the UI elements will fit together and interact with each other.

You can use a pen and a piece of paper to sketch the app, which sometimes is exactly what you need. You can also opt for one of the many wire framing and mockup apps available to give life to your amazing idea.

My personal favorite is MockFlow (`https://mockflow.com/`), which is a cloud-based app. It allows you design wireframes for virtually any platform and create UI interactions to roughly show how the app will work.

Figure 2-3 shows MockFlow in action. You can drag and drop the UI element to construct windows and forms.

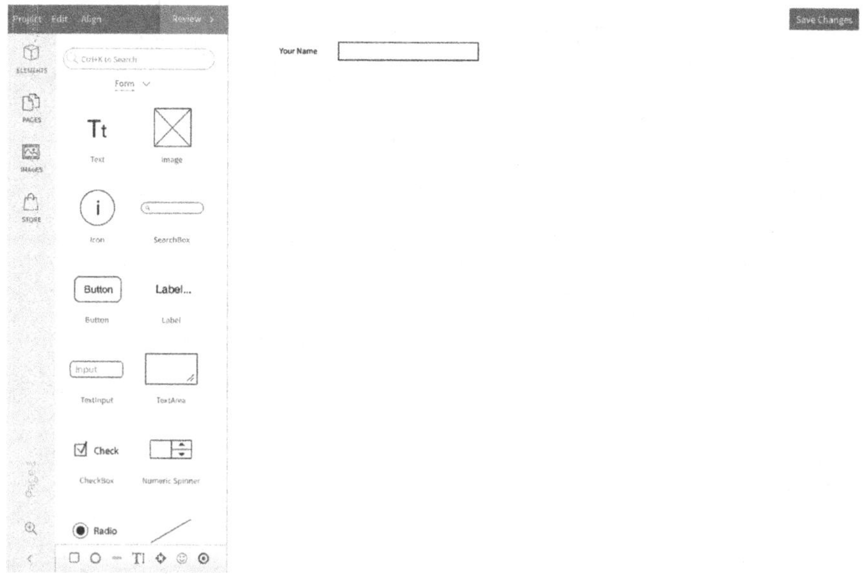

Figure 2-3. *Designing a great UI with MockFlow*

Suppose you are designing an inquiry form. The finished form might look like Figure 2-4.

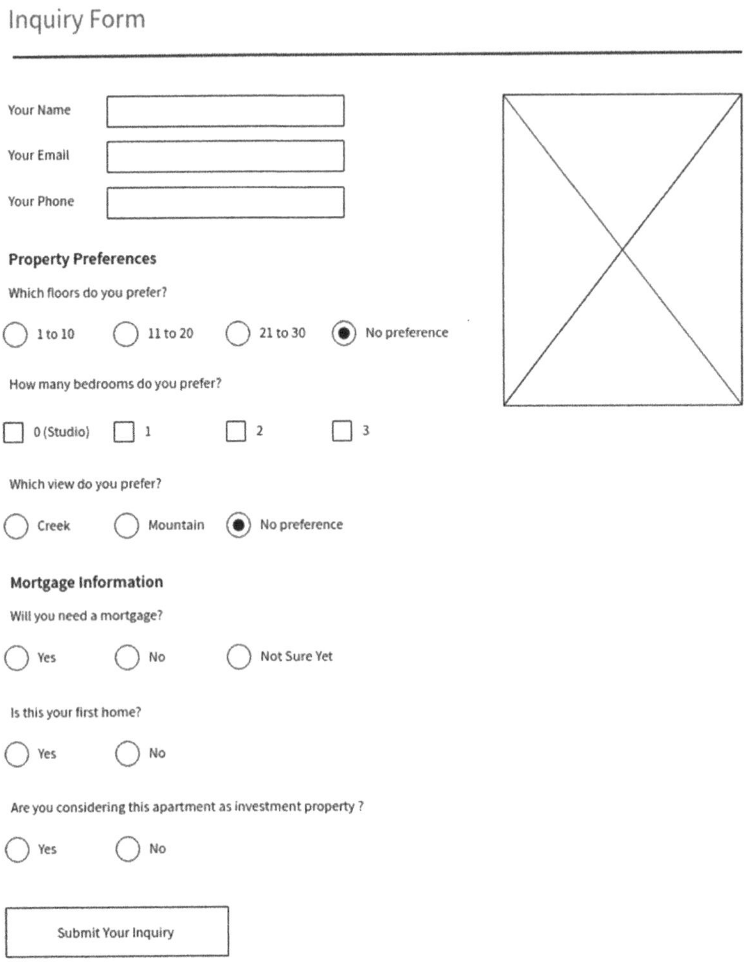

Inquiry Form

Your Name

Your Email

Your Phone

Property Preferences

Which floors do you prefer?

1 to 10 | 11 to 20 | 21 to 30 | No preference

How many bedrooms do you prefer?

0 (Studio) | 1 | 2 | 3

Which view do you prefer?

Creek | Mountain | No preference

Mortgage Information

Will you need a mortgage?

Yes | No | Not Sure Yet

Is this your first home?

Yes | No

Are you considering this apartment as investment property ?

Yes | No

Submit Your Inquiry

Figure 2-4. *Wireframe of an inquiry form*

This design prototype shows the type, order, and placement of the elements on the form. You can show this to peers, clients, and focus groups to get their buy-in or sign-off before designing the actual prototype.

Summary

In this chapter, you took a quick tour of some of the concepts and methodologies you need to consider when designing good software, including Zoho Creator apps.

You can start by designing and prototyping breathtaking (and useable) UI and then go deeper into creating logic and database, or you can start by designing a robust database and then building logic, and finally the UI, based on the underlying design.

The important point is to first take the time and design how the software will look and how it works and interact with the users. Fixing half-built software is not easy, nor is it pleasant or economically viable.

In the next chapter, you create your very first Zoho Creator App by using the tools and components available to you.

CHAPTER 3

Creating Your First Application

In the previous chapter, you got a bird's eye view of the fundamentals of software application creation. In this chapter, you get your hands dirty and create your very first cloud-based application on the Zoho Creator platform.

Creator provides you with a host of features and capabilities to help you create modern, usable, and functional apps in a fraction of the time it takes to build software from scratch.

In fact, if you wanted to recreate the simplest app created in Creator in any other modern programming language, such as Python or Ruby, it would take you thousands of lines of code and many days in testing and deploying your code.

To make it even easier, Creator also offers a set of application templates for most commonly used scenarios. These templates are ready-to-use real-life apps, such as order management and project management tools, that you can use in your day-to-day business dealings.

You can also customize them to match your specific requirements. Not only will these templates save you time, but they are also great ways to learn Zoho Creator.

In this chapter, you use one of these templates—a Contact Manager—to start learning about Creator and its essential capabilities.

Getting Started

To start with Zoho Creator, open your favorite browser and log on to: `https://creator.zoho.com/`.

I assume that this is your first time here, so before everything, you will create an account. This is a universal Zoho account that you can use to access other Zoho services, such as CRM, Campaigns, etc.

To create a user ID, follow these steps:

1. On the home page, type in your name, e-mail, and a strong password. You do this on the signup form on the right side of the page (Figure 3-1).

A. Shabdar, *Mastering Zoho Creator*, DOI 10.1007/978-1-4842-2907-1_3

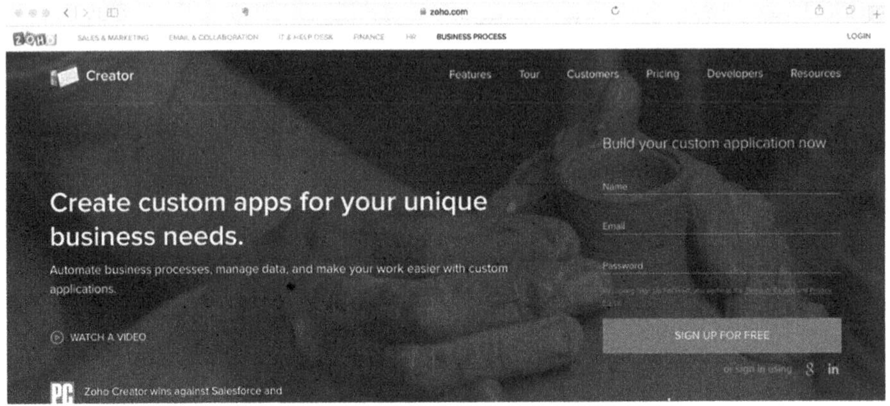

Figure 3-1. *Zoho Creator home page*

■ **Note** Building strong passwords for all your accounts, especially accounts in which you keep confidential business information, is paramount. You can use tools, such as Keychain Access for Mac OS, lastPass (`https://lastpass.com/`), or Zoho Vault (`https://www.zoho.com/vault/`) to create and manage your strong passwords.

---

2. Click on the *Sign Up for Free* button to initiate the signup process. Shortly, you will receive a confirmation e-mail from Zoho asking you to confirm your e-mail address.

3. In the e-mail body, click the *Confirm Your Account* button. Upon successful confirmation, you will be redirected to the login page.

4. On the login page, enter your e-mail address and the password you created in Step 1 and click *Login*.

5. On the next page, you will be asked for some basic information about yourself (Figure 3-2). Enter the following information:

   a. Your organization's name

   b. Your phone number

   c. A unique and relevant username

   d. Your operating time zone

   e. Your preferred date format

   f. You can also click *Profile Picture* and add a profile picture to your account.

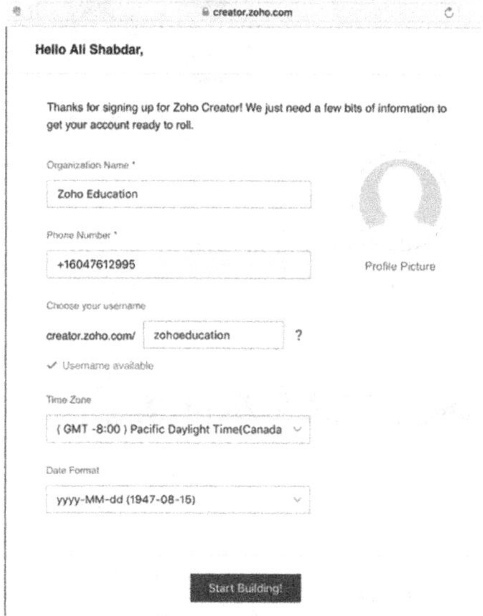

Figure 3-2. *Welcome screen after first login*

6. Click *Start Building!* to continue.

7. On the next screen, simply click the *Create Application* button to continue (Figure 3-3).

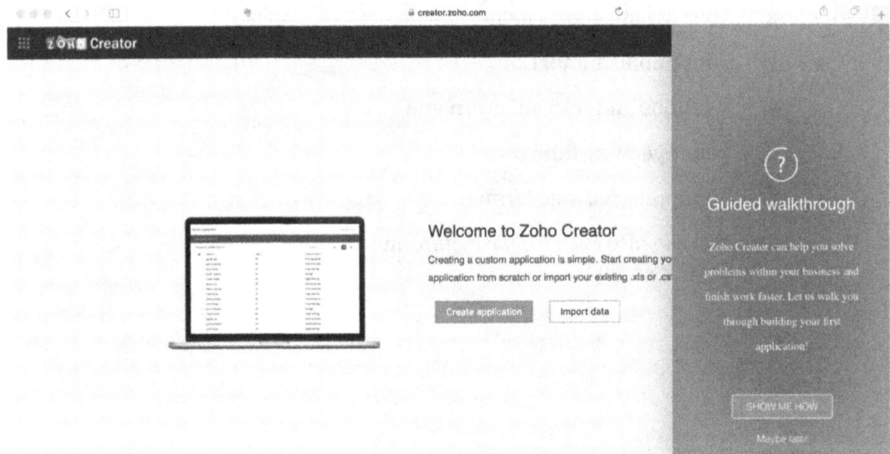

Figure 3-3. *Guided tour*

8. On the next page, you will see a list of application templates to pick from. Click on the *Contacts* (Figure 3-4).

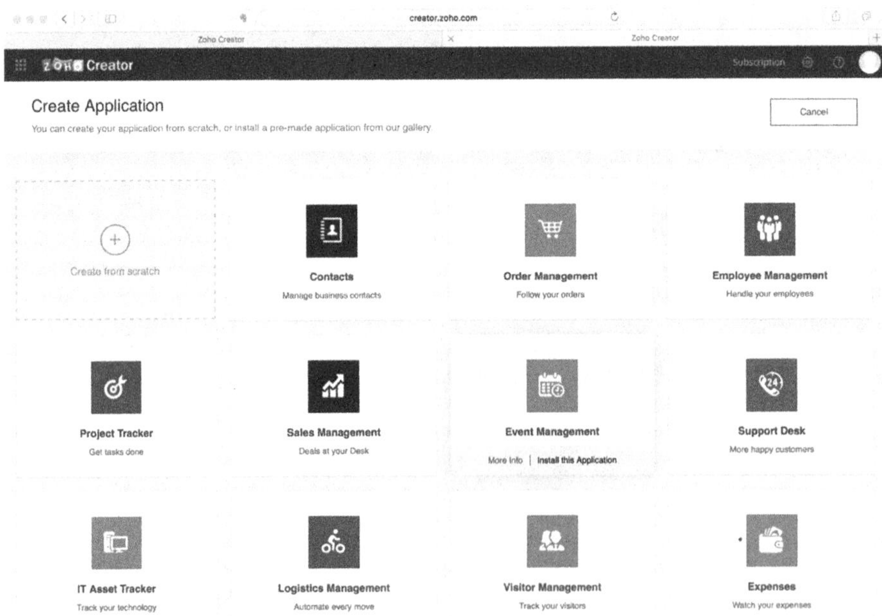

Figure 3-4. *Create Application page*

9. A dialog box will open showing you details about the *Contacts* app (Figure 3-5).

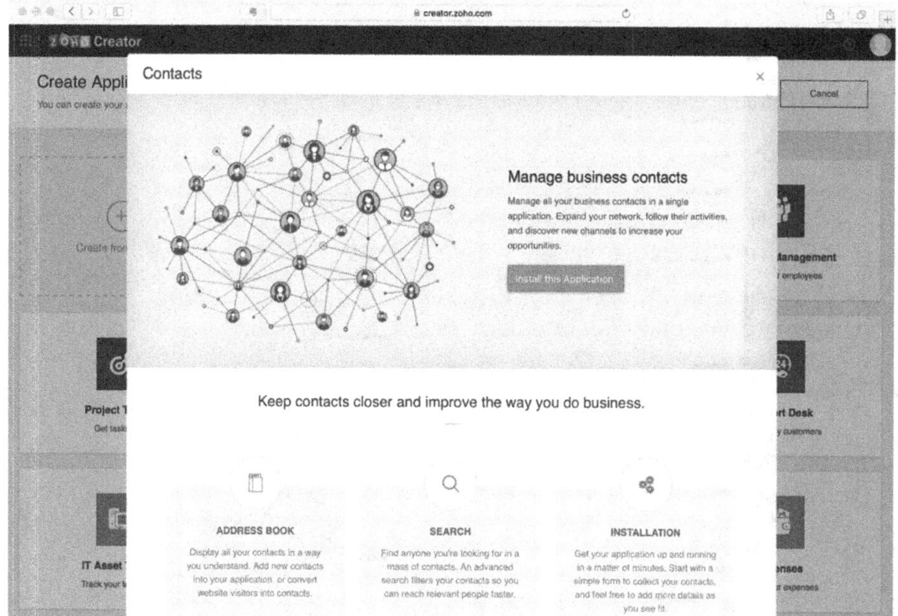

Figure 3-5. *Contacts app details page*

10. Take a moment and review the features listed in the details. Then click *Install this Application* to continue. It could take a few seconds for the application to set up (Figure 3-6).

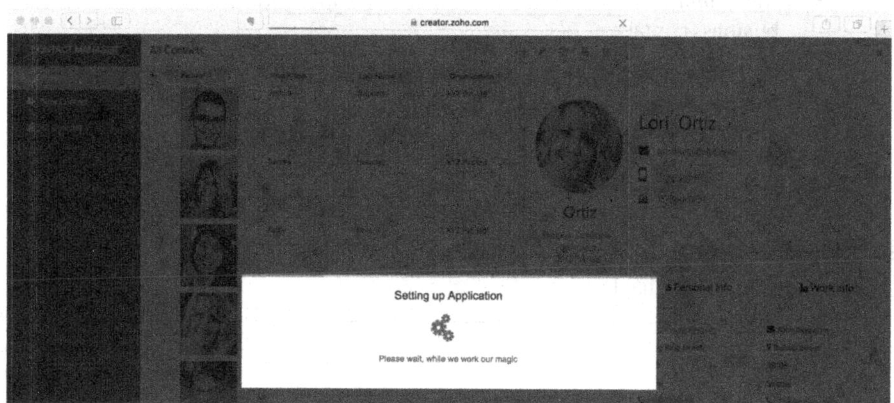

Figure 3-6. *Setting up the new application*

Once the setup is done, the newly created Contacts application will launch and be ready use right away (Figure 3-7).

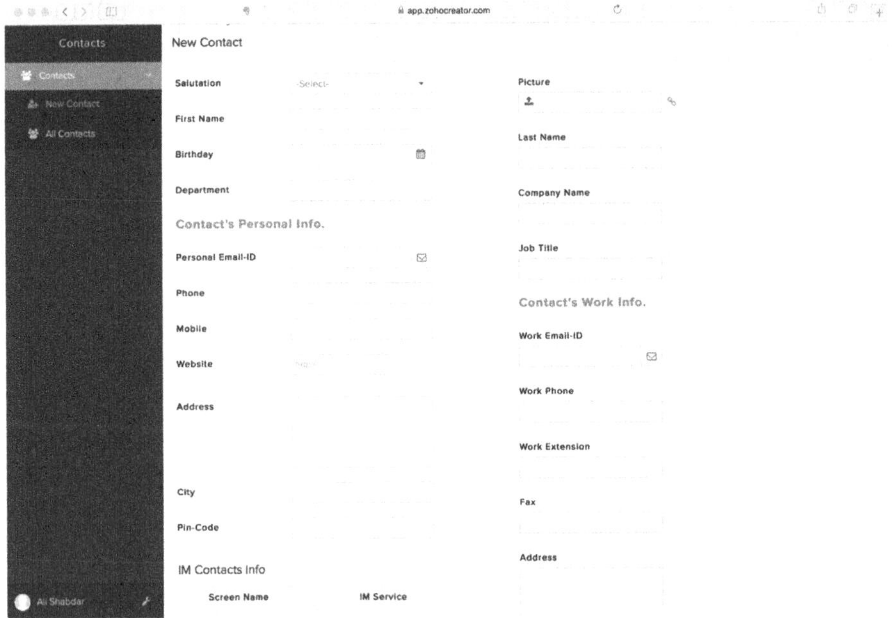

Figure 3-7. Brand new Contacts app ready to use

The app interface is minimal and easy to use. On the left side of the screen there is a sidebar with the navigation buttons aligned on top.

This simple app has only two pages:

- *New Contact*—A form in which you can add and store new business contact.
- *All Contacts*—Shows a list of all contacts stored in the app. You can manage existing contacts in this page, performing tasks such as search, view, edit, and delete.

■ **Note** You may notice that your name appears on the bottom of the sidebar. This is a shortcut that allows you to access your user profile, log out, and perform a couple of other tasks, covered in a later chapter.

Adding a New Contact

Now you'll see how to add your first contact:

1. With the *New Contact* page open, enter as much information in the relevant boxes as you like, such as *Salutation*, *First Name*, Last Name, and *Phone Number* (Figure 3-8).

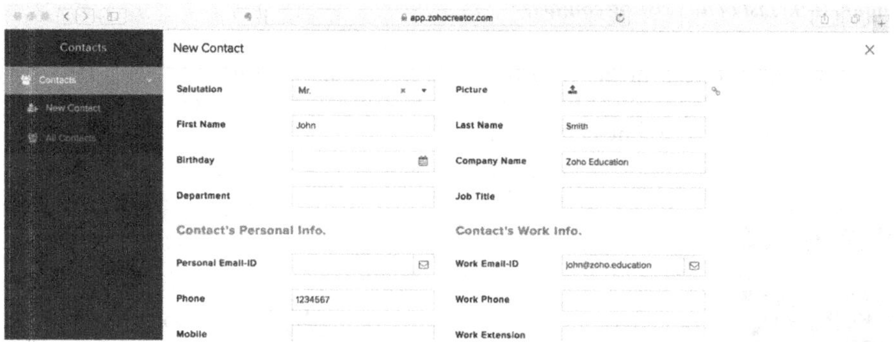

Figure 3-8. *Adding a new contact*

2. When you're finished entering information, click *Submit* on the bottom of the page (you may need to scroll down), or simply press *Enter* on your keyboard. A message will briefly appear on top of the screen indicating that the contact was added successfully.

After a successful contact entry, the form will be cleared and ready for another contact to be entered. Go ahead and add more contacts. Notice that the field validation and formatting present for some of the fields, such as phone numbers and e-mails. Data validation and formatting ensure the data entered is as clean and as easy to search and retrieve as possible.

Searching for Information

One of the essential features of all good software is the ability to search in the information stored in it. With the number of contacts growing, browsing through the long list of contacts to find the information you are looking for is simply not feasible.

Fortunately, Creator offers powerful search features out-of-the-box. Let's check a few of these features out:

1. On the sidebar, click on *All Contacts*. A page will load with a list of all the existing contacts (Figure 3-9).

Figure 3-9. *List of all existing contacts*

2. Click on one of the contacts in the list. A contact pane will appear on the right side of the page showing all the details of the selected contact (Figure 3-10).

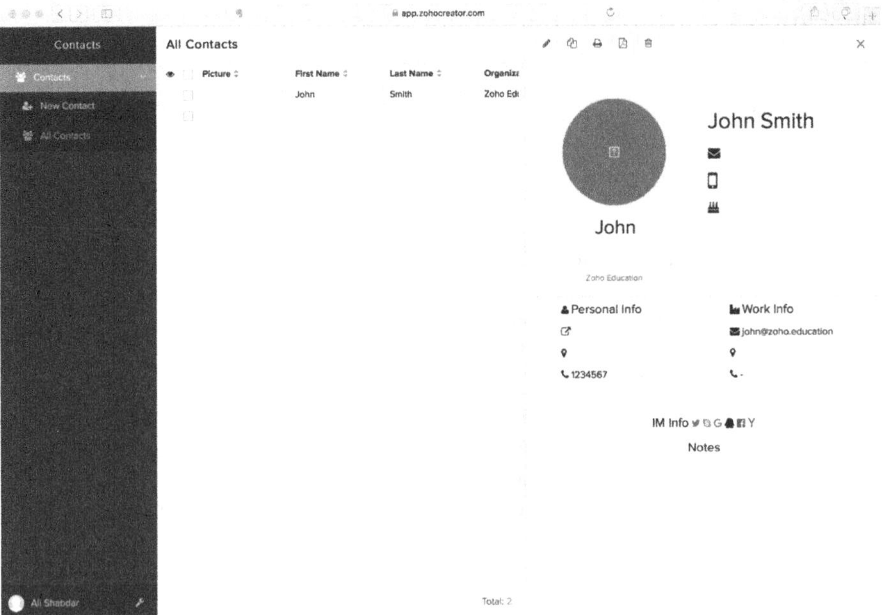

Figure 3-10. *Contact details*

On top of this pane, there are five icons that allow the following operations:

- *Edit*—To modify the information of the contact
- *Duplicate*—To create another contact with the exact same information
- *Print*—To print a copy of the contact on paper

- *Export to PDF*—To save a copy of the contact information to a PDF file
- *Delete*—To permanently remove the contact from the app

3. Click the × on top right of the page to close the pane and go back to the Contacts list.
4. There are three buttons on top right of the screen. Click the first one, the magnifier, to open the *Search* box.
5. You can search in the contacts based on a number of fields, including name, number, and organization name. To find all contacts whose first name is John for example, click the checkbox in front of *First Name* and enter "John" in the text box appearing below it (Figure 3-11).

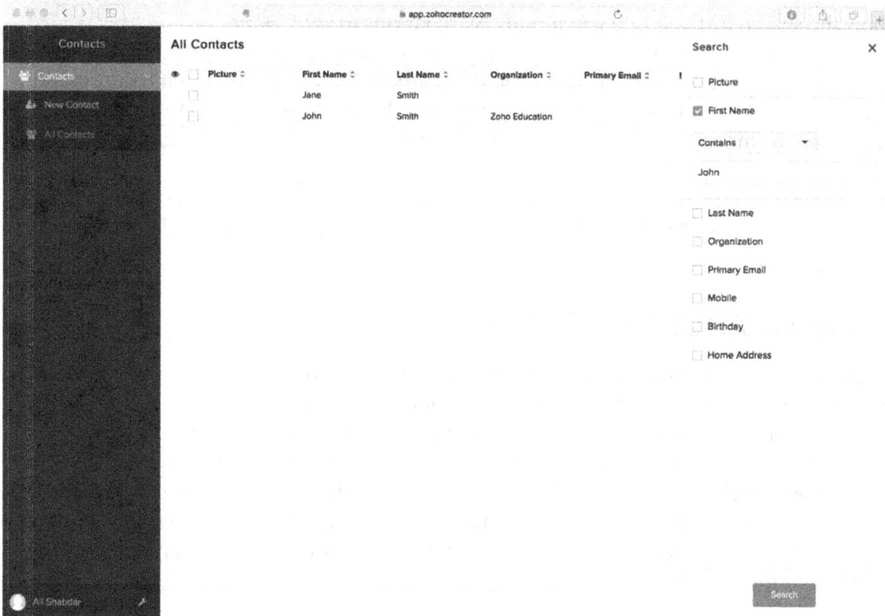

Figure 3-11. *Searching for a contact by first name*

6. Click the *Search* button at the bottom. The contacts list will reload and list only the contacts whose first name is John (Figure 3-12).

Figure 3-12. *Search results showing the only John in the contacts*

You will notice that right above the list on the left side, a new *Search button* appears, next to which another button labeled *John* is displayed. Clicking on either of these will show the search form, letting you modify search terms to your liking.

These shortcuts come in handy when you have many records (rows) in the search results and more refinement is needed in the search term in order to find the information you need. For example, you can combine terms and find all people working for the same organization whose birthday is the next month, so you can send birthday cards to their e-mail addresses.

To clear out the search terms and have the entire list of contacts, you can either click the small red × next to each term or open the search box and uncheck all the terms.

Zoho Creator on the Go

Zoho Creator offers native mobile apps for iOS, Android, and Windows Mobile. These mobile apps allow you to access all your Creator apps on the go.

Installing the mobile apps is as easy as installing any other app on your phone. During the first run, Creator app will ask for your Zoho credentials. Once you are logged in, all apps associated with the account will be listed under the *Personal Apps*, *Shared Apps*, or *Workspace Apps*. I discuss the latter two categories later, but suffice it to say that you can find any app you create yourself, including this little Contacts app, under the *Personal Apps* option (Figure 3-13).

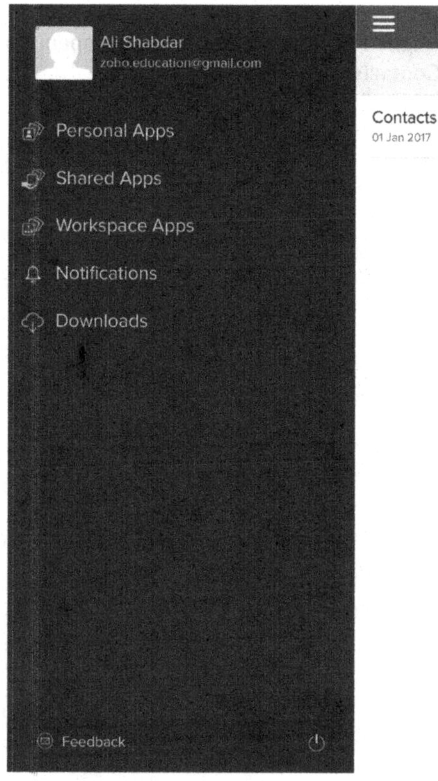

Figure 3-13. *Creator mobile app*

To open the Contacts app, you simply tap on its name in the list.

A minimal and usable version of the app designed specifically for mobile will open with all the elements and functionalities of the Contacts app (Figure 3-14).

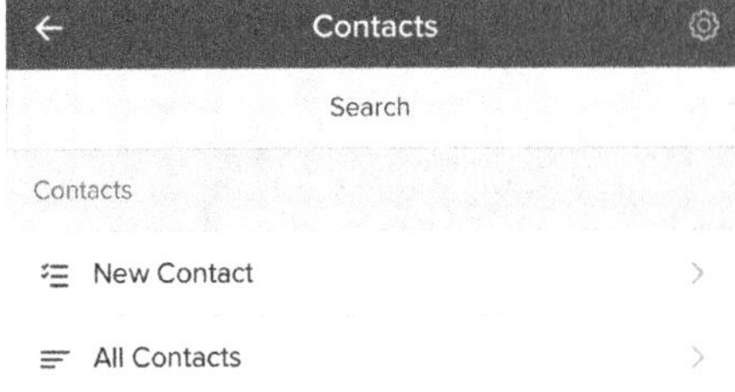

***Figure 3-14.** Mobile version of the Contacts app*

Tapping on the *Add New Contact* button will open the familiar contact form awaiting your input (Figure 3-15).

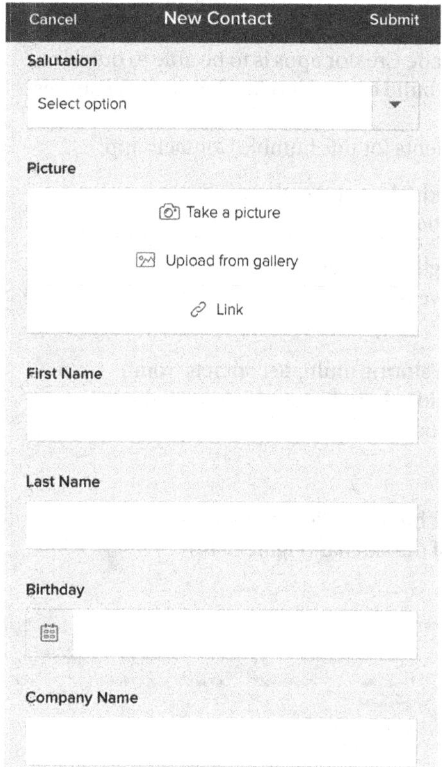

Figure 3-15. *The New Contact form on the mobile version*

The mobile form is designed in a way that utilizes the little screen real estate available on mobile devices as well as the special features available to phones, such as taking a photo with the camera to assign as profile picture for a contact.

Again, all of this happened somehow magically for you without you actually worrying how the app and its elements will look like on mobile devices. Zoho Creator allows you to focus on creating an app that works, without getting entangled in designing the user interface elements and losing sleep over degraded user experiences.

Editing the Application

This little contact manager seems powerful enough for many and can certainly manage all your business contacts in one place. However, what if you need more, or even fewer, features for your specific needs?

As mentioned, the point of using ready-made Creator apps is to be able to quickly get started with the essential features and then build on and modify the existing features according to your business requirements.

As it happens, there aren't many requirements for this humble Contacts app:

- No personal information is required. The app needs to collect only work-related contact information.
- No fax number is required. Although some people still put fax numbers on their business cards, we refuse to acknowledge such technology exists in 2017.
- Distinguishing key contacts. When storing multiple contacts from the same organization, it is a good idea to indicate which one calls the shots or at least influences major decisions.

Now you see how to customize this app:

1. With the Contacts app open in your browser, click the tool icon next to your name on the bottom of the sidebar (Figure 3-16).

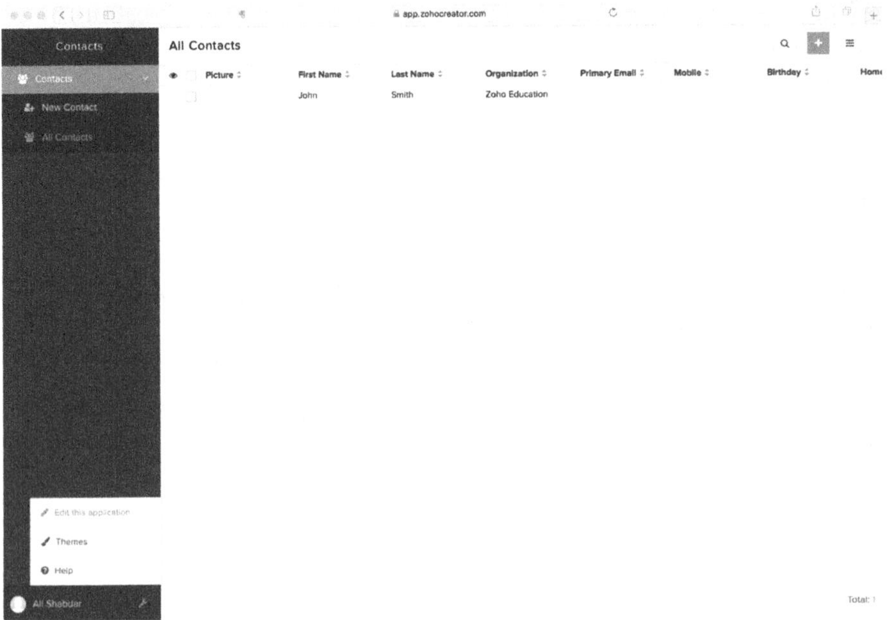

Figure 3-16. *Tools context menu*

2. Click the *Edit this Application* item in the context menu.
   The app will open in *Edit* mode (Figure 3-17).

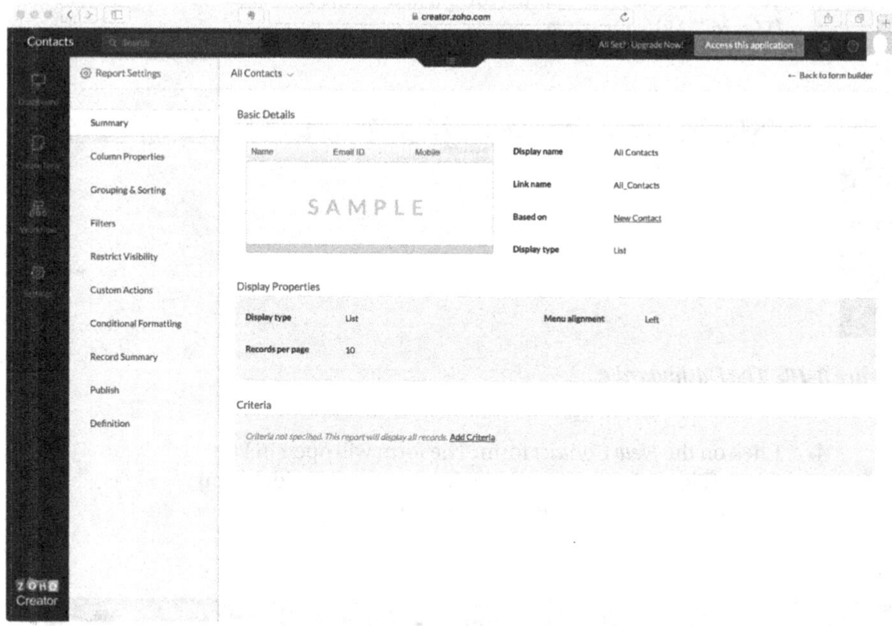

Figure 3-17. *Edit mode*

■ **Note** Edit mode is under the hood of your application and is where you can customize (almost) all aspects. This means that you may intentionally or unintentionally modify elements and behavior, delete features, and worse, data, in the process. Make sure you are certain of your actions and take backups before doing so. You will learn about backups later in this book.

---

3. By default, Edit mode shows the only report in the app—that is, the *All Contacts* list. Ignore this page for a moment and click on *Dashboard* on the sidebar. In the *Dashboard* page, you can see the *New Contact* form listed on the *Forms* tab (Figure 3-18).

Figure 3-18. *The Dashboard*

4. Click on the *New Contact* form. The form will open in Edit mode (Figure 3-19). Apart from the ever-present sidebar on the left, the page is divided into three areas:

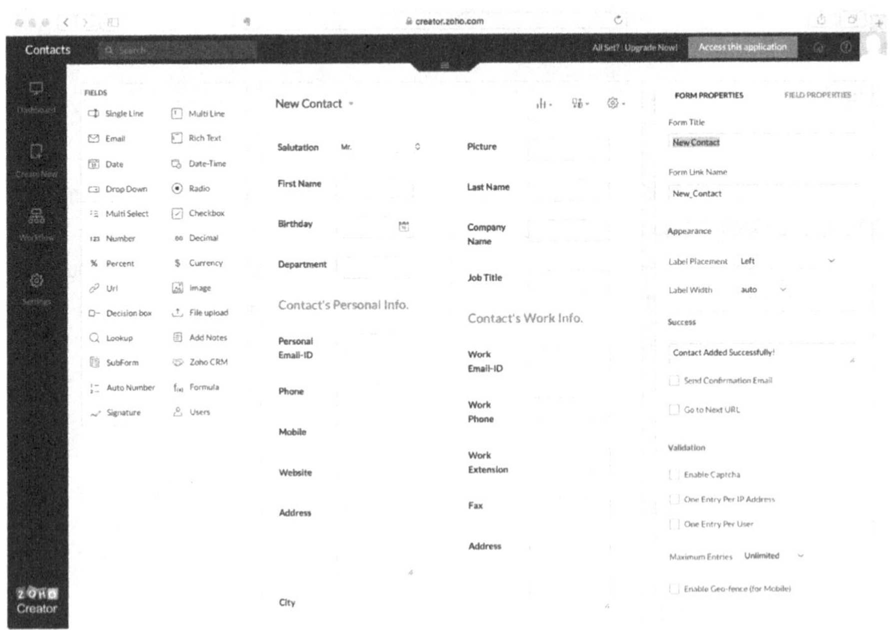

Figure 3-19. *New Contact form in Edit mode*

a. There is a list of fields on the left side, which you can drag and drop on a form. These fields are building blocks that offer various ways of inputting, or showing, information on a form.

■ **Note** A form is a combination of input elements that allow users to enter specific values. When a form is submitted, the values are validated and stored together as a data row (or record). A data record (row) is an ordered combination of data fields (columns) forming a virtual table. Each table represents a set of information about a specific entity, such as Contacts. These concepts will sound familiar if you have used database systems, such as MySQL, or spreadsheets, such as Microsoft Excel. Otherwise, don't worry. You will learn about these concepts in more detail in upcoming chapters.

---

b. In the middle of the page is the form itself, ready to be modified.

c. On the right, there is a pane showing the properties of the form, or the fields on the form. Clicking on each field will show the properties of that particular field, thus allowing you to modify it as needed.

If you recall, the first requirement was that the Contacts app doesn't need to collect personal information, so you need to remove the fields that do this:

1. In Edit mode, select each one of the following fields listed under the red text *Contact's Personal Info* and click the little trash can button appearing next to them. This will remove them from the form. Click *Yes* when you are asked if you really want to delete this field (Figure 3-20).

   a. Personal Email-ID

   b. Phone

   c. Mobile

   d. Website

   e. Address

   f. City

   g. Pin-code

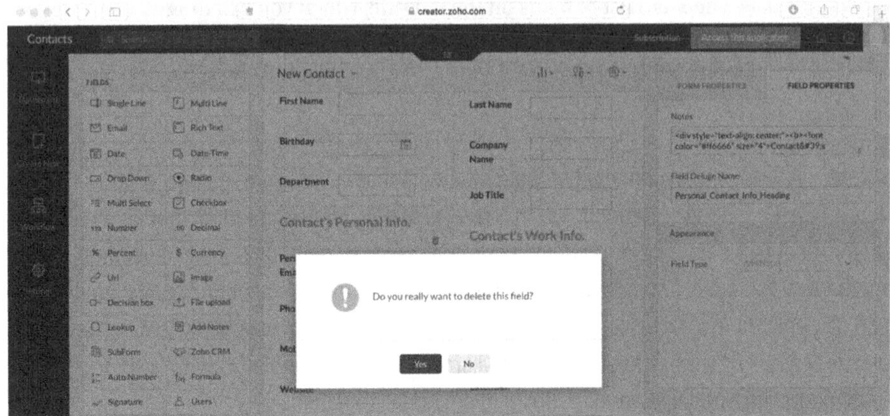

Figure 3-20. *Confirming removal of fields from the form*

2. Remove the red *Note* field *Contact's Personal Info* too.
3. Remove the *Fax* field under *Contact Work Info.*

The end result should look like Figure 3-21. The first and second requirements (no personal information and no fax number) are now met.

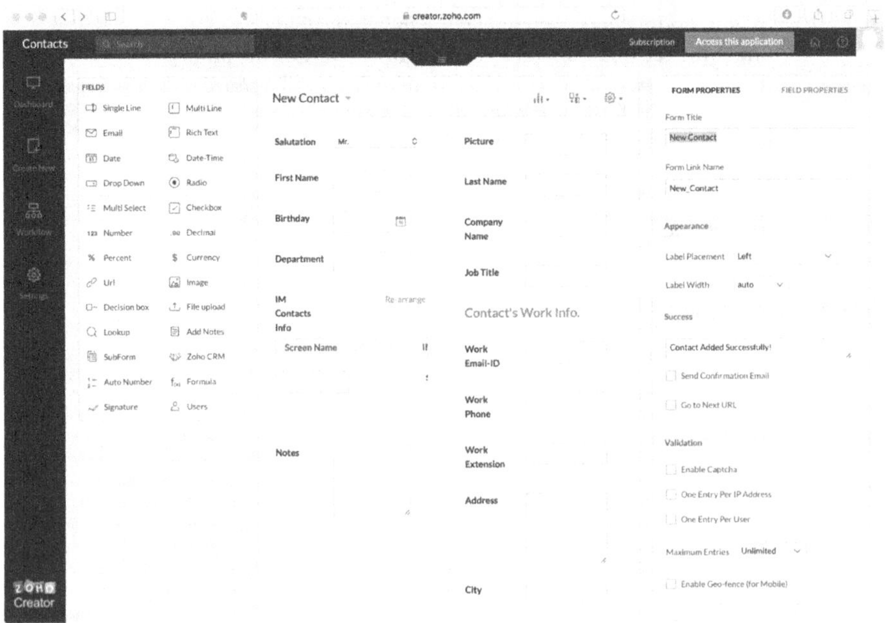

Figure 3-21. *Redundant fields removed from the form*

To see the changes in action, run the app by clicking *Access This Application*. The app looks cleaner and unnecessary information is not shown (Figure 3-22).

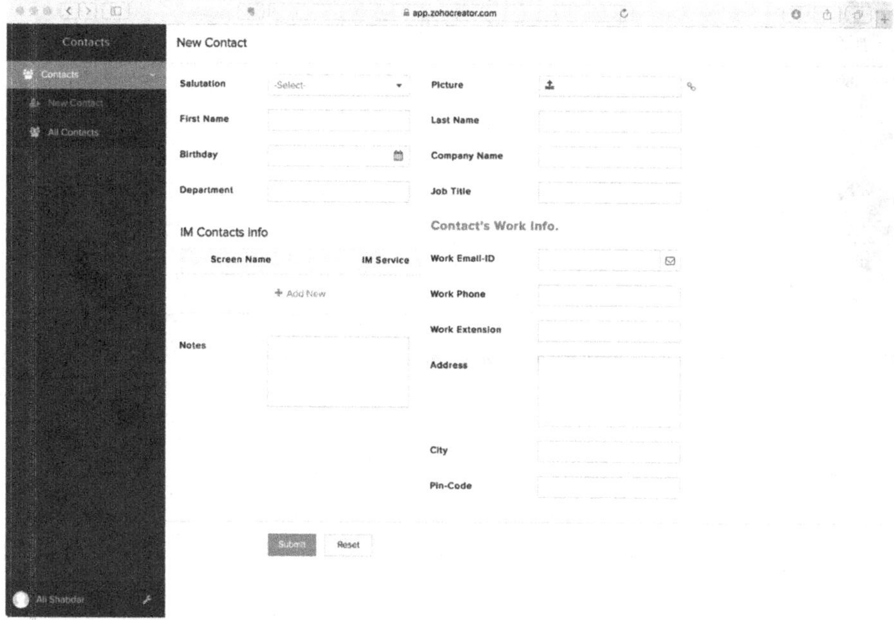

Figure 3-22. *Modified app in action*

■ **Note** One caveat of removing fields after saving some information in the app is that it will cause the data collected in the removed fields to be lost. In this example, if you have stored personal information, or Fax numbers, removing these fields will have caused the underlying data to be deleted as well. Adding deleted fields back to the form will not bring back the deleted data.

We are not quite done yet and still need to meet the third requirement, which is to indicate which contact is the key contact. For this purpose, you can use a checkbox field type.

Follow these steps to add a checkbox to the *Add New Contact* form:

1. If the app is not in Edit mode, enter Edit mode by clicking the tool icon on the sidebar and selecting *Edit This Application* in the context menu.

2. In Edit mode, drag a *Checkbox* field from the fields pane (on the left) and drop it between the *Department* field and *the IM Contact Info* fields (Figure 3-23). A new *Checkbox* field appears on the form with the default name of *Checkbox*. It has three choices (Figure 3-24). Notice the values in the *Field Properties* pane on the right side of the page.

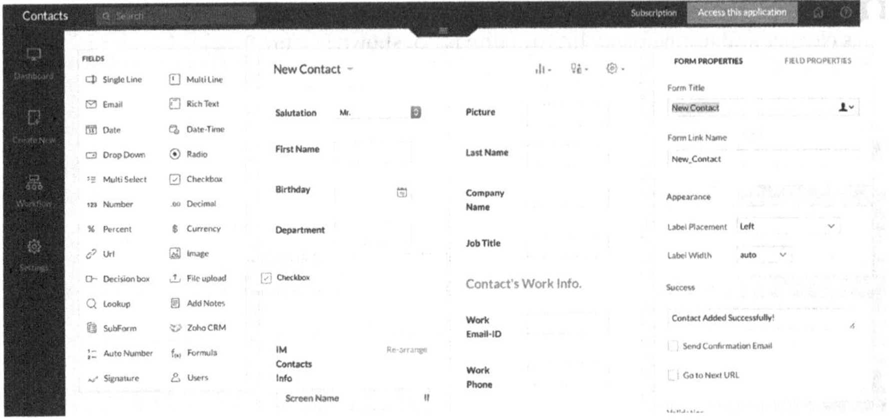

Figure 3-23. *Adding a checkbox field to the form*

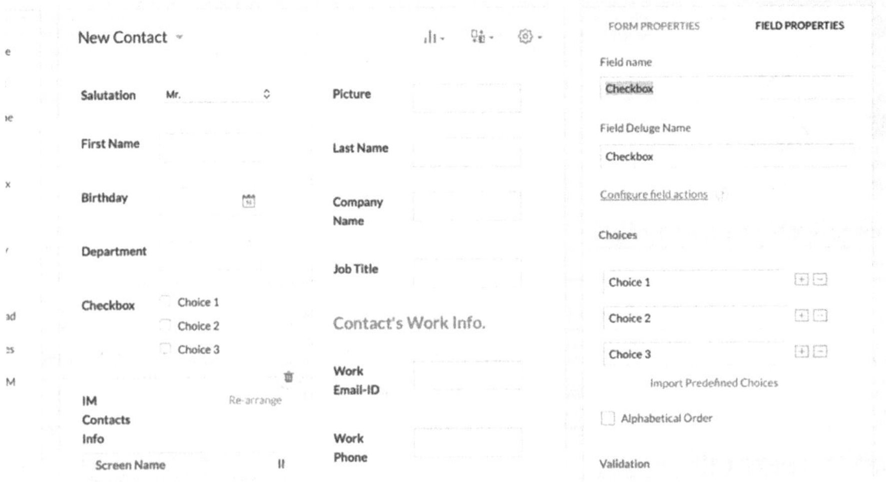

Figure 3-24. *New checkbox placed on the form*

3. With the checkbox fields on the form selected, change *Field Name* under *Field Properties* to **Key Contact**. Then change the first choice in the Choices to **Yes** and remove the other two choices: *CHOICE 2* and *Choice 3* (Figure 3-25).

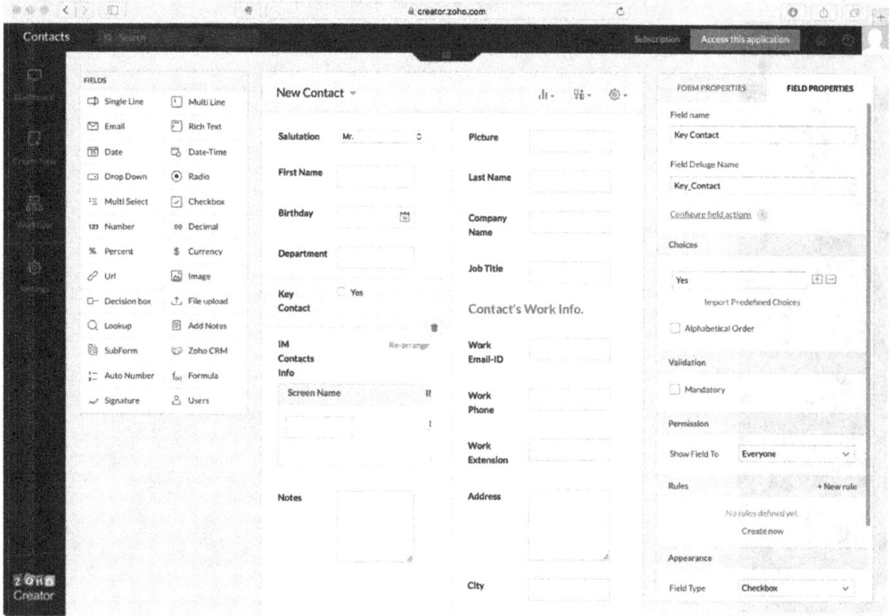

Figure 3-25. *Changing field properties*

4. Run the app by clicking on the *Access This Application* button on top right of the page. You will see the newly added *Key Contact* field displayed in the form and you can select it for any contact that is deemed a key contact (Figure 3-26).

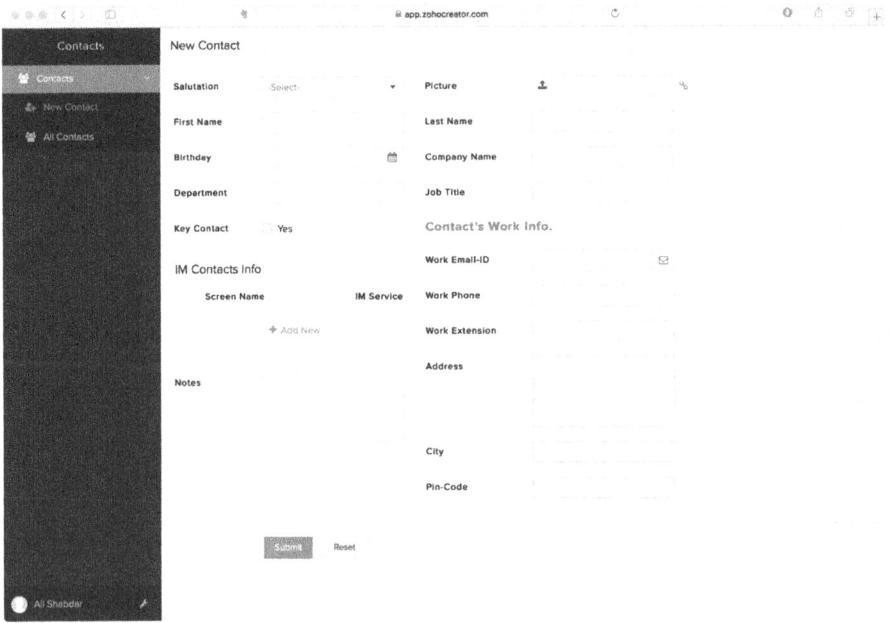

Figure 3-26. *Key Contact checkbox ready to be selected*

Great work so far! Now let's make sure that the *Key Contact* field is shown in the report as well. That way, at a glimpse of an eye, you can see who the key contact is.

Follow these steps to add the *Key Contact* field (or column) to the *All Contacts* report:

1. Enter Edit mode and click on the *Dashboard* button on the left sidebar. Make sure the *Reports* tab is selected (Figure 3-27).

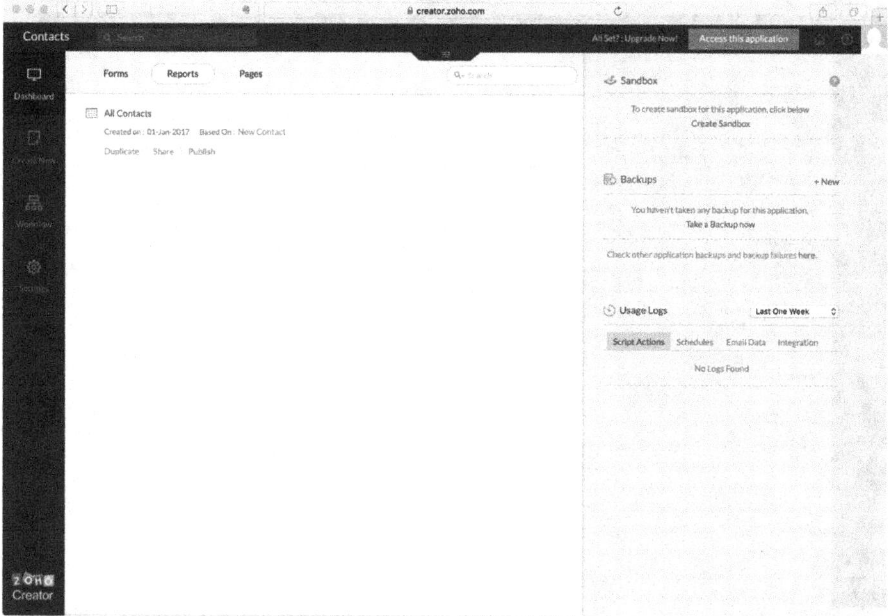

Figure 3-27. *List of reports in Edit mode*

2. Click on *All Contacts* in the *Reports* tab. The *Report Settings* page loads with the list of the display columns in the report (Figure 3-28).

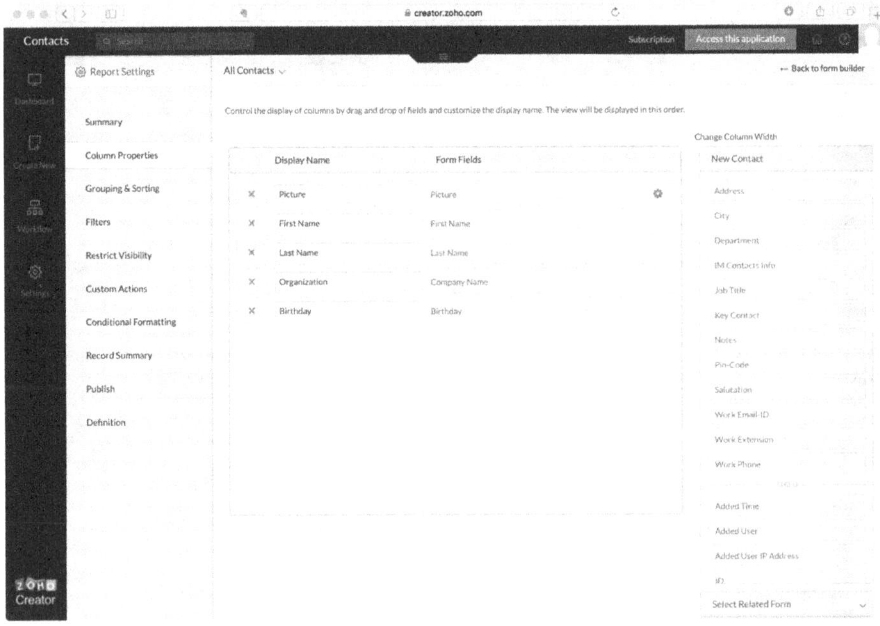

Figure 3-28. *Reports Settings page*

3. On the list of available columns on the right side of the page, find *Key Contact* and drag it to the middle of the page. Then drop it in the empty space after the last column. *Key Contact* will appear in the bottom of the list of display columns (Figure 3-29).

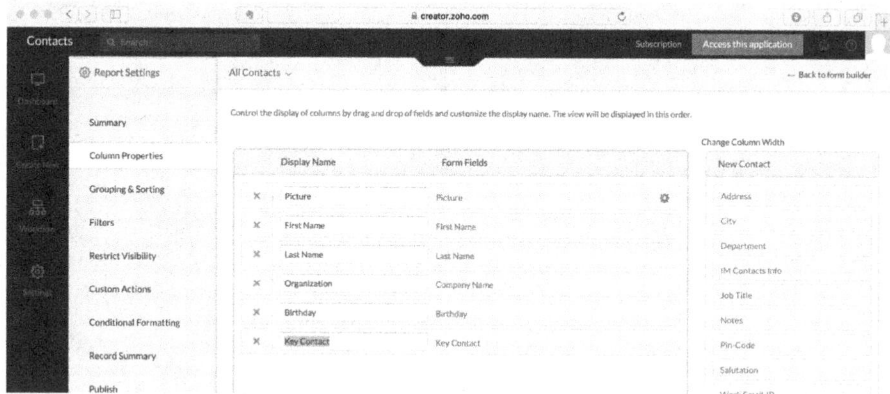

Figure 3-29. *Key Contact added to the display columns*

4. Run the app. You can see that the *Key Contact* column is added to the end of the list (Figure 3-30).

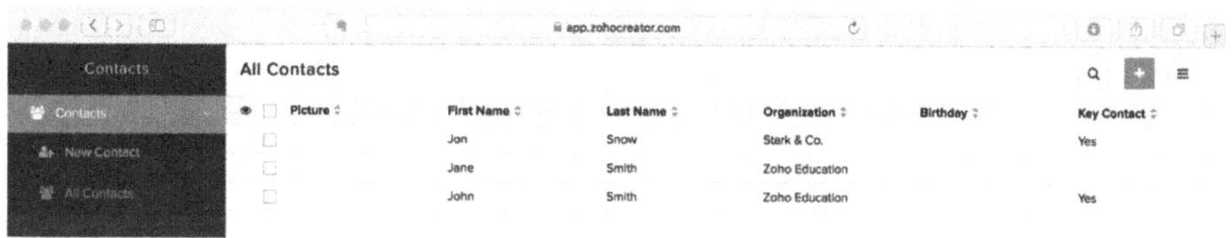

Figure 3-30. *Key Contact column added to the report*

Summary

In this chapter, you created your very first Zoho Creator application using one of the ready-made apps available in the gallery. You then customized it to your needs and learned the basics of forms, reports, search, Edit mode, and fields.

The next chapter delves deeper and builds on the lessons in this chapter.

CHAPTER 4

Adding More Features to Your Second Application

In the previous chapter, you created your first application in Zoho Creator by using a pre-made contact manager application and slightly customizing it. Working with pre-made applications is a very good way to start with Creator. You can learn the basics and best practices by looking at how different pieces fit together, tweaking and breaking it while referring to Creator help.

This chapter shows you how to create another application—this time from scratch—and you will learn more about the inner workings of Creator.

A Real Estate Project Inquiry App

Imagine you are working in the marketing department of a real estate development company. A new residential tower is about to launch. You speak with your team about providing a number of ways for potential buyers to reach your company and inquire about the upcoming project.

You suggest creating an inquiry form and placing it on a landing page on your web site. Then this landing page will be promoted online to your target audience (i.e., potential home buyers) in a three-month-long digital advertisement campaign.

Gathering Requirements

Interested people will click (or tap) on your online ad and land on the inquiry form. They will then will fill up the form and submit it back to you, so your sales team can contact them, provide more information, and hopefully make a booking.

You find out from your team that the inquiry form needs to collect the contact information of the visitors (i.e., leads), their property preferences, and basic information about their mortgage plans. The sales and finance departments both need to receive the inquiries immediately to be able to contact prospects without wasting any time.

The sales manager tells you that inquiries made via phone calls to the office or sales team should also be captured. This means that sales people need access to the inquiry form on their computers and phones.

A. Shabdar, *Mastering Zoho Creator*, DOI 10.1007/978-1-4842-2907-1_4

A last request from the Finance team indicates that they need a custom report for mortgage only inquiries.

To recap the requirements, you need an app that:

- Is available on desktop, phone, and web environments
- Has an inquiry form as the only way of inputting data
- Collects the contact information, property preferences, and mortgage information of an interested party
- Sends submitted information to the sales and finance departments
- Provides the Finance team with a customized report focused on mortgage-related inquiries

Mockup Design

Based on the requirements gathered from the concerned departments, you can work on a mockup (or wireframe), which is a rough idea of how the inquiry form should look.

■ **Note** Don't forget to obtain written agreements about the requirements and the mockup before proceeding. This way you ensure that the internal clients (the Sales and Finance teams) are on the same page regarding the features and basic elements of the app. This will minimize the time spent on needless changes to the app down the road, simply caused because the requirements were not defined and communicated to the concerned parties properly.

Figure 4-1 shows a mockup of the inquiry form.

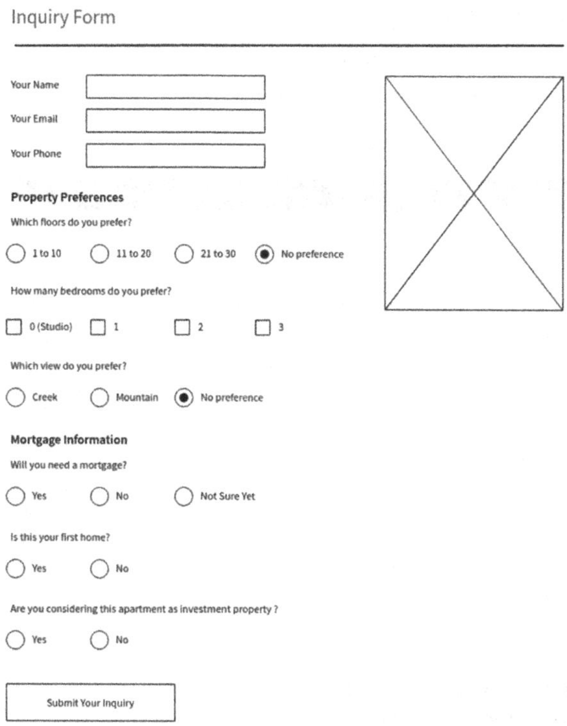

Figure 4-1. *Inquiry form mockup*

■ **Note** The mockup shown in Figure 4-1 was designed using MockFlow (`https://mockflow.com/`). You used MockFlow very lightly in Chapter 2. It's a good habit to prepare a mockup of the app. It gives you a visual representation of the real app so you can share it with colleagues and other stakeholders for review and sign-off.

Now that we have the requirements gathered and a mockup ready, let's get to work right away.

Creating a New Application

As mentioned in the beginning of the chapter, you will be creating an app from scratch this time. Although Zoho Creator has a host of useful apps to start with, there are times when it is easier and better to start from scratch.

This is especially true when you start with a small app, such as the inquiry form you'll be building here, and as your requirements grow, the complexity of the apps grow with it too, allowing you to add exactly what you need and avoid using existing features that you don't need.

To create an app from scratch, follow these steps:

1. Open Zoho Creator (if you haven't already) by opening `http://creator.zoho.com`. You will see a list of your applications (Figure 4-2).

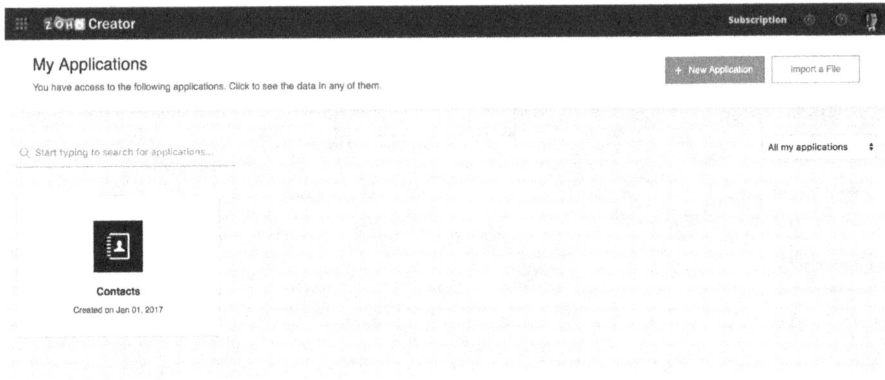

***Figure 4-2.** Zoho Creator home page (logged in)*

2. On the *My Applications* page, click on the (green) *New Application* button on the top-right side of the screen. A list of premade apps appears on the screen (Figure 4-3).

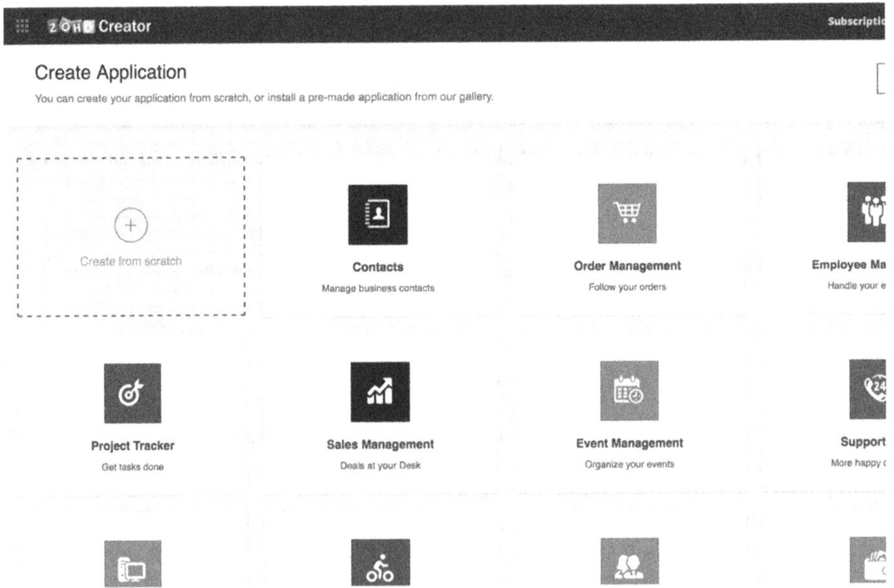

***Figure 4-3.** Creating a new application*

3. Click on the first button, called *Create from Scratch*. A small dialog box opens asking for the name of the new application (Figure 4-4).

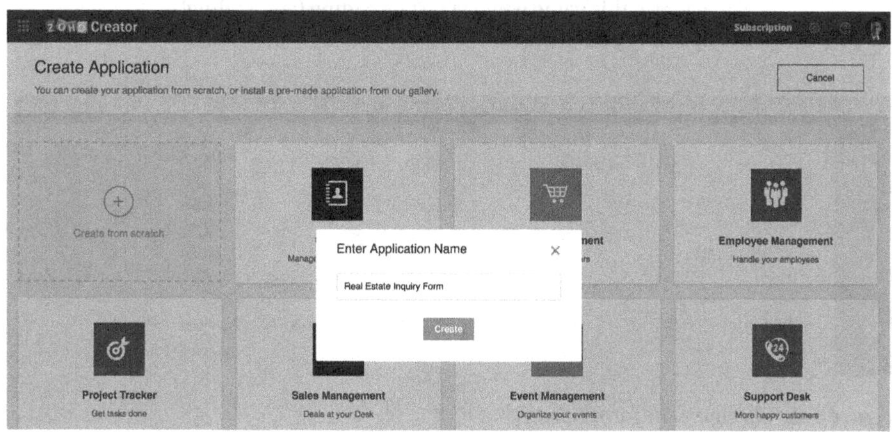

Figure 4-4. *Entering a name for the new application*

4. Type in *Real Estate Inquiry Form* and click *Create*. A new app gets created and will open in Edit mode (Figure 4-5). You used Edit mode in the previous chapter. This time, the form (in the middle) is empty and is waiting for you to add elements on it.

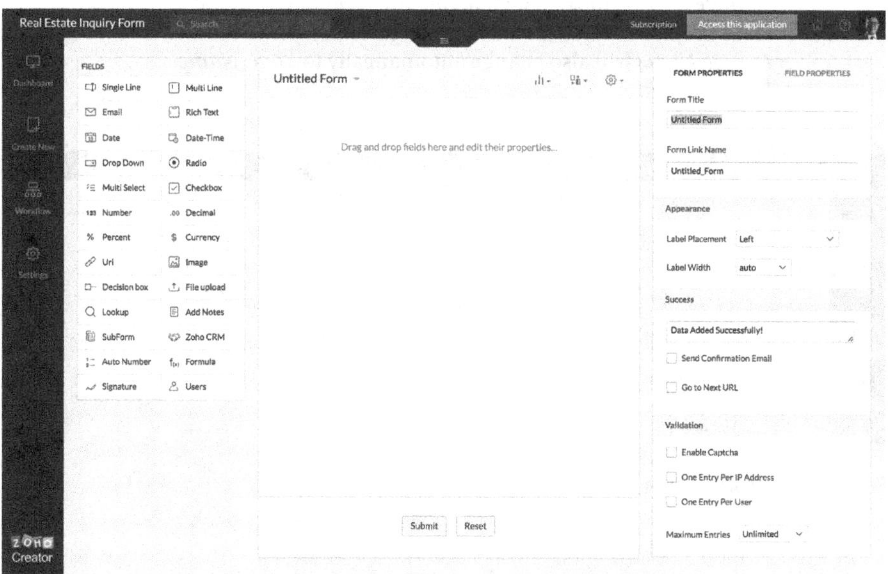

Figure 4-5. *New application in Edit mode*

5. First off, on the *Form Properties* tab (on the right), change the *Form Title* to *Inquiry Form*. Notice how the next field, *Form Link Name* changes to *Inquiry_Form* (Figure 4-6). Leave it as it is. You will use this value when you start coding (yes, coding!) in the upcoming chapters.

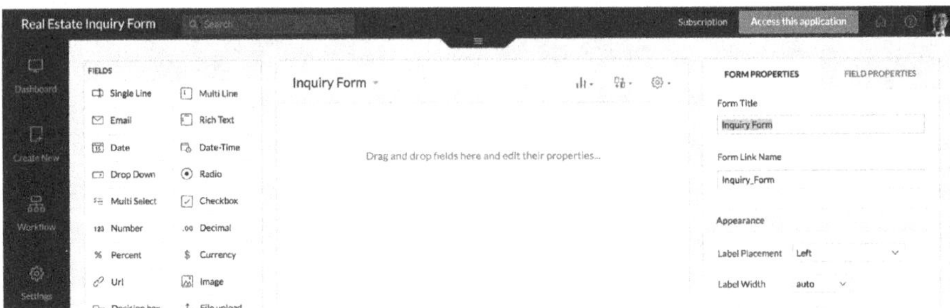

Figure 4-6. *Changing the form title*

Note When you change values, such as of the *Form Title* or *Form Link Name*, the changes are saved automatically. There is no *"Save"* button in Edit mode in Creator. This is rather handy, but be careful you don't change your values by accident.

---

6. Continue by dragging the first element (field) to the form, a *Single Line* textbox, and changing the *Field name* on the *Field Properties* tab to *Your Name* (Figure 4-7). The *Field Deluge Name* will also change automatically to *Your_Name*. Leave it as is.

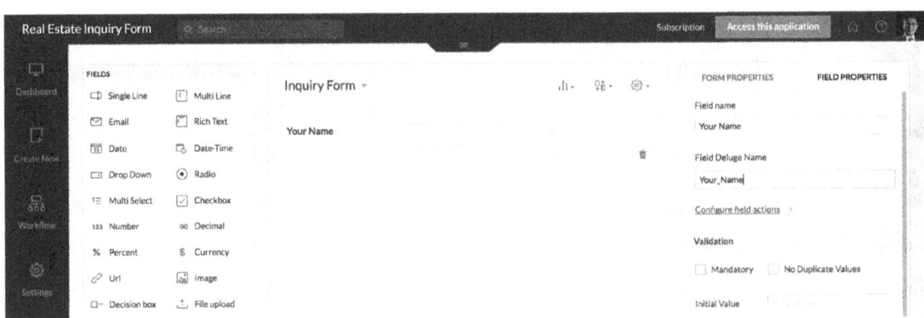

Figure 4-7. *Renaming the textbox*

7. You want the user to enter the name for every inquiry submitted, so you must make it mandatory. Check the *Mandatory* checkbox under *Validation*. A red asterisk will appear next to the textbox label on the form, which indicates that it's a mandatory field (Figure 4-8).

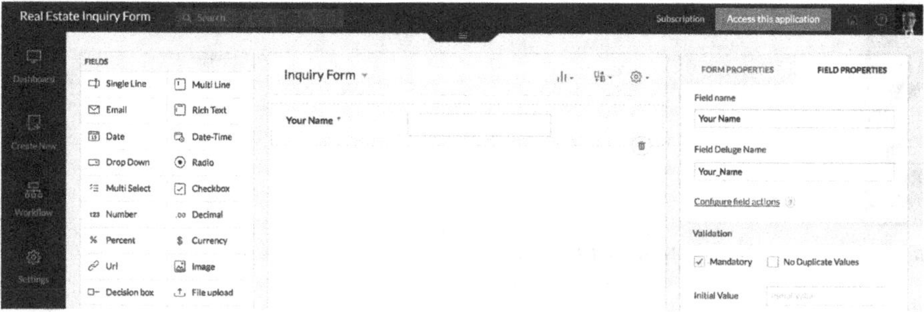

Figure 4-8. *Making the Your Name field mandatory on the form*

8. Next, add an *e-mail* field to the form, rename it *Your Email*, and make it *mandatory* (Figure 4-9).

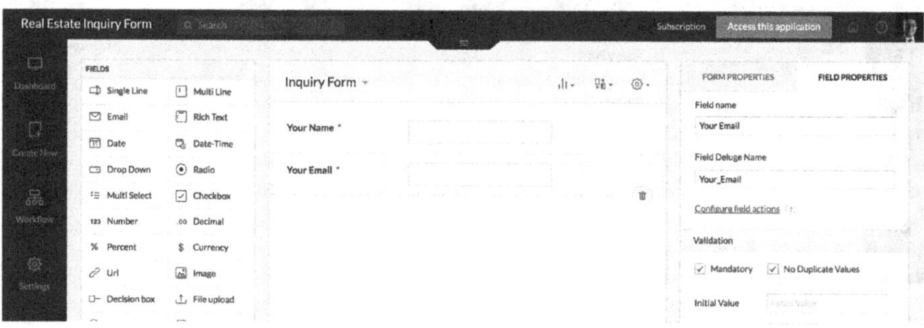

Figure 4-9. *Adding an e-mail field to the form*

9. Add another text field and name it *Your Phone*. This one doesn't need to be mandatory (Figure 4-10).

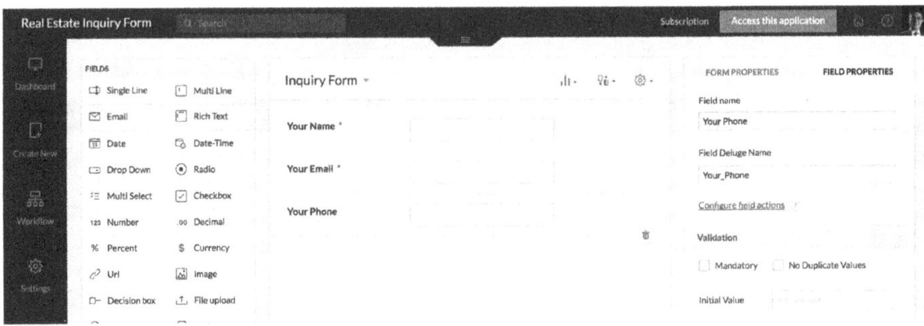

Figure 4-10. *Adding a phone field*

10. To create a separate section of the form where you ask property related questions, add an *Add Notes* fields to the form. A placeholder will appear on the form reading *Add your Note here...* (Figure 4-11).

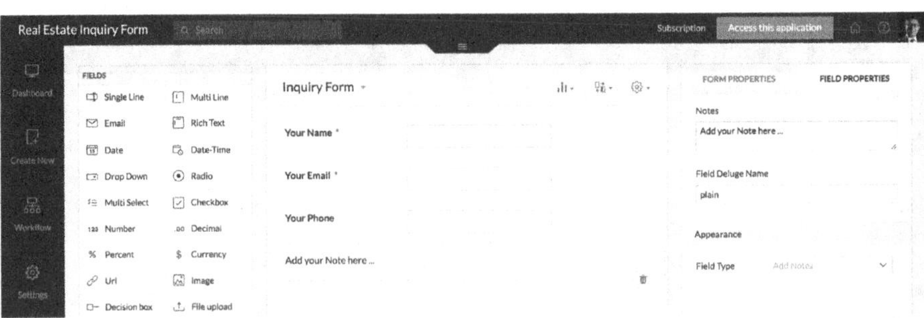

Figure 4-11. *Add Notes field*

11. Click on the Notes field or on the Notes box on the *Field Properties tab.* A text editor box will appear where you can enter formatted text. Enter *Property Preferences* and click the *B* (for bold) button on the toolbar to make the text bold (Figure 4-12). Then click *Done* to go back to the form.

Figure 4-12. *Adding note as a section separator to the form*

12. Now, add a *radio* field to the form. Radio fields allow users to pick only one option from a group of options presented to them.

13. Change the Field Name to *Which floors do you prefer?*.

14. Under Choices, enter three choices: *1 to 10, 11 to 20,* and *21 to 30.*

15. Add a fourth choice by clicking on the small plus (+) button next the last choice and enter *No preference.*

16. Click on the last choice to have it selected as the default option. This means that the users must choose a floor range only if they have a preference. The result should look like Figure 4-13.

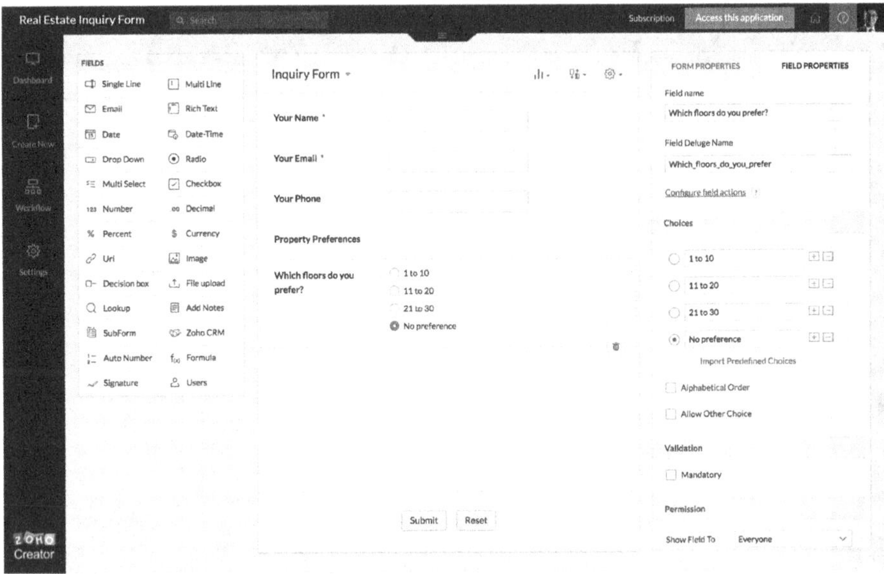

Figure 4-13. *Adding a radio field to the form*

17. Another way of collecting user input is via checkboxes. They allow users to choose multiple options from a list. Add a *checkbox* field to the form.

18. Change the field name to *How many bedrooms do you prefer?*.

19. Add four choices: *0 (Studio)*, *1*, *2*, and *3* (Figure 4-14).

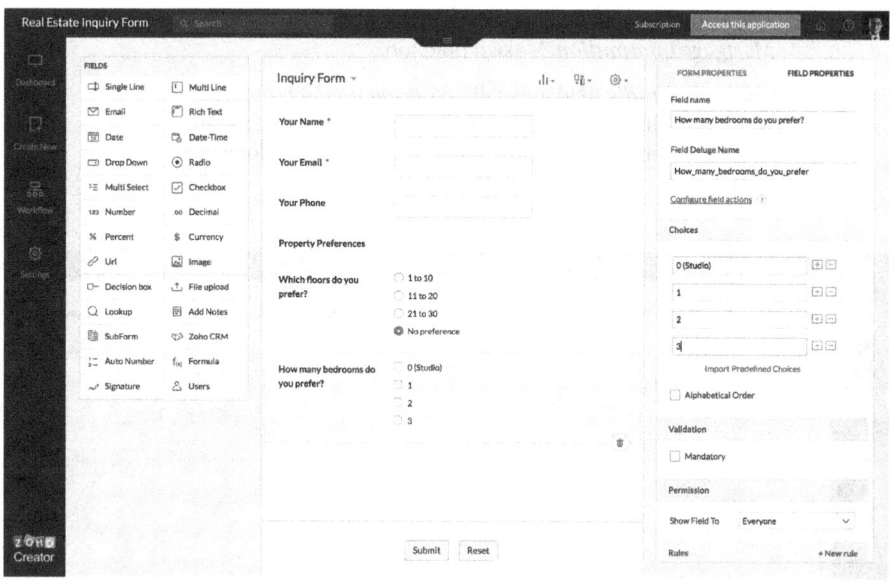

Figure 4-14. *Adding a checkbox field to the form*

20. Add another *radio* field, call it *Which View do you prefer?*, and add three choices: *Creek*, *Mountain*, and *No preference*. Select the last choice as the default (Figure 4-15).

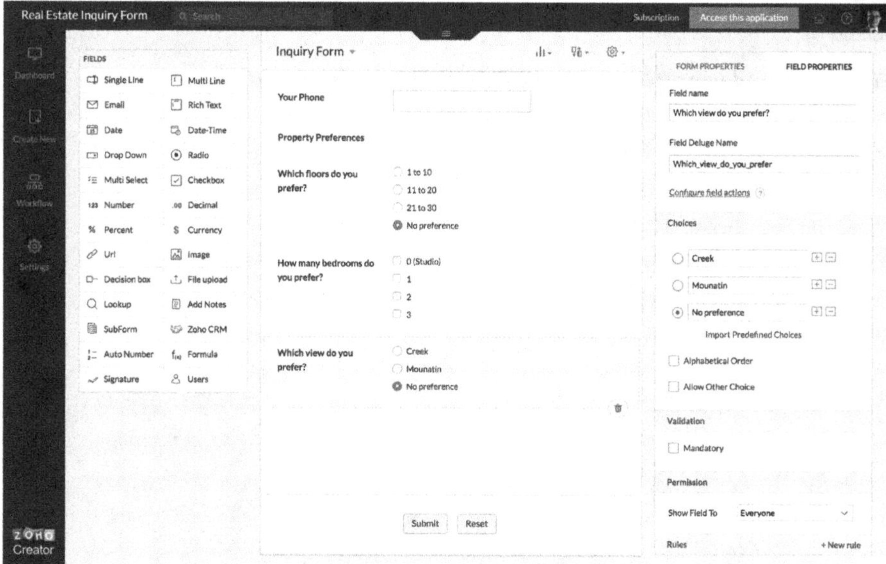

Figure 4-15. *Adding another radio field for the preferred view*

21. Add another *Notes* field as a separator and change the text to *Mortgage Information*. Make it bold too.

22. Then add a *radio* field and call it *Will you need a mortgage?* with three choices: *Yes, No,* and *Not sure yet*. None of them should be selected as the default. The result should look like Figure 4-16.

Figure 4-16. *Adding yet another radio field for the mortgage question*

23. Add another radio field and call it **Is this your first home?**. Add two obvious choices: **Yes** and **No** (Figure 4-17).

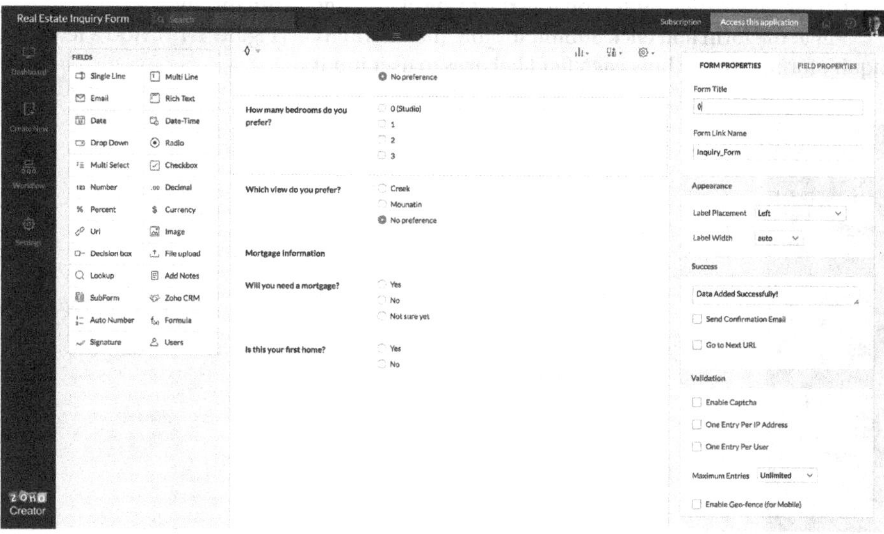

Figure 4-17. *And yet another radio field*

24. Finally, add the final element, which is another radio field. Call it *Are you considering this apartment as investment property?* and leave only two choices: *Yes* and *No* (Figure 4-18).

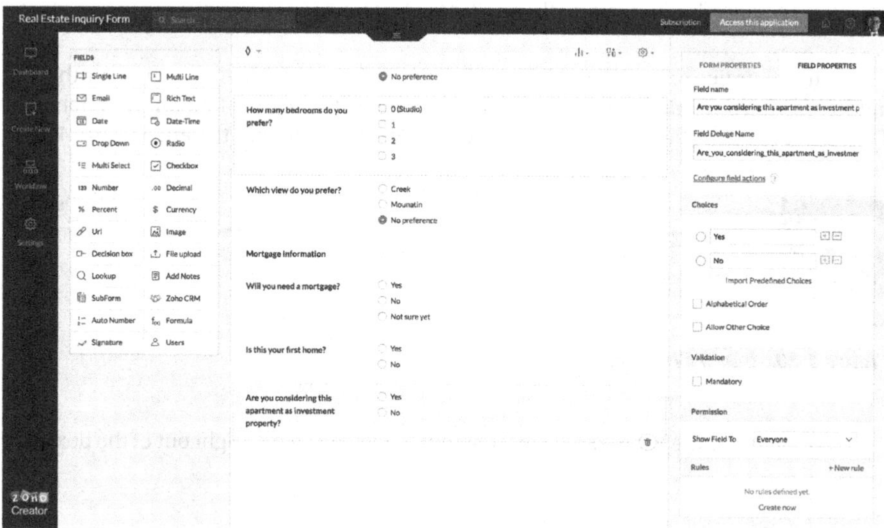

Figure 4-18. *Finally, the last radio field*

Testing the App

The form now has all the data fields required and is ready for a test run. Click the (green) *Access This Application* button on top-right side of the page to run the app.

Fill in the form and click Submit to store the information (Figure 4-19). Add a few inquiry forms and see how each field behaves to user input.

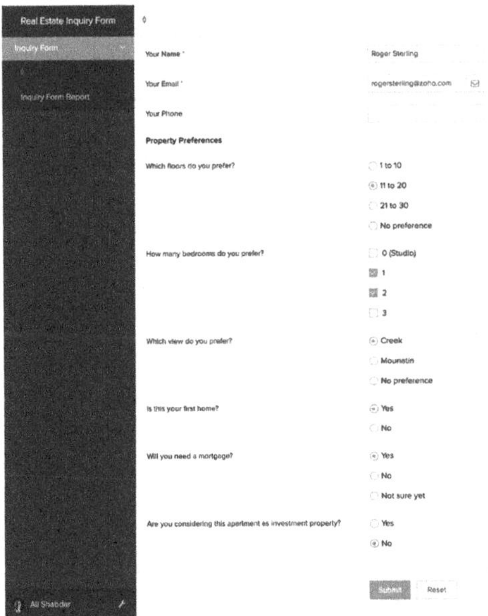

Figure 4-19. *Running and testing the app for the first time*

You will notice on the left sidebar that a report is automatically created for the inquiry form, conveniently called *Inquiry Form Report*. Click the link on the sidebar. The report opens with a tabular list of all the inquiries entered in the app (Figure 4-20).

Figure 4-20. *Inquiry Form Report*

You can order the list based on any column, filter, and search right out of the box.

Adding Basic Logic

Software can behave differently based on user actions (inputs). A simple action would be clicking a button, to which a generic software behavior performs an action, such as submits a form or opens a window.

In Creator, you can define actions to be performed based on various inputs and create complex behaviors that meet your business requirements. This is done by defining rules that trigger tasks, which automate actions based on certain logic. In this application, for example, you can have the form show or hide certain fields, based on user input, or have the application send a notification e-mail every time an inquiry is submitted.

The ability to add logic to your apps is what makes them very powerful; otherwise, they would be fancy means of entering and capturing data.

Now let's add some basic logic (rules, as Creator calls them) to the inquiry form.

To add a new rule to the inquiry form, follow these steps:

1. In Edit mode, click the field called *Will you need a mortgage?*, then on the *Field Properties* tab, click + *New Rule* under *Rules*. The New Rule dialog box will appear.

2. In the dialog box, enter *Show Investment Property* in the *Rule Name* field and enter a description about what the rule does (Figure 4-21).

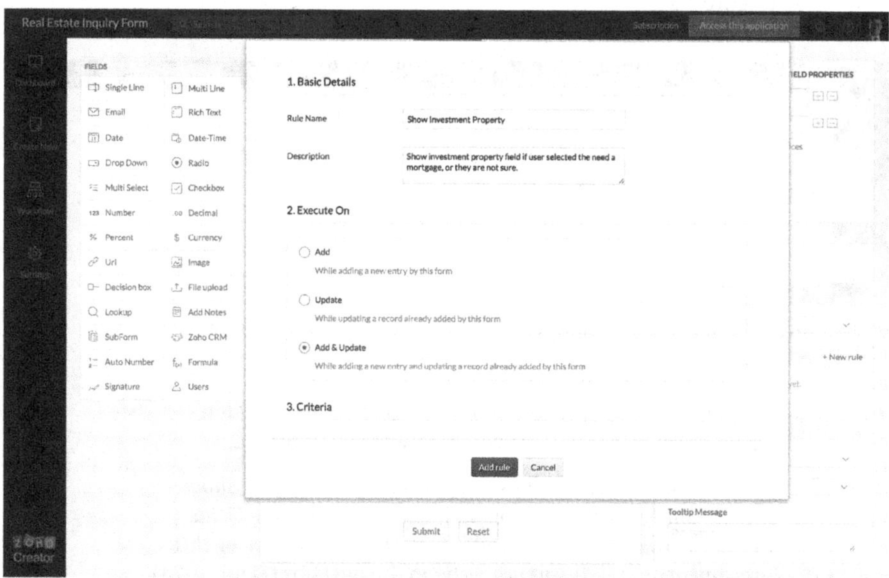

Figure 4-21. *Adding a new rule*

3. Scroll down a bit or simply click *Add Rule*. Under *Criteria*, select *Selected Records*. Then select *Will You Need a Mortgage?* in the dropdown list, *equals* in the second dropdown, and enter *Yes* in the value box.

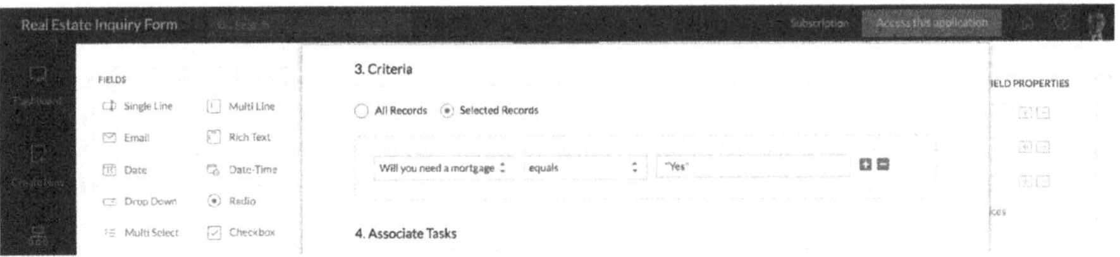

Figure 4-22. *Adding criteria*

4. Add other criteria by clicking the gray plus (+) button in front of the first one.
5. Select OR in the dropdown appearing under the first option.
6. Select *Will you need a mortgage?* for the first dropdown, *equals* for the second one, and enter *Not sure* in the value box (Figure 4-23).

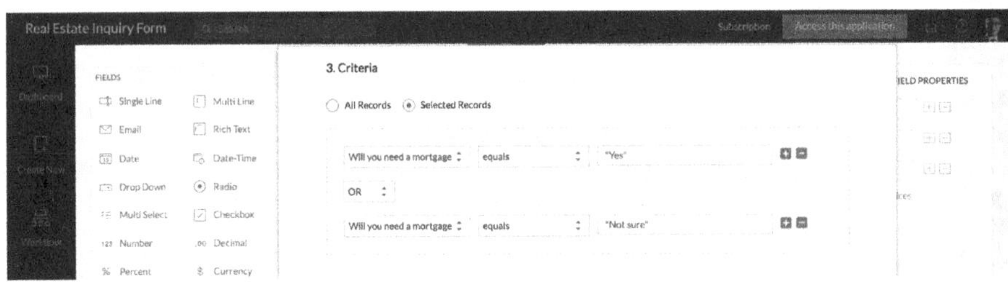

Figure 4-23. *Adding a second option*

This means if the user selected either *Yes* or *Not sure* when asked if they need a mortgage, a task will be performed.

7. Under Associate Tasks, click the plus (+) button. Enter *Show Investment Property Field* for *Task Name*, select *Show Fields* in *Choose Task dropdown*, and select *Are you considering this apartment as investment property?* in the next box (Figure 4-24).

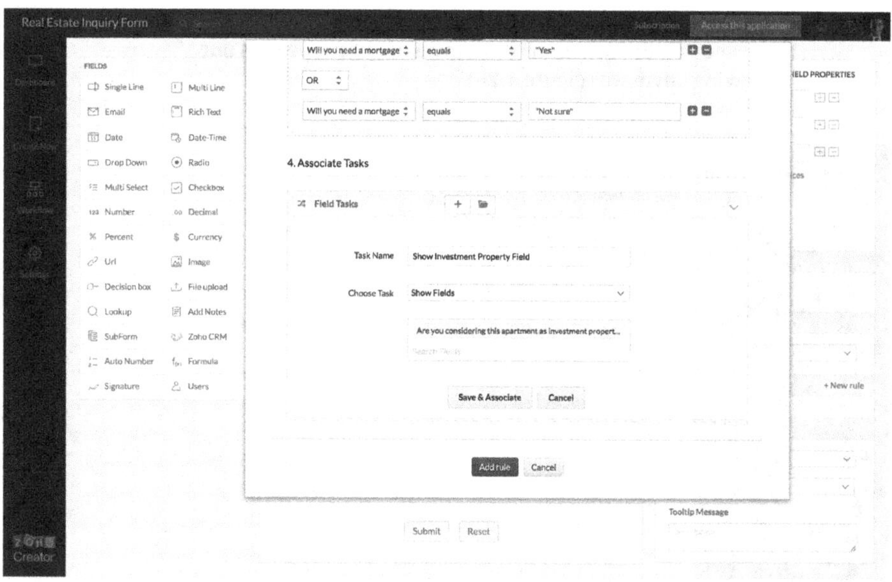

Figure 4-24. *Associating a task to trigger if the criteria is met*

8. Click *Add Rule*. The new task will be listed under the field tasks (Figure 4-25).

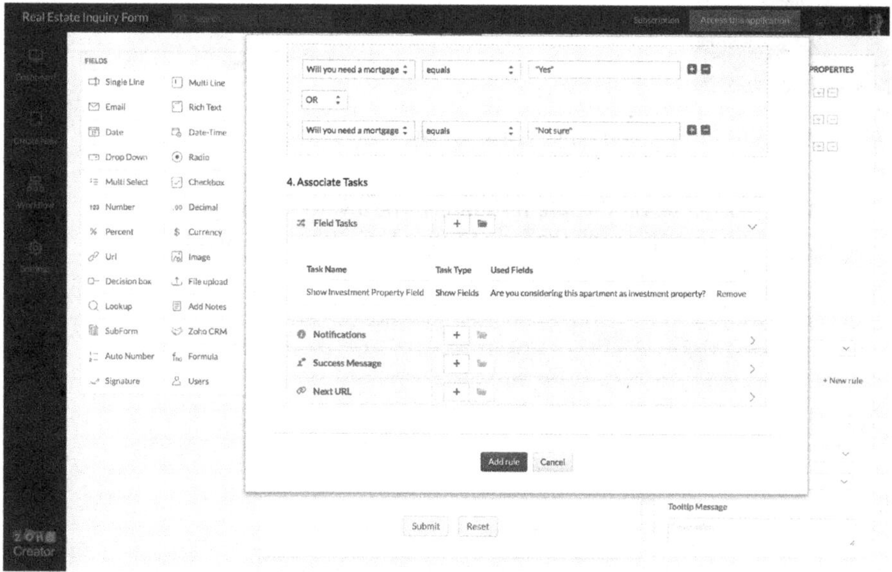

Figure 4-25. *Newly created task is listed*

9. Run the app again to test whether the rule works properly. You can see that the question about investment property is not showing anymore (Figure 4-26).

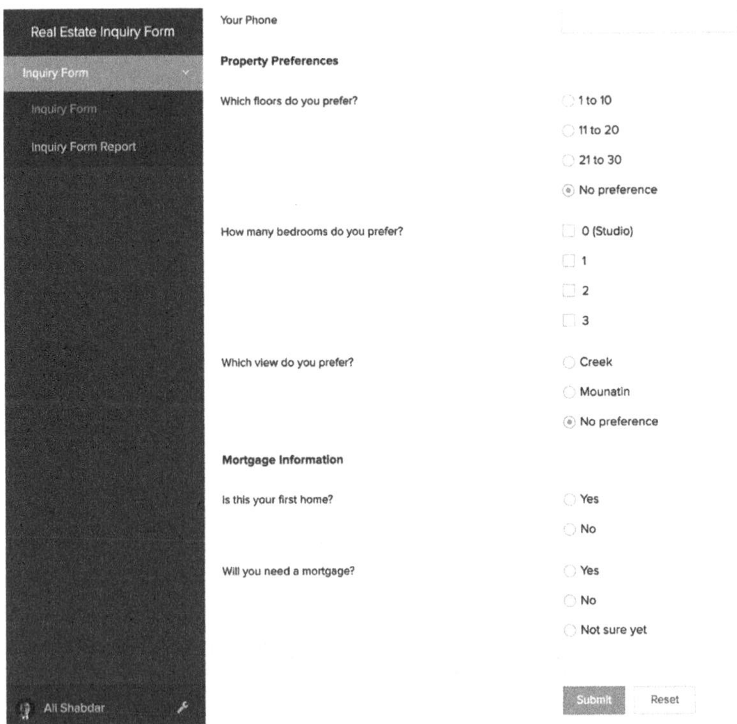

***Figure 4-26.** The investment property field is hidden by default*

10. Click the *Yes* or *Not Sure Yet* options. The investment property question appears on the form (Figure 4-27). Choosing *No* will hide the field.

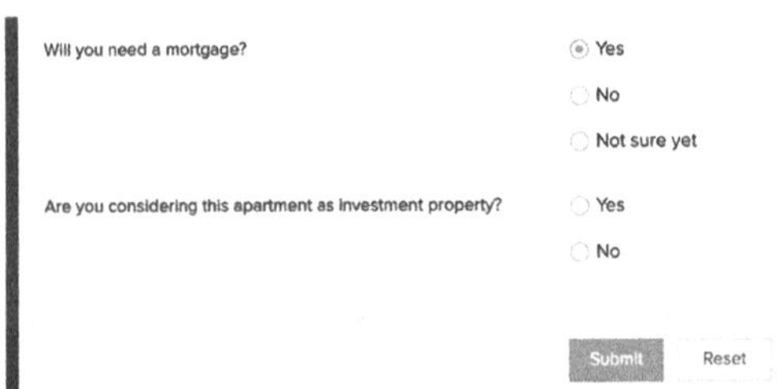

***Figure 4-27.** The investment property field appears depending on the answer to the previous question*

Showing and hiding fields based on user choice in the previous fields is very common and is used to improve usability of crowded forms and prevent users from filling in unnecessary information.

Next, you learn to enable e-mail notifications to be sent to sales and finance departments when a new inquiry is submitted.

1. In Edit mode, with the *Inquiry Form* open, click on the *Settings* (gear) icon and select *Notifications* ➤ *E-mail* (Figure 4-28).

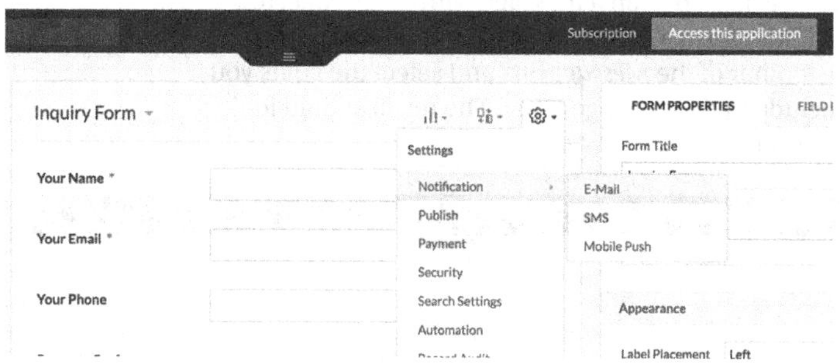

Figure 4-28. *Adding e-mail notifications to the form*

2. In the *E-mail* tab (Figure 4-29), you can compose an e-mail to be sent from a specific sender to one or more recipients with a set subject and fully customizable body.

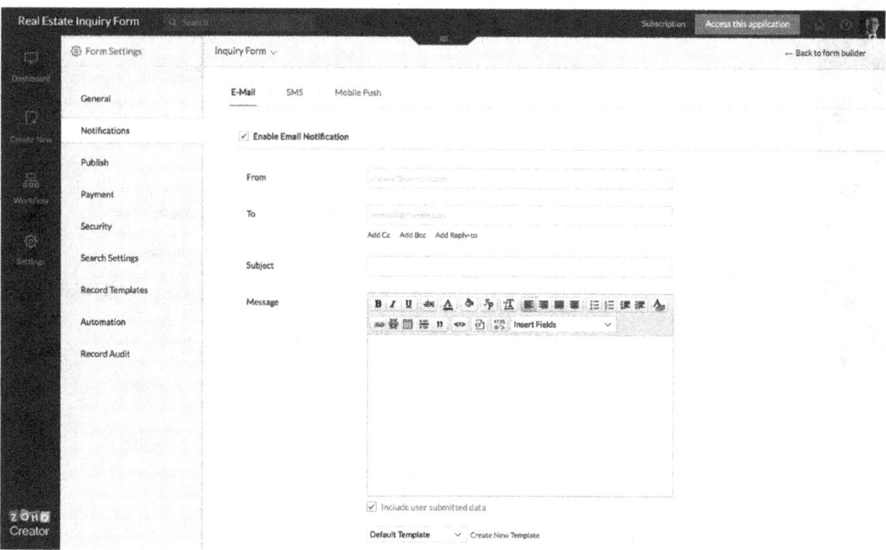

Figure 4-29. *E-mail notification creation tab*

3. Click on the *From* field and select *Admin User ID*. The current admin e-mail address will be placed in the box.

4. Click on the *To* field and type in a specific recipient for the e-mail, in this case the Sales department.

5. Since you need to send a copy to the Finance team too, add their e-mail addresses to the *Cc* field.

6. Type in *New Inquiry* for the Subject field.

7. In the *Message* box, you can a message with fields collected from the inquiry form. Click on the *Insert Fields* dropdown list on the toolbar of the *Message* box and select the fields you want to include in the message body. The result should look like Figure 4-30.

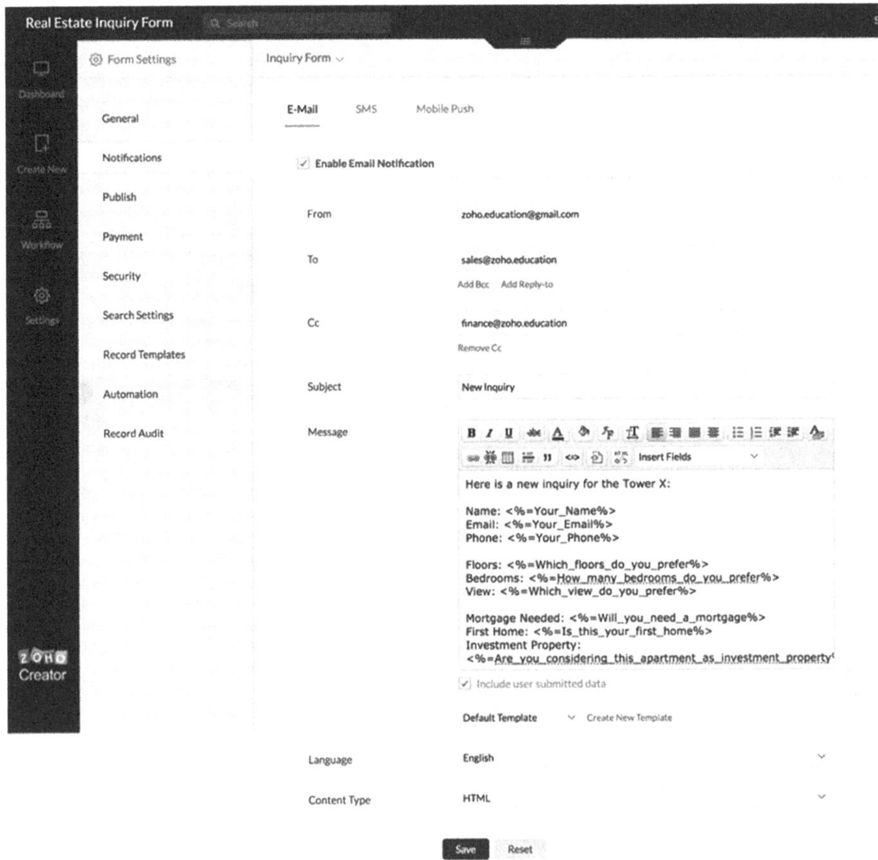

Figure 4-30. *E-mail notification ready*

8. Click Save to store the changes to the e-mail notification.

For now on, every time a new inquiry is submitted, an e-mail notification with all the information about the inquiry form will be sent to the Sales and Finance departments.

EXERCISE

Suppose you need to send different notifications to the Sales and Finance departments. The Sales team needs to see the contact information and property related fields. The Finance team, on the other hand, needs to receive the contact information and the mortgage related fields.

How do you implement this?

Hint: Use the Automation tab under Form Settings and create different sets of tasks for when a new record is submitted.

Publishing the Inquiry Form

One of the main requirements of the inquiry form application was for the visitors of your landing page to fill it in and submit the form directly on the page.

So far, the apps works perfectly on desktop and mobile devices. You now need to give Internet users access to the form. For this, you simply need to publish the form. That is it!

To publish the inquiry form, in Edit mode, open *Form Settings* ➤ *Publish*. A message will be shown indicating that the form is not published yet (Figure 4-31). Click the *Publish* button to publish the form.

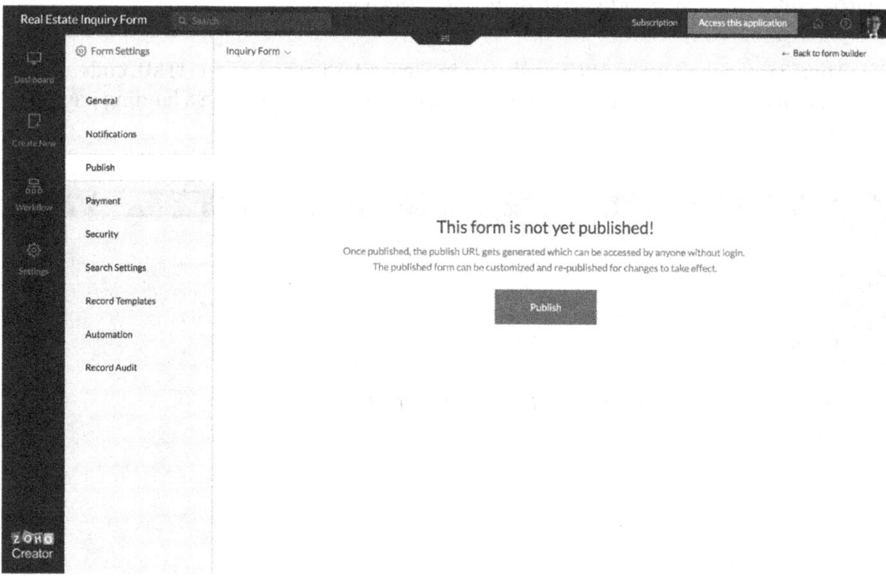

Figure 4-31. *Publishing a form*

Once the form is published, a pane will appear with two tabs—Publish URL and Embed URL. Below the link is a preview of how the form will look to the end user. You can copy this link under Publish URL (Figure 4-32) and distribute it to anyone. The link basically opens a page with the inquiry form in the middle. This is great for sending the form via e-mail (or other messaging service), similar to surveys, and asking recipients to submit forms easily.

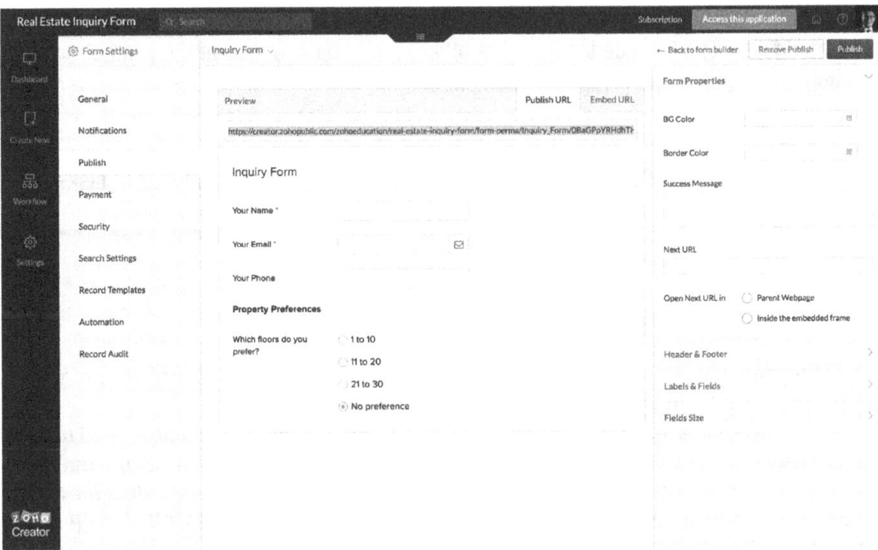

***Figure 4-32.** Accessing the Publish URL of a published form*

There is also the *Embed URL*, as shown in Figure 4-33, which is an HTML code snippet that you (or your web developer) can use to embed the form in a landing page or any web page for that matter.

***Figure 4-33.** Accessing the Embed URL of a published form*

Creating a New Report

One last thing you need to do is design a customized report for the Finance team, so that they can easily find relevant information.

To create a new report, follow these steps:

1. While in Edit mode, on the left sidebar, click the *Create New* button and select *Report* in the context menu. The *New Report* page opens (Figure 4-34).

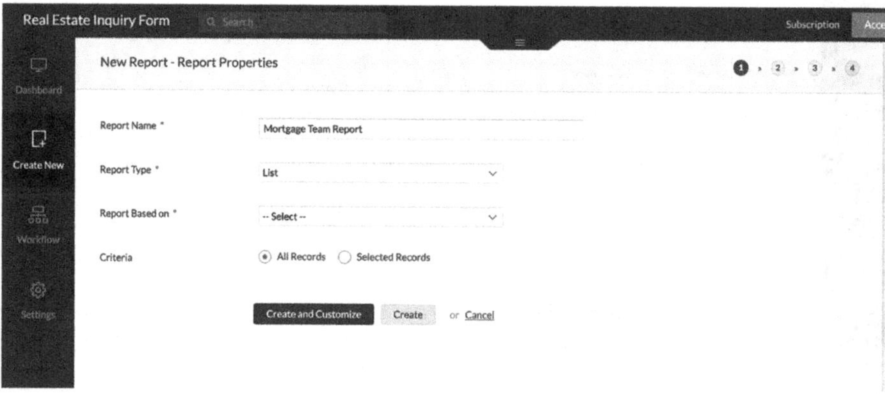

Figure 4-34. *Creating a new report*

2. Enter *Mortgage Team Report* in the *Report Name.*
3. Select *List* in the *Report Type* dropdown list.
4. Select *Inquiry Form* in the *Report Based on* dropdown. Another dropdown shows up called *Place This Report Under*. Leave it as is (Figure 4-35).

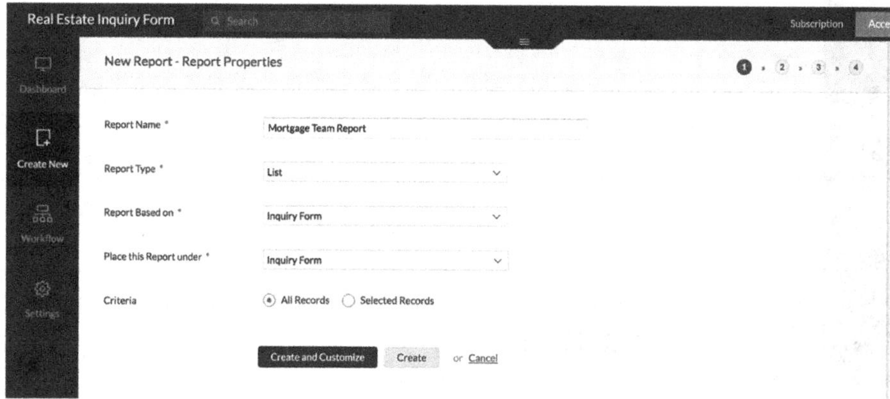

Figure 4-35. *Creating a new report, continued*

5. Click the *Selected Records* radio button. Criteria boxes appear (Figure 4-36).

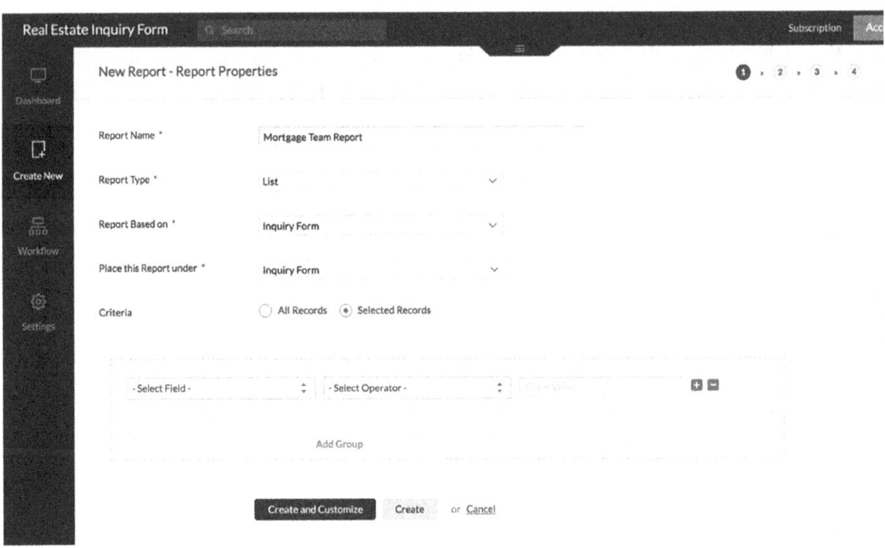

Figure 4-36. *Choosing to show the selected record in the report*

6. Select *Will you need a mortgage?* in the first dropdown, *not equal to* in the second one, and enter *No* in the value box (Figure 4-37).

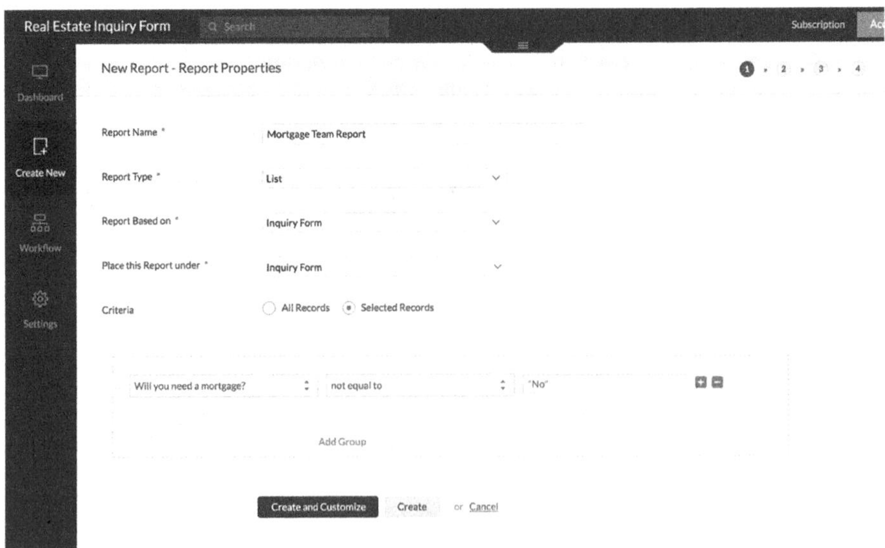

Figure 4-37. *Omit only the people who specifically indicated they are not interested in a mortgage*

7. Click *Create and Customize.* The column properties page will open and ask you to choose which columns to show in the report (Figure 4-38). You can also change the label for each column.

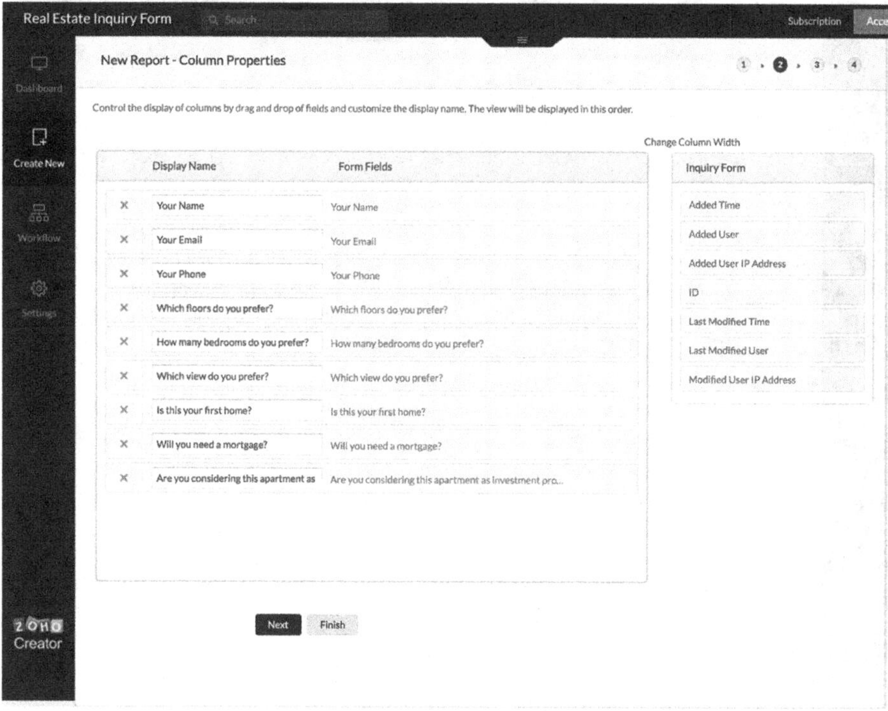

Figure 4-38. *Report column properties page*

8. Remove all the property-related fields and add *Added Time* to the columns from the list of columns available on the right side of the list. The result should look like Figure 4-39.

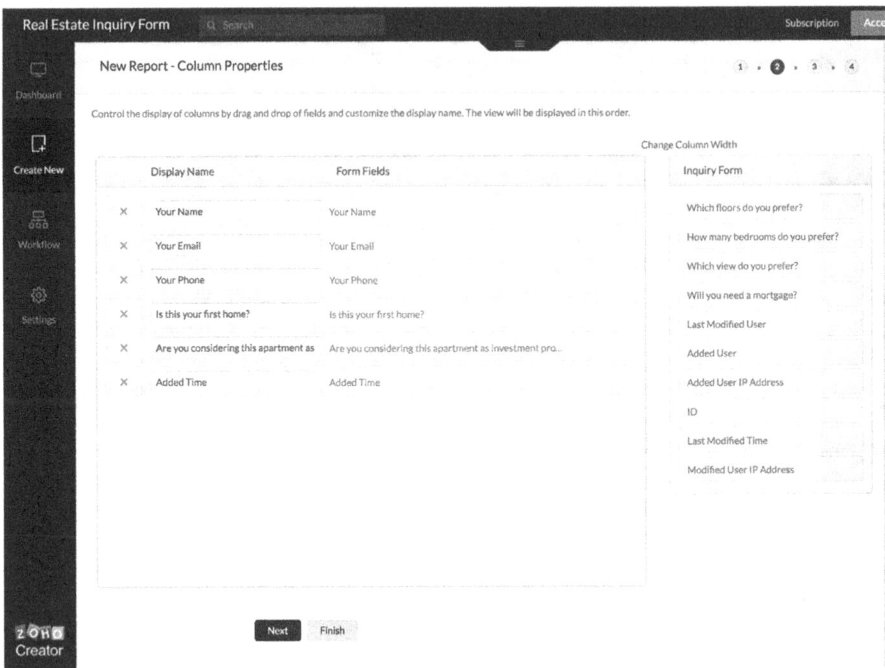

Figure 4-39. *Leaving only the columns relevant to mortgage*

9. Click *Next* to continue. The *Grouping & Sorting* page opens, as shown in Figure 4-40.

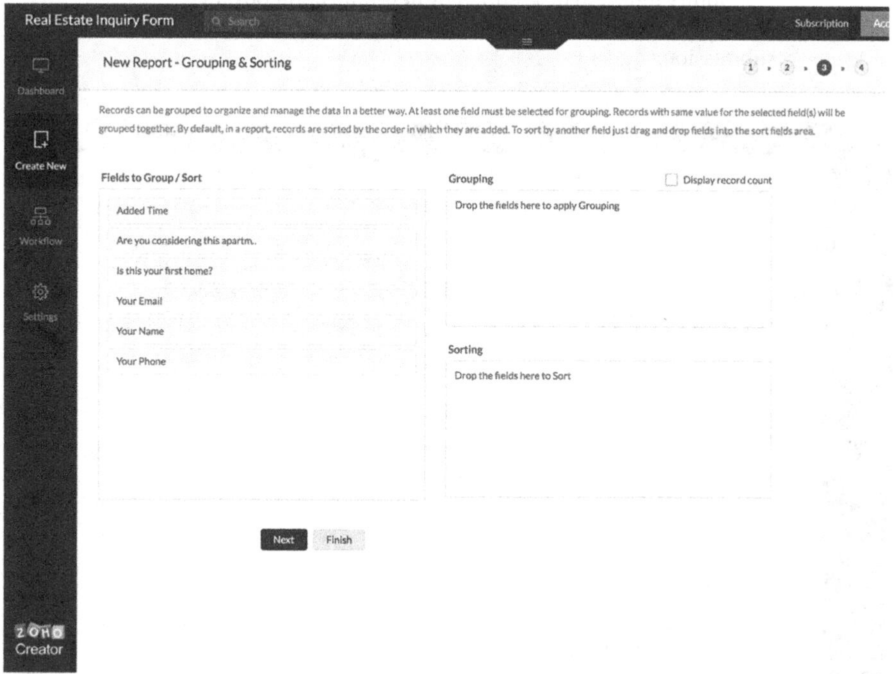

Figure 4-40. *Grouping and sorting page*

10. From the fields list on the left, drag the *Is this your first home?* field to the *Groups* box on the right. Also, drag and drop *Added Time* to the *Sorting* box (Figure 4-41). This will allow the inquiry report to be grouped by first-time homebuyers and the rest while being sorted according to the time of the submission.

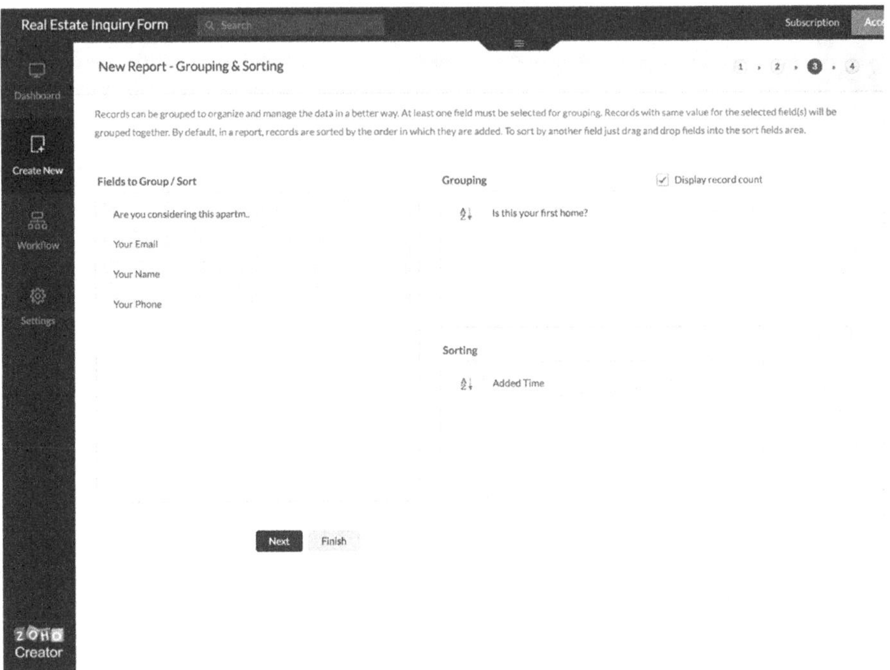

Figure 4-41. *Adjusting the grouping and sorting for the report*

11. Click *Next* to continue. The *Filters* page appears (Figure 4-42). On this page, you can indicate which columns to filter the report on.

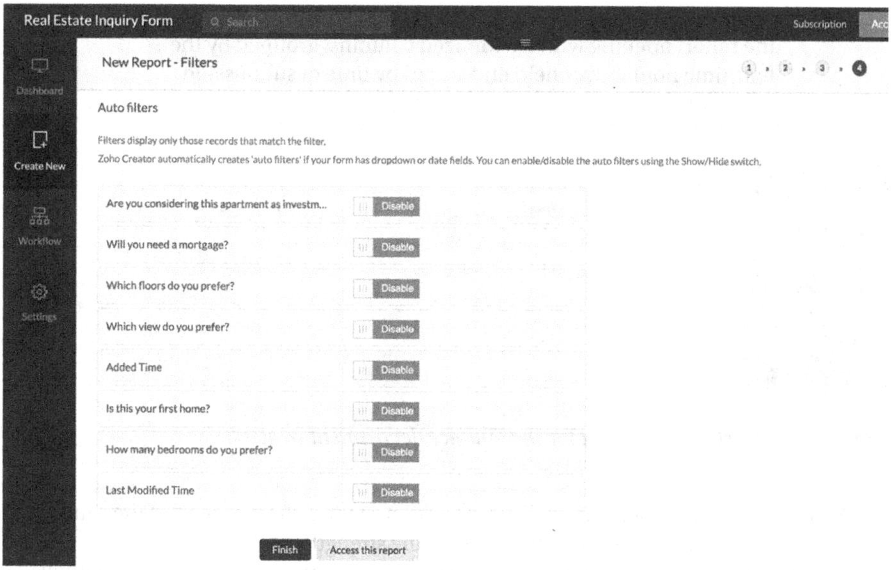

Figure 4-42. *Filters page*

12. Turn on one filter: Are you considering this apartment as investment property? (Figure 4-43).

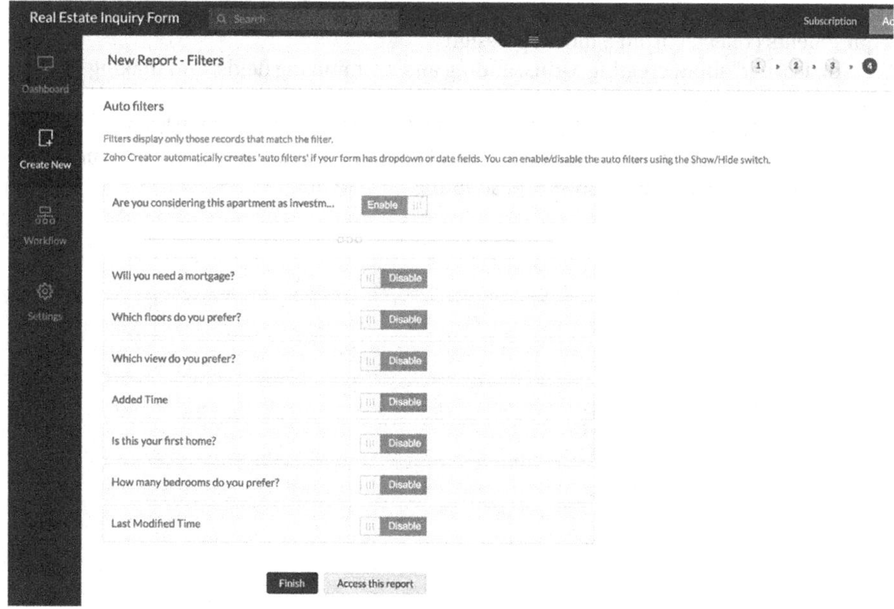

Figure 4-43. *Enabling filters for specific columns in the report*

13. Then click Access This Report to run the report. You can see the report opening with customized columns, grouped by the first-time homebuyer field and sorted by time of submission (Figure 4-44).

Figure 4-44. *Customized report for the Finance department in action*

You can create many customized reports and provide different views of the same data to different target audiences. This is one of the strengths of Zoho Creator.

You start by creating forms that collect structured information via various channels. Then you create complex reports, each meeting the needs of specific groups of people or departments in the organization.

Summary

In this chapter, you created your send application, this time from scratch, based on the requirements collected from a mockup design.

You learned about creating forms, adding and customizing fields, and making your app smarter using rules.

You also learned how to make a form available to the world via publishing.

The next chapters cover about security and data access, and then delve into more advanced topics, such as workflows and scripting.

CHAPTER 5

Taking Your Application to the Next Level

In the previous chapter, you created a simple app sporting a single form and two reports to help a real estate company collect potential customer inquiries. The app did a good job managing information (it enabled you to add, edit, find, and show information) and notifying the sales team upon submission of a new inquiry.

However, a real-life application should perform more than just one task. It should help users manage complex datasets and automate daunting tasks. For instance, for a real estate company, such an app would maintain all property listings, client, and sales information, while providing sophisticated reports to different roles (sales executives, managers, etc.) in the company.

Although building complex apps is not easy, Zoho Creator promises that people with little to no programming experience can build business apps that address the needs of SMEs.

You learned about some of the tools Creator offers to deliver on this promise, such as forms and reports. You also learned basic automation.

In this chapter, you continue your journey of making useful apps and learn a few more essential skills in the process. You will start dipping your toes into programming and learning about Zoho's easy-to-learn scripting features.

But first, let's start getting acquainted with the tools.

Deluge

Deluge (Data Enriched Language for the Universal Grid Environment), as Zoho puts it, is an online scripting language and is the backbone of Zoho Creator. In fact, if you look behind the visual design of a Creator app, all you get is pure Deluge code and nothing else.

If you want to go beyond mere basics and create exciting Creator applications suitable for medium to large enterprises, sooner or later you will need to use Deluge.

It is a powerful and easy to learn and use scripting language and in this chapter, you will use it a little bit. In the next chapter, you learn more about Deluge.

A. Shabdar, *Mastering Zoho Creator*, DOI 10.1007/978-1-4842-2907-1_5

Listing 5-1 shows a small piece of Deluge code.

Listing 5-1. A Sample Deluge Code Snippet

```
on edit
{
  update
  (
    type  = submit
    displayname  =  "Update"
  )
  cancel
  (
    type  = cancel
    displayname  =  "Cancel"
  )
}
```

For those with previous programming experience, the good news is that Deluge is easy to read and easy to learn. For the rest of us, the great news is that most of the time you either won't see the actual code as it remains in the background, or you don't need to write most of it. Creator comes with a user-friendly Code Editor and powerful *Script Builder*. It's a visual scripting tool that helps you generate code using drag-and-drop techniques and requires minimal typing.

You will see some of these in action in a bit and will learn more about it when you delve into Deluge in the next chapter.

Form Actions

Creator apps are comprised of forms and reports. The responsibility of collecting data from the user is on forms. Forms also contain application and business logic, i.e. the rules and interactions that are designed to make the application work as intended.

You (the app developer) can tell the forms how to act or what to do in different scenarios. For instance, you can tell the form, when it loads, to populate specific fields automatically or to hide some fields if a specific value is entered in another field.

■ **Note** Form actions for DB forms (that store data in CRM) are covered in this chapter. To learn about form actions for stateless forms (that don't store data in Creator), refer to the official documentations at `https://www.zoho.com/creator/help/script/form-actions-stateless-forms.html`.

Form actions are triggered for each one of the three data interactions: *Add, Edit,* and *Delete.* You can tell Creator what to do when a new record is added, or when an existing one is modified or deleted.

For each one of these, there are three actions available:

- **On Load**—Triggered when a form loads (opens)
- **On Validate**—Triggered when a form is about to get submitted, right before the actual submission
- **On Success**—Triggered when the operation is successfully done

This combination of nine places where you can put your custom code and instruct Creator what to do in each situation gives you a lot of flexibility to create complex applications. You will see how to use some of these actions in the upcoming sections.

Field Actions

To give you (the developer) more flexibility to control the behavior of your app, Field actions allow you to perform tasks at the field level. For instance, you can modify the value of a field based on a change in another field, or validate a field before the form gets submitted, even before the validation action of the form is called.

Field actions are divided into two types:

- **On user input script**—Triggered every time a user, or another script (code), changes the value of a field
- **On update script**—Triggered when the value of a field is updated in the database (the app)

Automating Operations

You got a quick look at how automation works in the previous chapter by setting up e-mails to be sent to the sales team once an inquiry was submitted by a user. In this section, you take a closer look at this important feature.

In Creator, automation is done by using rules and tasks. Tasks are the actions that need to be automated (e.g., sending an e-mail) and rules tell Creator to perform the tasks (e.g., upon a successful record addition).

Rules can be triggered (executed) in these occasions:

- Once a new record is added
- Once an existing record is updated

You can specify rules to execute these occasions based on predefined criteria, i.e. when a set of conditions is met. Each rule can execute one or more tasks.

There are three types of tasks:

- **Field tasks** allow you to:
    - Show/hide form elements (fields and buttons)
    - Enable/disable form elements
    - Set the value of forms fields

- **Form tasks** allow you to:
  - Send e-mails, text messages, or push notifications to specific users
  - Show customized success messages after the form submission
  - Redirect users to a specific URL after form submission
- **Subform tasks** allow you to hide/show the subform

Schedules

Zoho Creator offers yet another powerful tool, the *Scheduler,* which provides you with tools to set automated, timed actions for tasks that need to be repeated at certain intervals.

Scheduler can make an app shine. For example, using a Creator app, it can send daily e-mail reporting to the team, send and receive data from external data sources to interact with third-party software, and send people in the client database birthday messages on their birthdays.

There three types of schedules in Zoho Creator:

- **Form schedules**, which are event schedules based on date/time information found in a form, e.g. a birthdate, an appointment date, a date range, etc.
- **Report schedules**, which are scheduled based on a report, e.g. to send monthly sales reports to an accountant or a weekly list of appointments to a doctor.
- **Custom schedules**, which are custom events with set dates and intervals, e.g. monthly database cleanup, nightly data import from an external source, or meeting reminders.

Note You'll see how to use the Report Schedule later in this chapter. To learn more about the other types of schedules, refer to the official documentation at: `https://www.zoho.com/creator/help/schedules/scheduler.html`.

A Smart(ish) Careers App

To see these automation capabilities in action, you are going to create a simple Careers app. The Careers app lists the current job openings at your company and provides job applicants with an efficient means to apply for their favorite position.

What sets the Careers app apart from other simple single-form apps is that it has a couple of neat features, thanks to Creator's automation tools. It will ask the applicants questions relevant to the job they are applying for, acting as a mini-interview.

Also, if applicants indicate that they have skills that are more interesting to the HR department, the app sends an immediate notification to HR, so they can act accordingly.

Finally, it will send a daily report of the applicants to the HR department.

Creating the Careers App

Let's get to work and create the Careers app.

1. On the Creator home page (*My Applications* page), click on the *New Application* button. Then on the *Create Application* page, click *Create from Scratch.*
2. Enter *Careers* in the *Enter Application Name* dialog box and click *Create* (Figure 5-1).

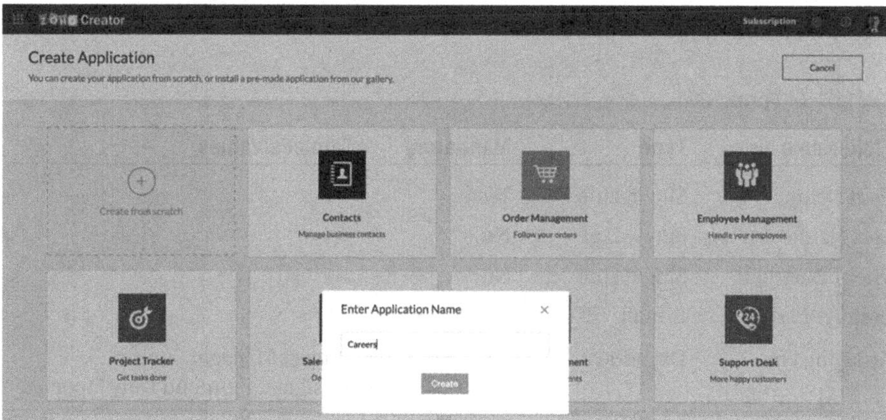

Figure 5-1. *Creating the new Careers application*

3. In Application Edit mode, add five fields to the form in the form designer (Figure 5-2). The five fields are listed in Table 5-1.

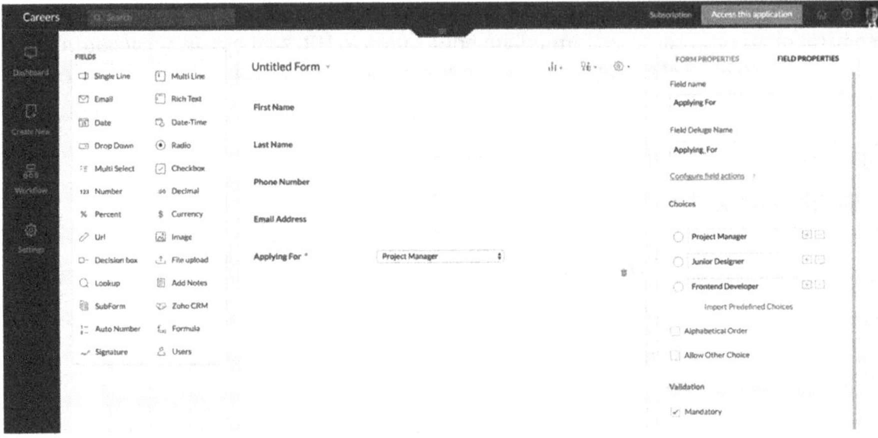

Figure 5-2. *Adding fields to the form*

Table 5-1. *Form Fields*

Field Name	Type	Mandatory	Choices/Values
First Name	Single Line	Yes	--
Last Name	Single Line	No	--
Phone Number	Single Line	No	--
Email Address	E-mail	Yes	--
Applying For	Dropdown	Yes	Project Manager, Junior Designer, Frontend Developer

4. Add a decision box to the form and set the *Field name* to *Are you a PMP (project Management Professional)?* Then change the *Field Deluge Name* to *is_PMP* (Figure 5-3).

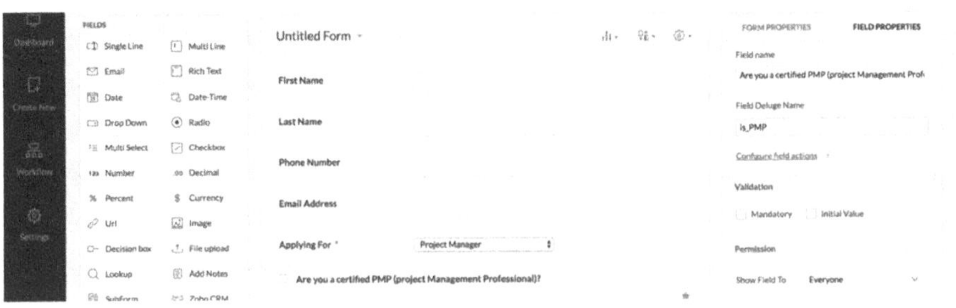

Figure 5-3. *Adding a decision box field to the form*

5. Add a radio button to the form and name it **How good are you with Adobe Creative Suite?** Then change the Field Deluge Name to **knows_Adobe** and add three choices, as shown in Figure 5-4.

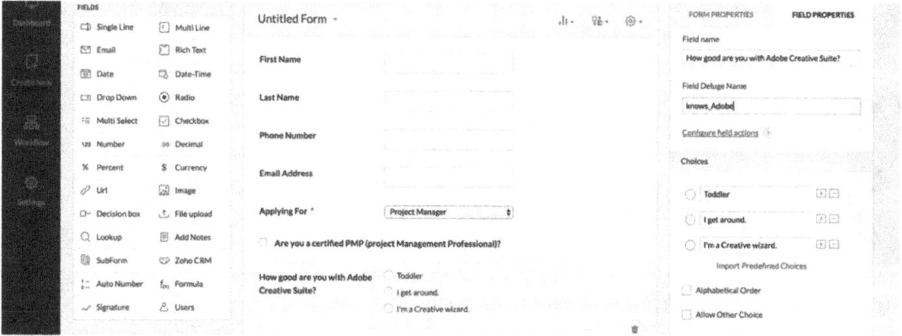

Figure 5-4. *Adding a radio field to the form*

6. Add a *Multi Select* field to the form and name it *Your Toolbox.* Then add a few options to the *Choices*, as shown in Figure 5-5.

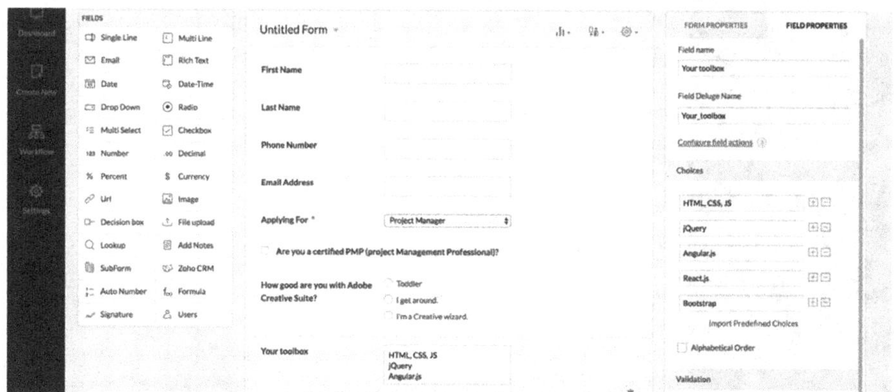

Figure 5-5. *Adding a multi-select field to the form*

7. Add a file upload to the form and name it *Upload your resume,* then change the *Field Deluge Name* to *resume* and make the field *Mandatory* (Figure 5-6).

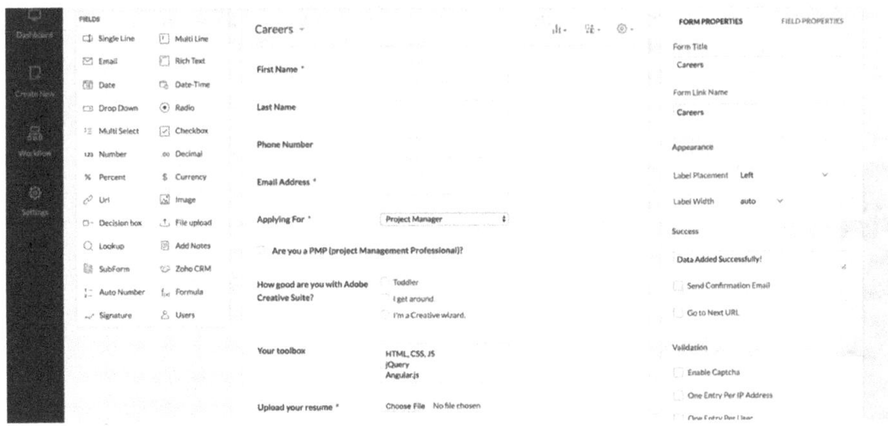

Figure 5-6. *Adding a file upload field to the form*

8. Run the application by clicking the *Access this Application* button on the top right of the screen. The application works and is ready to accept new job applications (Figure 5-7).

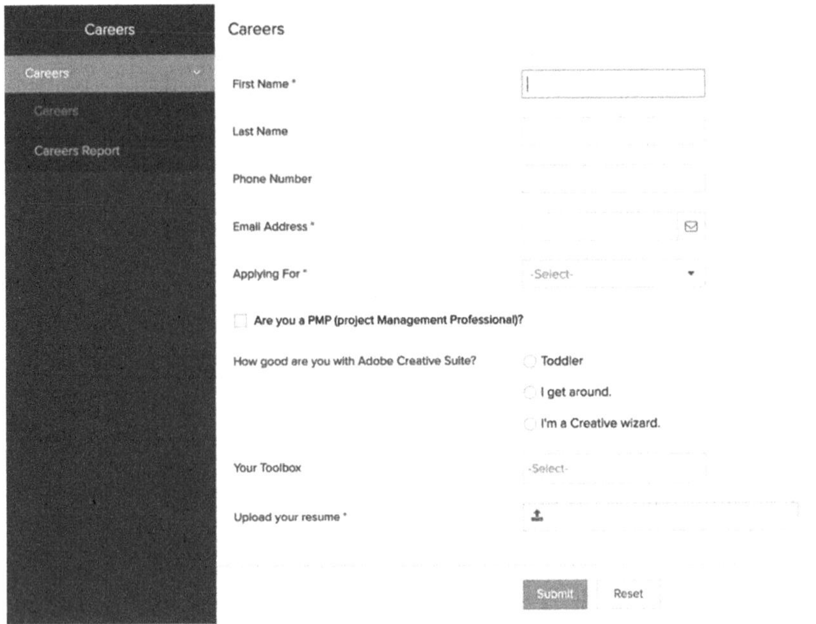

Figure 5-7. *Application running for the first time*

The app works, but there is something that is bothersome. Can you guess what it is? Read on to find out what impacts the user experience and how automation can fix it.

Go back to Edit mode after you are finished testing the first iteration of the app.

■ **Note** When building a new app or editing an existing one, run the app often to see how the app behaves and if the changes you make turn out as you intended. Switching between Edit mode and Run mode often is a simple way of debugging apps and will help you find issues as soon as they arise.

Adding Form and Field Actions

The careers app works, but there is a problem. It shows questions irrelevant to the job posting selected by the use. For instance, when an applicant applies for the Project Manager job, the user can still see the two questions intended for Junior Designer and Frontend Developer candidates. This is a design flaw and needs to be addressed.

You can fix this quite easily with *Form Actions* and by hiding the irrelevant questions based on user input.

First, all the questions must be hidden when a form loads. Then relevant question must be shown only when users select a job opening in the *Applying For* dropdown list.

Let's get to work:

1. In the form builder (Edit mode), select *Form Settings* ➤ *On Add* ➤ *Actions on Load* (Figure 5-8).

Figure 5-8. *Opening form actions when the form loads*

2. The *Workflow* page will open (Figure 5-9). From the left, you can see the Creator sidebar, a list of available actions to code for, design tools that help you write scripts, and the Code Editor (the large whitespace), where you will place/write the actual code. Drag a *hide|show* Construct from the *Design Tools* (under *Client Functions*) and drop it in the Code Editor.

Figure 5-9. Workflow environment

3. The code construct appears in the Code Editor. Select *hide* from the dropdown list (Figure 5-10).

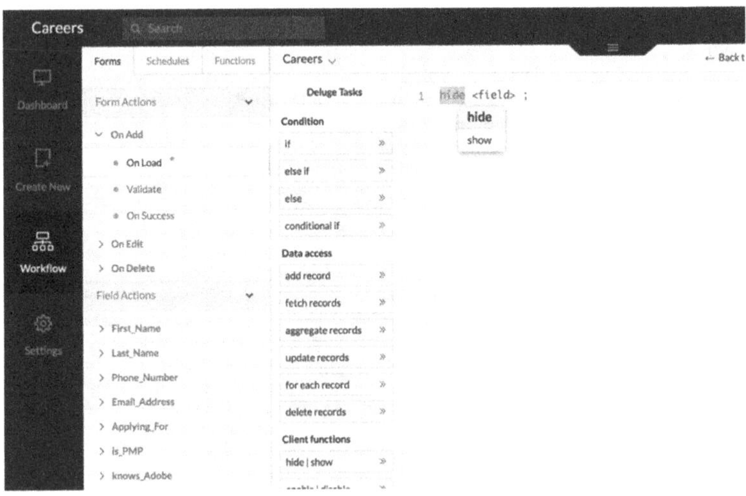

Figure 5-10. Adding a hide|show code snippet to the code

4. Then select *is_PMP* in the `field` dropdown (Figure 5-11). The code should read. `hide is_PMP;` . This tiny line of code tells Creator to (not surprisingly) hide the field called *is_PMP* in the form.

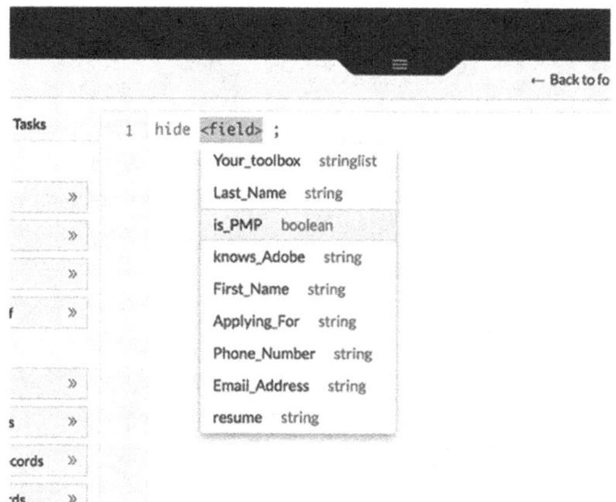

Figure 5-11. *Selecting which field to hide*

5. Similarly, place code to hide the other two fields—*knows_Adobe* and *Your_toolbox*. You can drag and drop Hide|Show Constructs or type the corresponding code for each field directly in the Code Editor. The result should look like Figure 5-12.

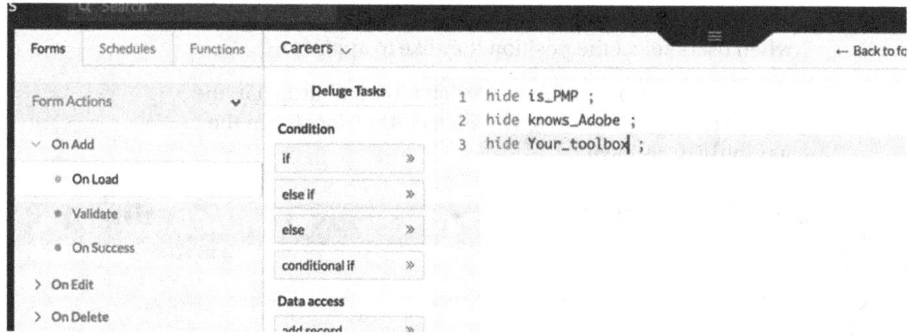

Figure 5-12. *Writing code to hide the other two fields when the form loads*

6. Now, click on the *Save* button on the bottom of the page and then run the app to see how those three lines of code affected it. All questions are hidden when the form first loads (Figure 5-13).

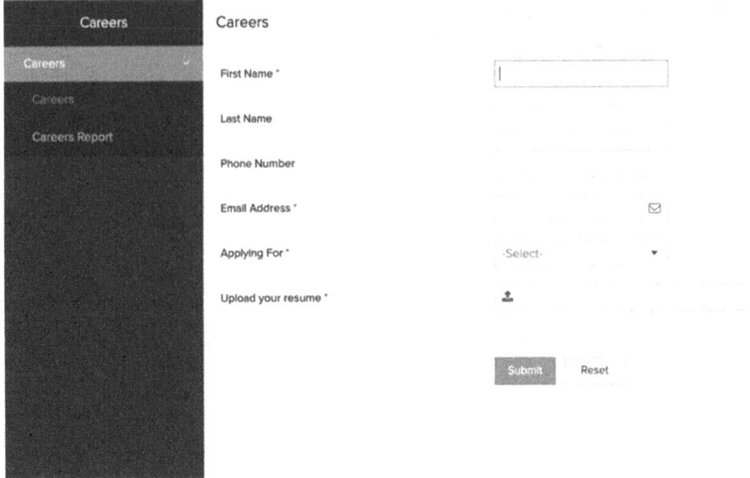

Figure 5-13. Questions are hidden by default when the form loads

7. Return to Edit mode and open the Code Editor by clicking on the *Workflow* button on the left sidebar.

8. In the form builder, under *Field Actions*, click on *Applying_For* ➤ *On User Input*. This will open the action that will trigger when users select the position they like to apply for.

9. Drag an *If* construct from the Design tools and drop it in the Code Editor (Figure 5-14). Then select *Applying_For* in the `variable` dropdown.

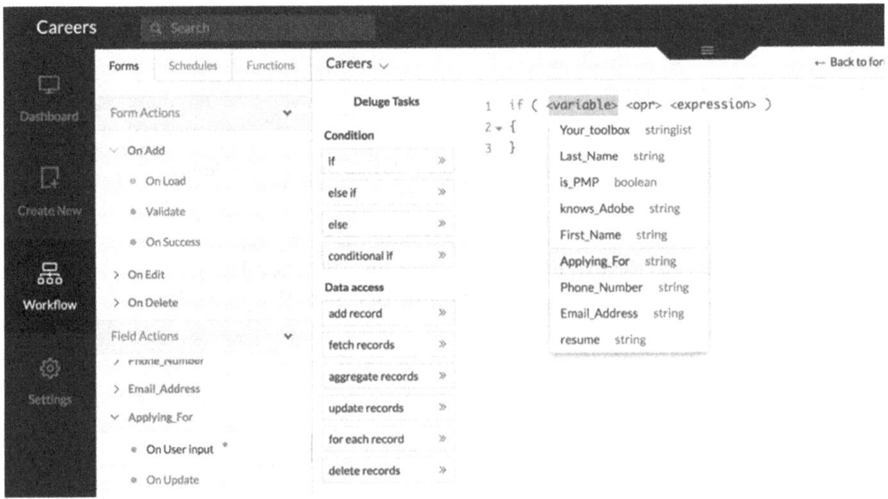

Figure 5-14. Adding a condition code to the field action

10. Click on the *<opr>* in the code and select ==. Then click *<expression>* and type *Project Manager*. The finished code should look like Figure 5-15. This line means that the code within the braces will run only if the value of the *Applying_For* field equals "*Project Manager*" letter by letter.

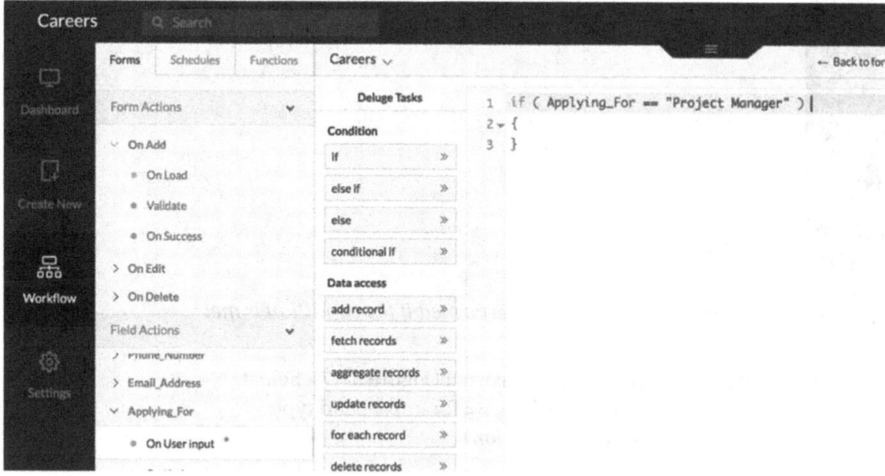

Figure 5-15. *Writing the condition part of the code*

11. Type the following lines inside the braces, as shown in Figure 5-16:

```
show is_PMP;
hide knows_Adobe;
hide Your_toolbox;
```

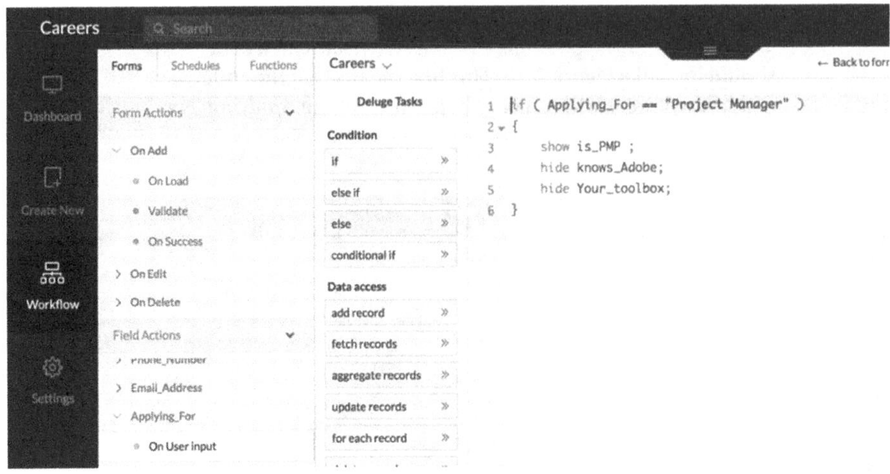

Figure 5-16. Writing the actions to be performed if the condition is met

12. Drag and drop an *else if* construct (Figure 5-17). Select *Applying_For* for <*variable*>, == for <*opr*>, and type *Junior Designer* for <*expression*>.

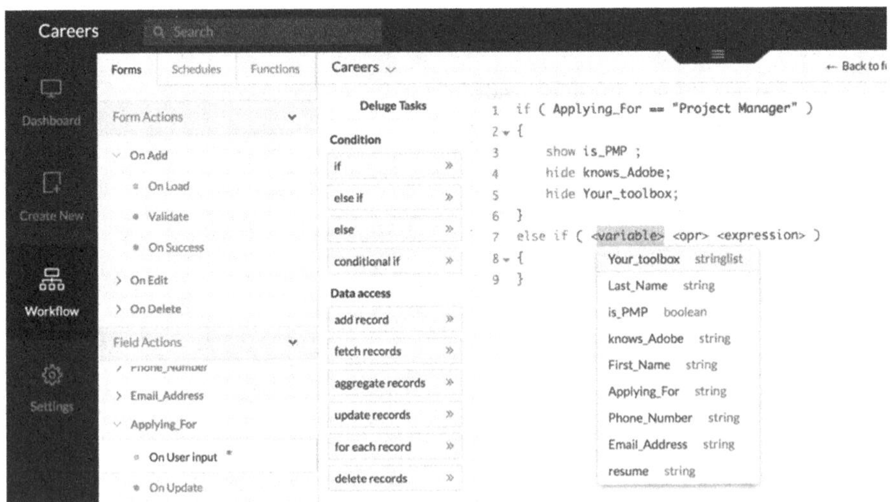

Figure 5-17. Adding a secondary condition

13. Similar to the previous step, add another `else if` construct. Select *Applying_For* for <*variable*>, == for <*opr*>, and type *Frontend Developer* for <*expression*>. The finished code should look like Figure 5-18.

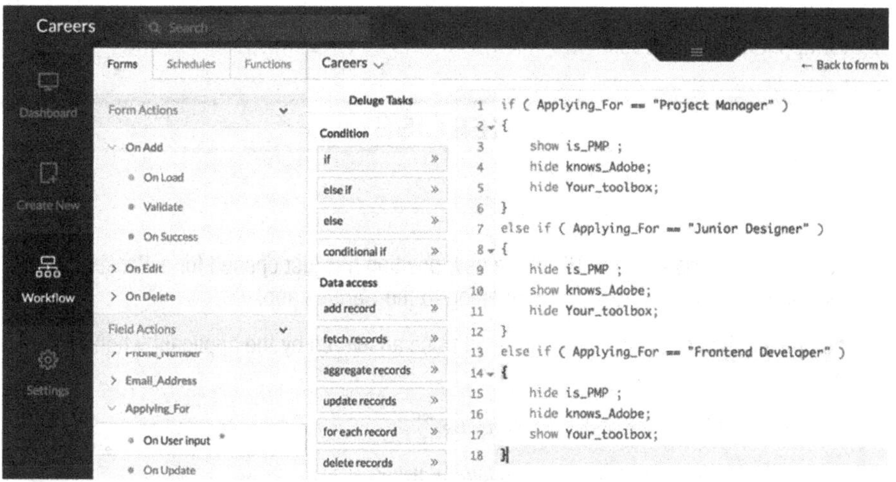

Figure 5-18. *All conditions and their actions are complete*

14. Click the *Save* button to apply the changes. Then run the app.
15. In Run mode, select each one of the three available options in Applying For to see how the relevant question appears, while other two questions remain hidden (Figure 5-19).

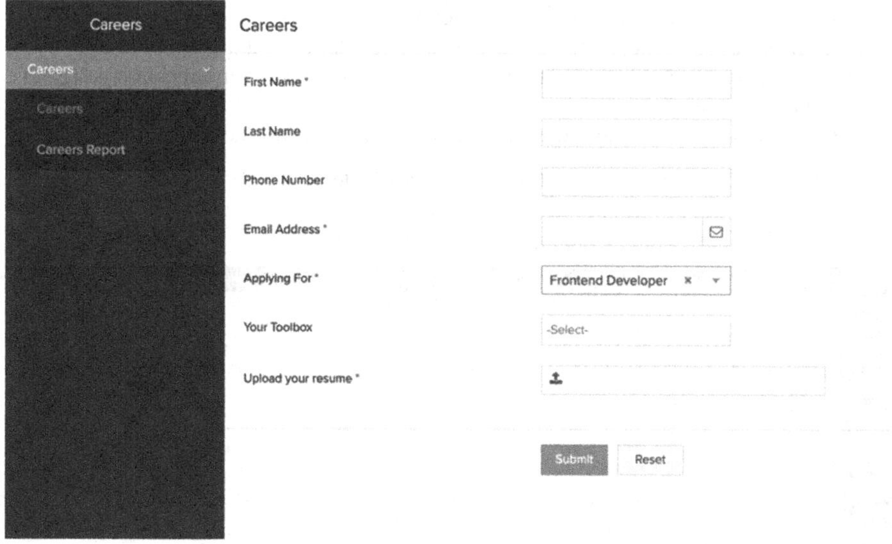

Figure 5-19. *The questions that aren't relevant remain hidden*

You just wrote your very first piece of Deluge code and added business logic to your Creator app. Congratulations!

EXERCISE

One More Opening

You receive a message from HR that a new position has just opened for a *Backend Developer*, so you need to add this opening to the *Careers* app.

The opening has two questions that need to be answered by the applicant when applying:

- "*What backend frameworks do you use?*"
- "*What code repositories are you familiar with?*"

Add these two questions to the form and write the necessary code to hide and show them when appropriate.

Adding Rules and Tasks

So far, this little app provides a dynamic UI that changes based on user input. There is one more requirement that needs to be implemented.

The HR department is keen on giving interview priority to Project Managers who hold a PMP® certificate. You, as the developer, need to make sure that as soon as an applicant submits an application with the PMP question checked, a notification is sent to the HR person in charge.

For this, you will use automation rules. Let's see how this can be done:

1. In Edit mode, open the *Careers* form and select *Automation* from the *Settings* menu (Figure 5-20).

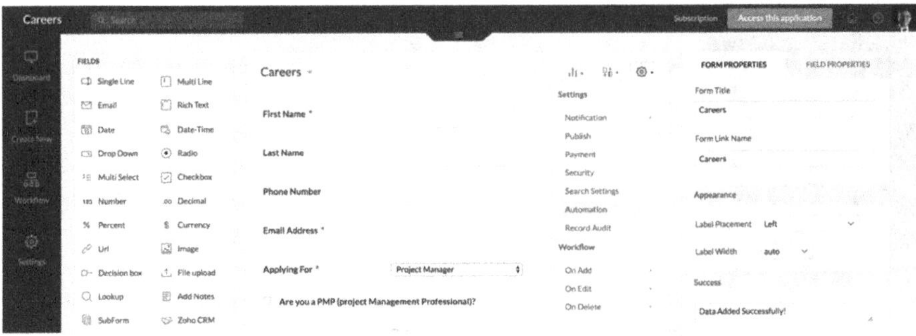

Figure 5-20. *Opening form automation page*

2. The Automation page opens (Figure 5-21). Under the *Rules* tab, click on the *Create Rule* button.

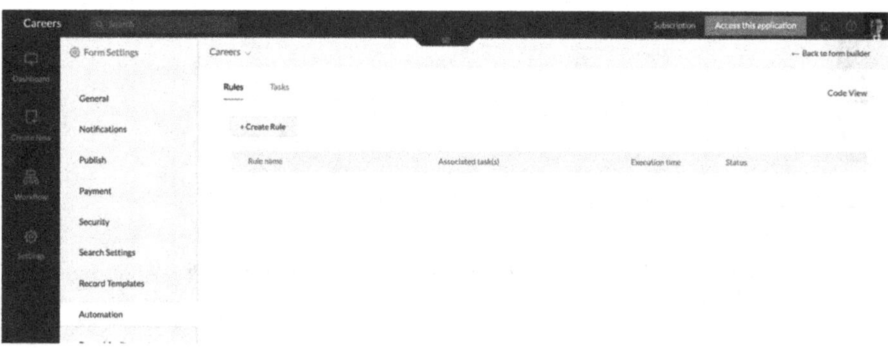

Figure 5-21. *Creating a new automation rule*

3. Under *Basic Details*, add a *Rule Name* and *Description*, as shown in Figure 5-22.

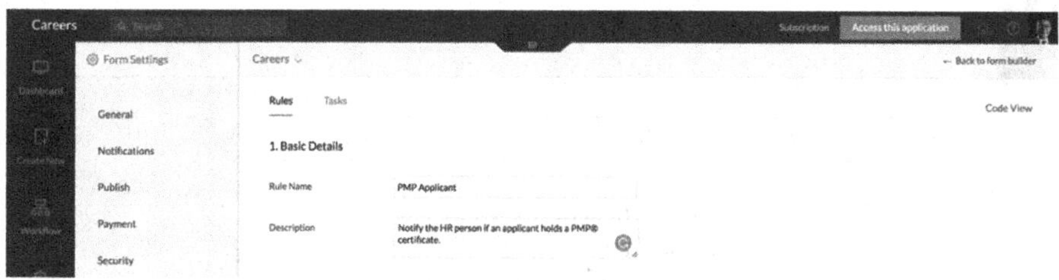

Figure 5-22. *Entering basic details for the rule*

4. Under *Execute On*, select *Add* (Figure 5-23). This will cause the rule to execute only when a new record (a new job application) is added.

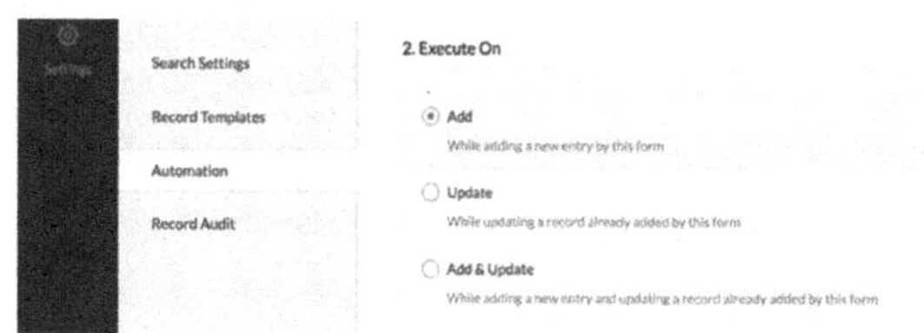

Figure 5-23. *Setting when the rule should execute*

5. Under *Criteria*, click the *Selected Record* radio button. Then select *Are you a PMP ...* in the first dropdown list, *equals* in the second one, and *true* in the third (Figure 5-24).

Figure 5-24. *Choosing the criteria under which the rule will execute*

6. Under Associated Tasks (Figure 5-25), click on Notifications and Create New Task.

Figure 5-25. *Adding a notification task*

7. For the new task, enter a task name, then select *Email Notification* for *Choose Task*. The form will expand showing more fields for the e-mail notification (Figure 5-26).

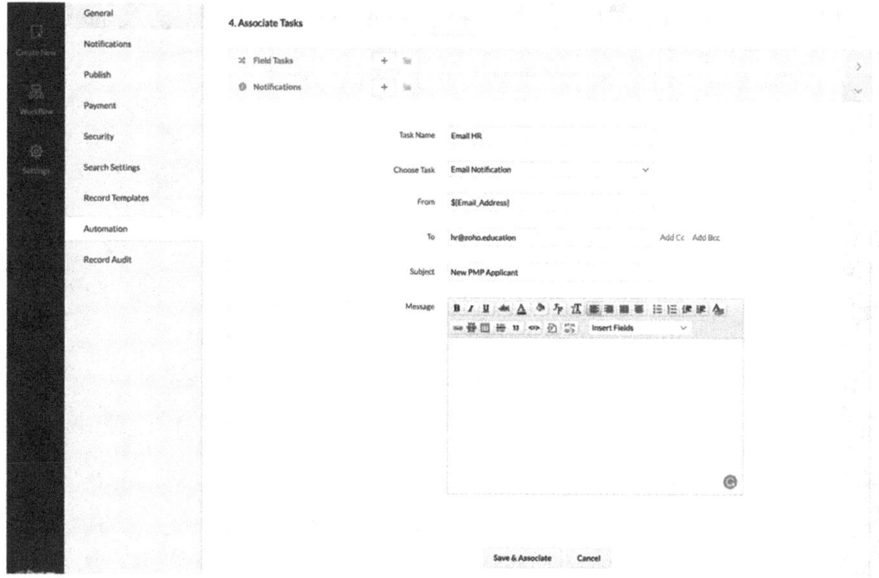

Figure 5-26. *Creating an e-mail notification field*

8. Set the *From* field to *${zoho.loginuserid}*, then type the e-mail address of the HR person in charge in the *To* field.

9. Type in the e-mail *Subject*.

10. In the *Message* body, you can enter formatted text and embed field tags, so information about the current record is sent in the e-mail body as well. Type in the message shown in Figure 5-27.

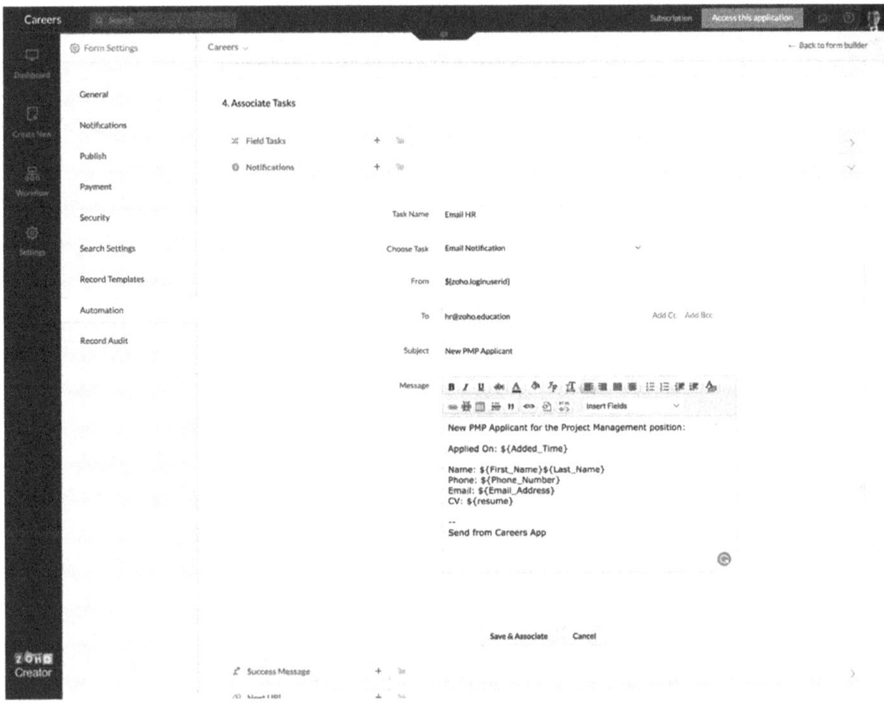

Figure 5-27. *Typing in a dynamic message body with field merge tags*

11. Click on the *Save & Associate* button to proceed. The newly created task is shown in the *Notifications* list (Figure 5-28). Notice that you can add more tasks, such as an SMS notification, to the same rule.

Figure 5-28. *The task is created and listed under Notifications*

12. Add another task, called *Next URL*, which redirects the form after submission to your home page (Figure 5-29). Click *Save & Associate* to proceed.

Figure 5-29. *Adding a Next URL task to the rule*

13. You can see the newly created task listed under *Next URL* (Figure 5-30). Click *Save* to create the rule and the corresponding tasks.

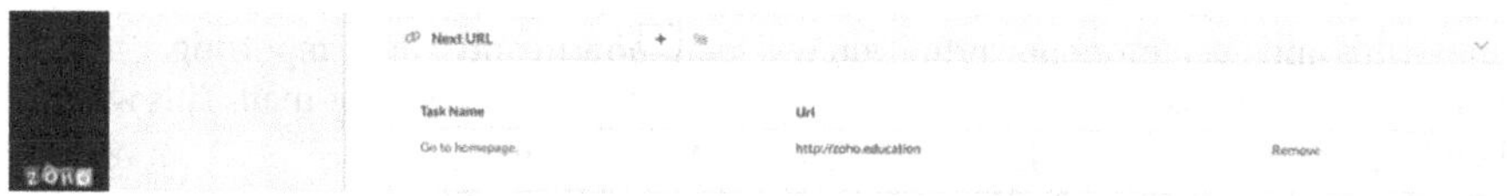

Figure 5-30. *The task is created and listed under Next URL*

After successful creation of the rule and its tasks, you will be redirected back to the Rules page, where the newly created rule is listed (Figure 5-31).

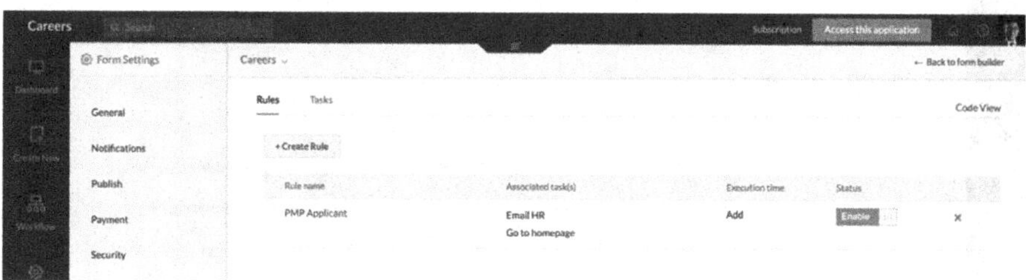

Figure 5-31. *New rule is created and enabled*

The rule is active by default, as indicated by the *Enable* switch under the *Status* column. You can disable it any time by clicking the switch. You can also edit or delete the rule permanently.

Similarly, the tasks created for the rule are listed under the *Tasks* tab (Figure 5-32). You can edit or delete them and also reuse them for other rules.

Figure 5-32. Tasks are created and listed in the Tasks tab

Adding Schedules

To make this app even more powerful, you will learn how to add a daily reporting mechanism that sends a list of all applicants to the HR department via e-mail. This way, HR doesn't need to use the app. Everything is done by e-mail.

Follow these steps to schedule a daily report of the applicants:

1. In Edit mode, click on the *Workflow* button on the sidebar. Then click on the *Schedules* tab (Figure 5-33).

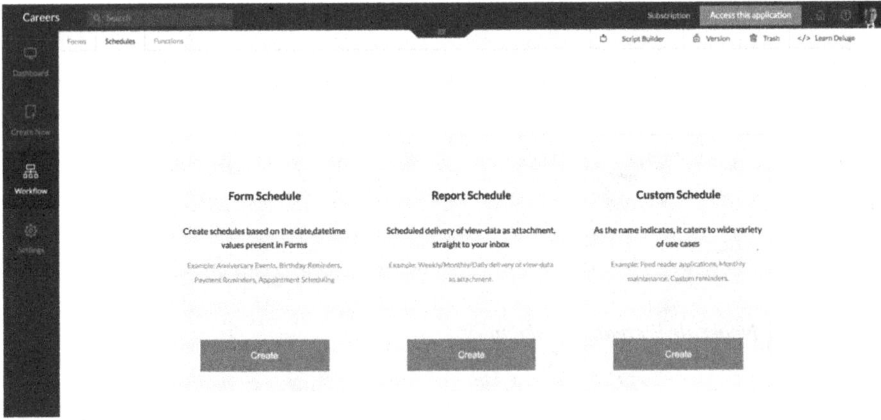

Figure 5-33. The Schedules page opened for the first time

2. Click on the *Create* button for the *Report Schedule.*

3. In the *When to do*? tab (Figure 5-34), enter a *Title* for the schedule, then set the *Date* and *Time* to run the schedule. Click *Next* to continue.

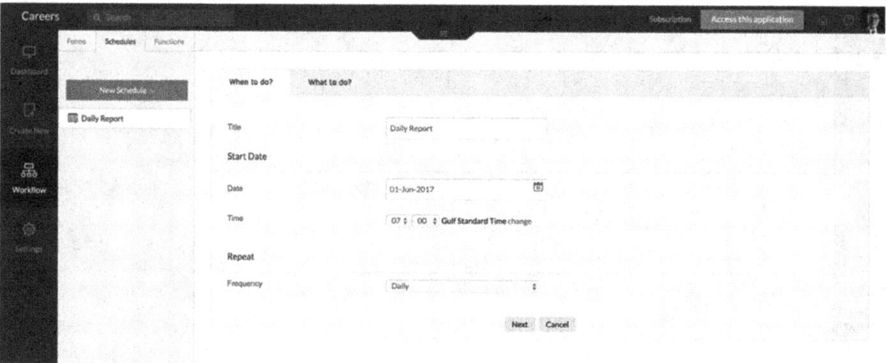

Figure 5-34. *Setting the schedule to run the report*

4. In the What To Do? tab (Figure 5-35), type in the e-mail recipient in the *To* field, select which report needs to be attached to the e-mail, and then type in the e-mail *Subject* and *Message*.

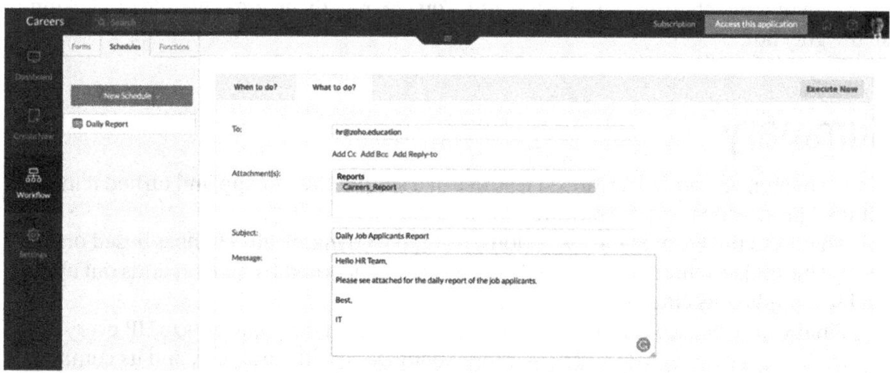

Figure 5-35. *Telling the app which report to run*

5. Click on the *Save* button at the bottom of the page to apply the changes.

6. Click on the *Execute* button on the top right of the page to test the schedule. The click *Close* in the *Execute Script* dialog box (Figure 5-36).

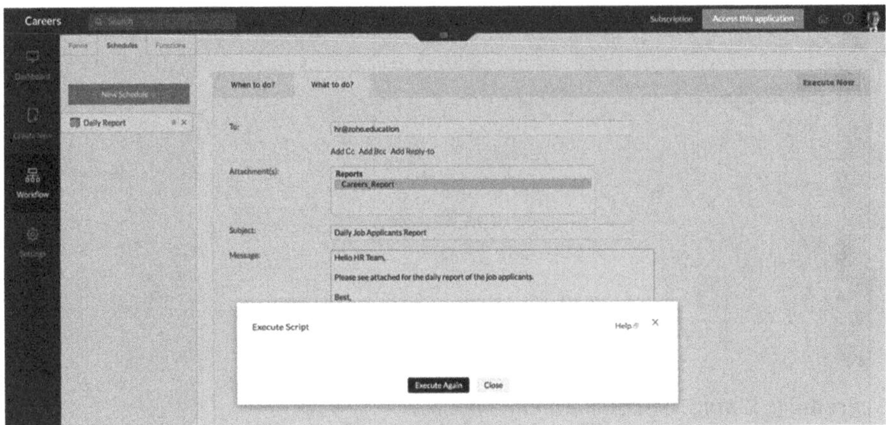

Figure 5-36. *Manually executing the schedule for testing purposes*

Notice under the *Schedules* tab that the newly created schedule is listed with a green dot in front of it. This green dot indicates that the schedule is active and will send e-mails every day until you deactivate it. You can deactivate the schedule by clicking on the green dot, which turns it into a gray dot. You can reactivate the schedule by clicking on the gray dot.

Summary

In this chapter, you added advanced features to a simple Creator app and turned it into (almost) professional-grade software.

Thanks to the Form and Field actions, the app UI dynamically changes based on user input. This makes it more intuitive to use. Also, the concerned HR person finds out about qualified applicants almost immediately.

Finally, you learned how to send scheduled reports of the applicants to HR every day.

In the next chapter, you will learn more about Deluge, its structure, and its common statements.

CHAPTER 6

More Deluge

In the previous chapter, you were introduced to Deluge, Zoho's data-oriented scripting language. Deluge gives Zoho Creator its real power and flexibility to perform complex tasks, including automation, data processing, and connecting to external data sources and services.

In this chapter, you get a closer look at Deluge's building blocks and learn to use some of the most common elements of the language.

The Joy of Making Software

Computers were created to help people perform repetitive and complex tasks faster and better without having to put in long working hours.

From breaking the Enigma code, to landing humans on the surface of the moon, computers were at the center of most of the great achievements of the past century. Today, computers transcend beyond the bulky, noisy machines of the past and fit into our pockets, fridges, and even in our bodies. Ubiquitous and intertwined with modern civilization and pop culture, it is hard to imagine a day without them.

However, a computer, as a machine, needs to be programmed (at least until Skynet takes over completely) to perform as intended. A computer program is nothing more than a set of instructions that tell the machine to perform various tasks. These instructions can be as short as a few lines of code for simple programs, to millions of lines of code in the case of complex software (`http://www.informationisbeautiful.net/visualizations/million-lines-of-code/`).

To simplify, a typical computer program does three things: inputs data, processes data, and outputs the results. Most programs store data for later use one way or another.

For instance, a simple calculator takes two numbers (input), adds them together (processing), and shows the results on the screen (output).

Similarly, although in a much bigger scale, an accounting software, or a CRM, can input, process, store, and output data.

Making software programs as a hobby or as a full-time gig is a great joy. Not only does it help solve problems of different sizes, it also satisfies the human thirst for creativity, creation, and innovation.

However, like any love story, there is an insufferable amount of pain that comes with creating good software. You can ask any seasoned software engineer, developer, or programmer and they will have a horror story or two in their career that they can share with you.

A. Shabdar, *Mastering Zoho Creator*, DOI 10.1007/978-1-4842-2907-1_6

Reducing the Pain

Creating software requires many skills (in addition to having nerves of steel and a few superpowers), one of which is programming. As mentioned, complex software is made of thousands upon thousands of lines of code, which means it is time consuming and prone to all sorts of errors (bugs).

There are many tools available to make the job of creating software easier, such as templates and frameworks; however, you still need to write a considerable amount of code.

There are also tools, such as Microsoft Access and Apple FileMaker, that allow you to build data-centric business applications with no or minimal amount of programming.

Similarly, online platforms such as Zoho Creator offer an efficient way of creating cloud-based business applications with minimum effort and a high degree of reliability.

Most of these tools, including Zoho Creator, offer the means to write code to address more complex scenarios and make your business app more powerful. Zoho Creator's answer to a programming (more accurately, a scripting) language is Deluge.

Getting Started with Deluge

Deluge (Data Enriched Language for the Universal Grid Environment) is Zoho's proprietary scripting language and the backbone of Zoho Creator. In fact, if you export a Creator app for archiving or other purposes, all you get is a file containing pure Deluge code and nothing else.

Deluge is designed with the average user in mind. Zoho has worked hard to make it is as easy as possible to use. *Deluge Script Builder* is a visual tool built into Creator that lets users drag and drop code snippets and speed up the scripting process.

If you are new to programming, fear not—Creator and Deluge will help you build the logic you need in your application. If you are experienced in programming, you are in for a treat. It is really easy to code in Deluge.

■ **Note** Deluge, with all its power and fun character, is not a full-fledged scripting language. It is, by design, focused on getting the work done with minimal fuss and coding. If you come from JavaScript, Python, Ruby, or other languages, you will appreciate its nimbleness. It's best if you lower your expectations and give it a chance to grow on you. That said, you can connect Creator to the outside world (and your awesome code out there) using HTTP requests and Zoho's REST API.

In terms of syntax, Deluge borrows mostly from JavaScript, but it is simpler and easier to understand. It has all the common features of a scripting language, such as blocks, operators, control statements, and functions, plus a few extras specific to Creator. There are also limited debugging features.

In general, you can use Deluge to create the following in a Creator app:

- **Form actions**—Change the content of a form at runtime, validate data, run tasks before and after a form is submitted, and respond to events, such as clicking a button on the form.
- **Field actions**—Change the value of a field on the form, or run tasks based on the changes to a field.
- **Formula fields**—Auto calculate values in a field based on a specific formula.
- **Complex filters**—Show specific datasets in reports.
- **Functions**: Custom pieces of code that can be called and executed multiple times.
- **Mashups**: Send and receive data between Creator and external services and applications.

You have used Deluge to create Form and Field actions in the previous chapter. Using a few lines of code, you were able to control how various elements on a form behave and improve the user experience of the form.

Deluge Names

To refer to various objects (forms, fields, reports, and the application itself) in a Creator app, Deluge uses a name for each object. This is called a *Deluge Name.*

Deluge Names are allocated automatically when you create a new application, or new objects, e.g. forms and fields, in an application. When writing code, you refer to these objects using their corresponding Deluge Names.

For the application, the Deluge Name can be found on the Settings page. Simply switch to Edit mode and click on the *Settings* icon on the left sidebar. Then find the *Application Link* (Figure 6-1).

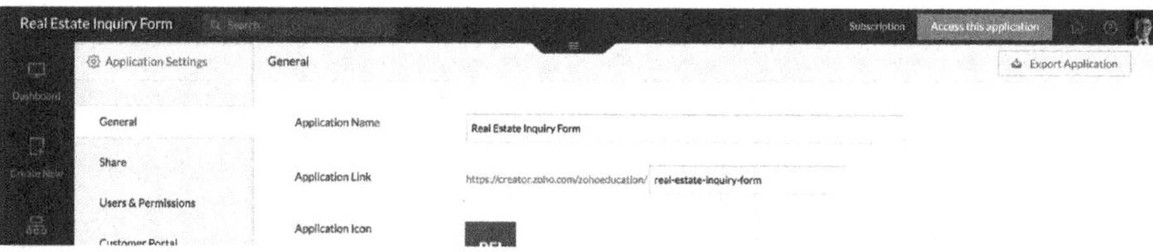

Figure 6-1. *Deluge Name (application link) of an application*

To see the Deluge Name of a form, in Edit mode, simply find the *Form Link Name* under the *Form Properties* tab on the right sidebar (Figure 6-2).

Figure 6-2. *Deluge Name (form link name) of a form*

Similarly, each field has its own Deluge Name allocated in *Field Deluge Name* under the *Field Properties* tab (Figure 6-3).

Figure 6-3. *Field Deluge Name*

Writing Deluge Code

As you saw in the previous chapter, to write Deluge code, you need to open the Workflow page and write code for each Form or Field action (Figure 6-4).

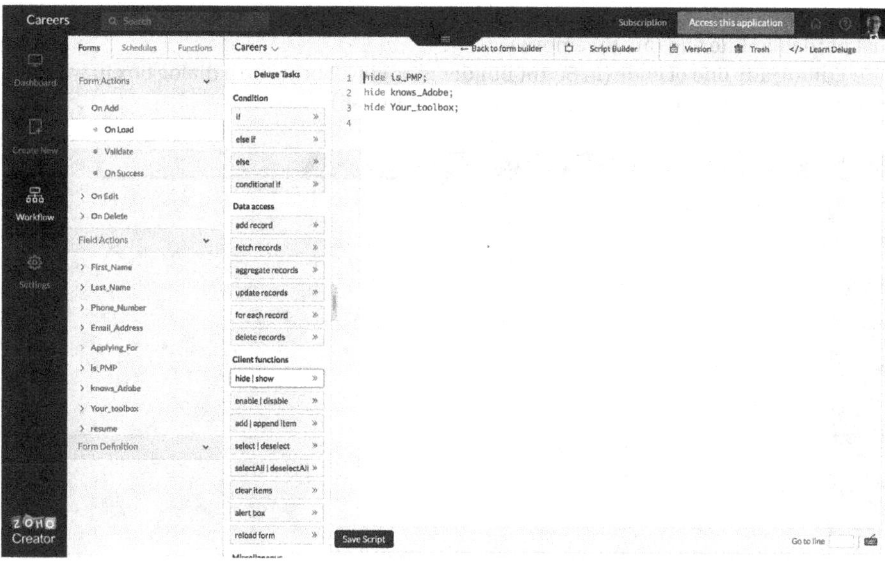

Figure 6-4. Workflow page

You can either type the entire code or drag code constructs (e.g., an `if` statement) from the *Deluge Task Pane* (sidebar with a list of code constructs), drop them into the Code Editor, and then add more code to it.

Script Builder

For the "cod-o-phobe" (my made-up word for people who don't want to touch code), there is a more sanitized way, using the *Script Builder*.

Simply click the *Script Builder* button on the top toolbar and the editor will change face a bit and will no longer let you freely modify code (Figure 6-5).

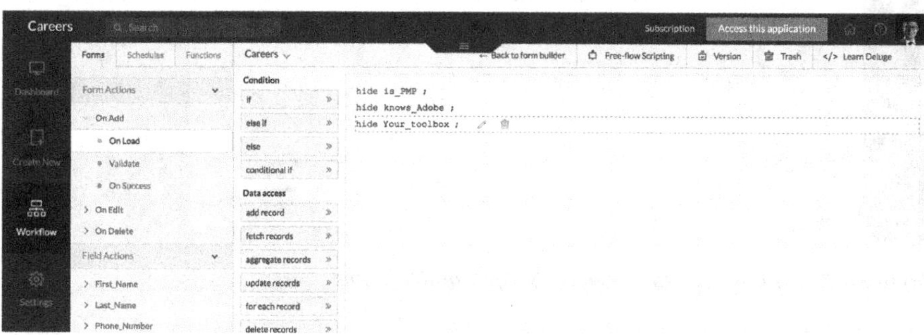

Figure 6-5. Activating the Script Builder

If you hover the mouse cursor on a line of code, two icons will appear—one to edit that particular line and one to remove it.

Editing any line of code (in Script Builder mode) will bring up a dialog box in which you can modify the code in a guided manner (Figure 6-6).

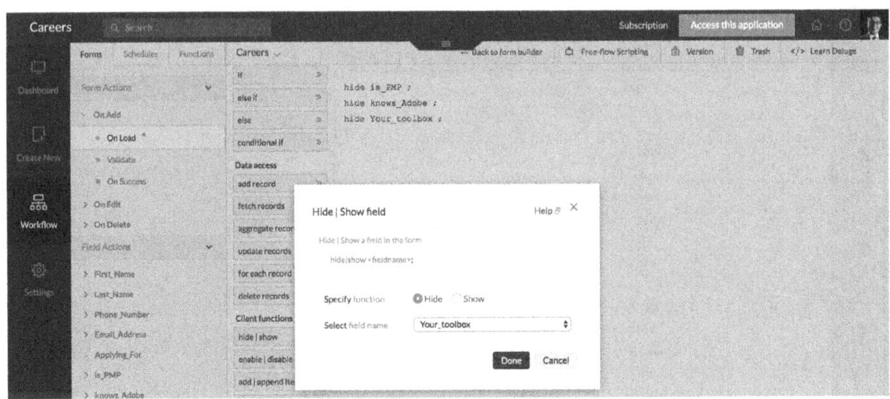

Figure 6-6. *Modifying code in Script Builder mode*

Similarly, when you're adding a new code construct, e.g., an *if* statement, Script Builder will show a dialog box where you can build the code and then paste it into the rest of the code (Figure 6-7).

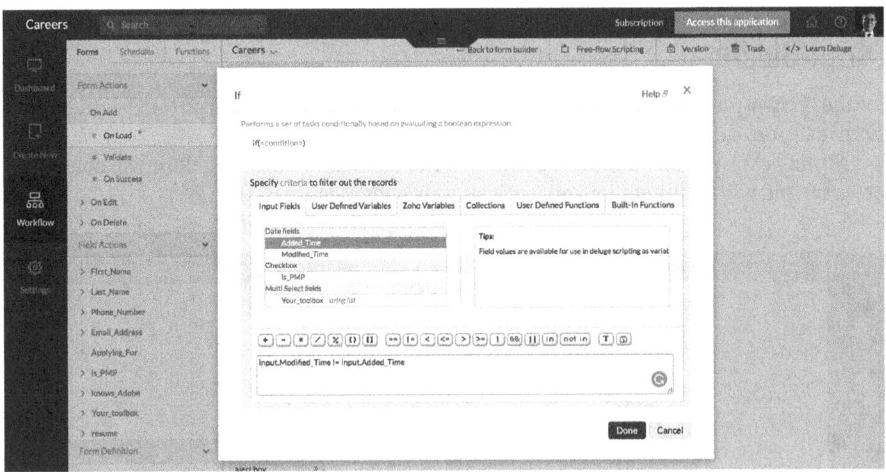

Figure 6-7. *Adding an if statement in Script Builder mode*

Jokes aside, it is a good idea to enable the Script Builder when you are just starting. It helps you avoid errors and typos in syntax and code more efficiently in the beginning. When you get more comfortable with Deluge, you can switch to *free-flow scripting* (accessible on the toolbar) and get back to typing.

Code Versioning

When you write code, sometimes you make changes that break the code (i.e., cause errors or bugs). In those cases, you'll want to go back in time, see what change caused the problem, and roll it back to a previous version.

In the programming world, there are many sophisticated tools that help you maintain your code and keep a meticulously accurate history of all the changes.

Fortunately, Creator offers its own simple and easy-to-use alternative, which does the job just fine. Every time you press the Save button (while editing code), Creator creates a snapshot of the code and adds it to the version history.

To see the previous versions of your code, simply click Version on the top toolbar. In the *Version History* dialog box (Figure 6-8), you can open older versions and copy and paste them back into the code.

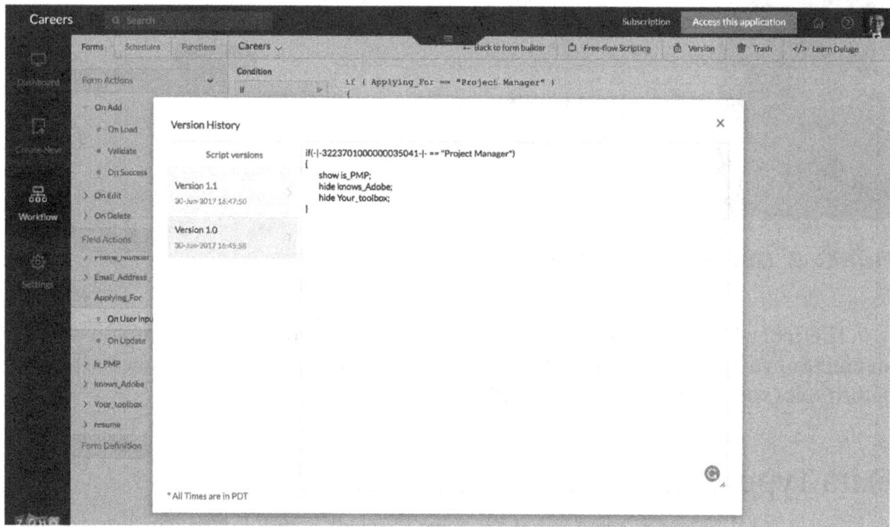

Figure 6-8. *Accessing previous versions of the code*

Basic Elements of the Language

Now, let's learn about Deluge language elements. You can create a new app and then test your knowledge in the workflow area of the default form, or use one of the apps created in this book before.

Before we proceed, I want to make honorable mention of a nifty tool by Zoho, called *Learn Deluge*. It's accessible from `https://creator.zoho.com/learndeluge/` (Figure 6-9).

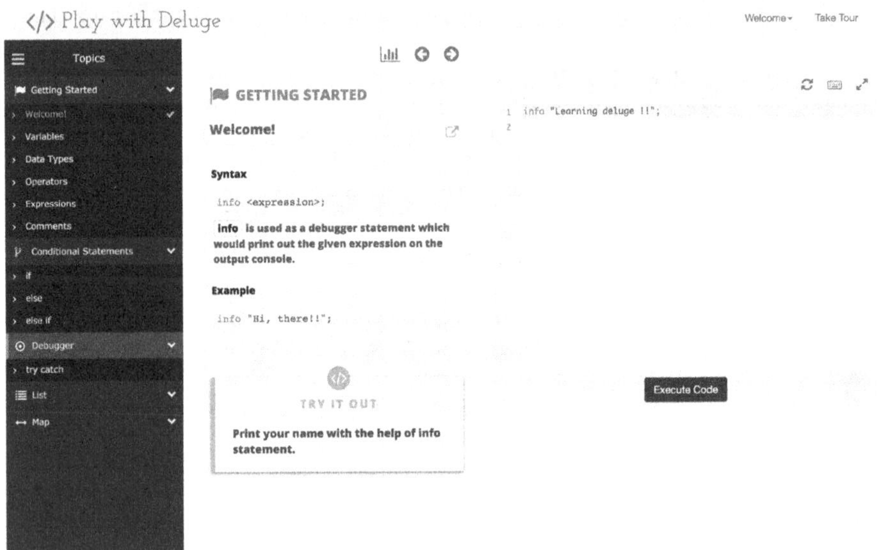

Figure 6-9. *Learn Deluge environment*

This tool will take you through step-by-step coding practices and provide you with an online environment to write and test code. You can also use this tool to practice most of the topics you learn about in this chapter.

Data Types

At the core of any computer program there is data, so obviously handing data is one of the key elements of any programming language, including Deluge.

Depending on the language, data comes in a number of shapes and forms, i.e. types. In Deluge, there are several types of data:

- **String**—Textual data, such as `"Vancouver"`, `"Charles Darwin"`, or `"Catch 22"`
- **Integer and Decimal**—Numeric data, such as `10000`, `3.14`, or `0`
- **Date and Date-Time**—Chronological data such as `"2017-07-01"`, `"April 13, 1949"`, or `"11/9/34"`

- **Boolean**—Data that is True or False
- **List Collection**—A collection that can contain values of different data types, such as `("2001", "A Space Odyssey", 1968)`
- **Map Collection**—A collection of key/value pairs, such as `{"id": 123, "fname": "Carl", "lname": "Sagan"}`.
- **Form Object**—A special data type used to pass to custom functions representing a collection of records in a form, such as *Careers* (representing all the records of the *Careers* form).

Without getting into too many of the technical details, one of the reasons there are different data types goes back to the early days of computing, when managing precious computer resources, such as processing power and memory space, was very important. Also, different data types have their own specific features that help you build better software.

■ **Reference** You will learn about most of these data types in the remainder of this book. You can also refer to the official documentations at: `https://www.zoho.com/creator/help/script/deluge-datatypes.html`.

Structured Data Types

To manipulate datasets more efficiently, Deluge comes with two types of structured data types: lists and maps.

Lists

Lists, similar to single dimensional arrays in math, can hold a collection of values. In Deluge, lists can hold values of the same type (e.g., all numbers), or a mix of numbers, strings, and other data types.

Here are some examples of lists in Deluge:

```
Goods = {"Bread", "Cheese", "Eggs", "Milk"};
Prices = {1.3, 3.25, 4.25, 2.99}
Some_List = {True, 3.14, “Tennis”}
```

Lists have a number of useful functionalities (methods) that allow you to perform advanced tasks, such as sorting, adding, removing, and finding elements in a list.

For instance, to get a value at a specific index (position) in the list, you can use the *get* method:

```
Price = Prices.get(2); //will return 4.25; index start at 0
```

■ **Reference** To learn more about lists, refer to the official documentation at: `https://www.zoho.com/creator/help/script/list-manipulations.html` and `https://www.zoho.com/creator/help/script/built-in-functions/built-in-function-list.html`.

Maps

Maps are similar to lists, except that they are collections of key/value pairs. That means that each item in a map has a key by which the value of that item can be referred to.

For instance, if you want to store the goods and their prices, you could use a single map:

```
Goods_Prices = {"Bread": 1.3, "Cheese": 3.25, "Eggs": 4.25, "Milk": 2.99};
```

Similar to lists, to access to a specific element in a map, you can use the *get* method, but instead of a numeric index, you will pass the *key* to the method to find the corresponding value:

```
Price_of_Cheese = Goods_Prices.get("Cheese");
```

■ **Reference** To learn more about maps, refer to the official documentation at: `https://www.zoho.com/creator/help/script/map-manipulations.html` and `https://www.zoho.com/creator/help/script/built-in-functions/built-in-function-map.html`.

Variables

So where does all the data go? Computers store data temporarily for processing and permanently for storage and later extraction. Variables are used to store data temporarily.

Remember the parameters in Algebraic equations from high school (e.g., $2x + 5 = 9$)? Variables are much like those parameters, but with the ability to store various data types. You can allocate values to Deluge variables and use them in the code as representations of the values they hold.

Form Fields and Other Automatically Created Variables

Deluge itself uses variables to send data around in the background in Creator apps. This means there are many predefined variables for you to use. When you add a new form to the Creator, the form itself and all the fields on it are represented by a variable created automatically as soon as the form is created.

For instance, if you add a form called *Users* to an app and then add three fields for first name, last name, and e-mail, Creator will create four variables in that form for the form and the three fields on it.

Each of these variables will bear the Deluge Name of the corresponding form or field, e.g. *Users, First_Name, Last_Name,* and *Email.* These are actually the Deluge Names of these components, which you learned about in the previous chapter.

This is how these fields should appear in the code:

- `Users`, for the form
- `input.First_Name`, for the *First_Name* field
- `input.Last_Name`, for the *Last_Name* field
- `input.Email`, for the *Email* field

The types of these variables will match the types of the respective form fields, i.e. if a form field contains a string (e.g., a *single-line* textbox), the variable will also be of type string.

The extra `input.` prefix added to each viable name indicates to Creator that this is a form field variable.

User-Defined Variables

In addition to the variable created by Creator itself, there are also user-defined variables, which are the variables you create when writing action scripts to store temporary values in your code.

For instance, if you want to concatenate a first name and last name and to construct a full name, you would write a code similar to this:

```
Full_Name = input.First_Name + " " + input.Last_Name
```

Full_Name is a user-defined variable and automatically becomes type *String* because at the time of creation, a string value was set to it.

Similarly, if you need to make an Address field out of Street, Postal Code, City, and State, you would write:

```
Address = input.Street + ", " + input.City + ", " + input.State + ",
" + input.Postal_Code
```

Deluge System Variables

Deluge also comes equipped with a set of variables that hold key information, such as today's date, the name of the logged in user, and the address (link) of the app itself.

For example, if in an app you want to look for records entered by specific users, you should use `zoho.loginuser` and `zoho.loginuserid`. Or, if you want to know where (geographically) your users connect to your app, you can use `zoho.ipaddress`.

Here are all Deluge system variables:

- **zoho.currentdate**—Returns the current date.
- **zoho.currenttime**—Returns the current date and time together.
- **zoho.loginuser**—Returns the username of the user currently logged into the app. For public apps, this value is null.
- **zoho.loginuserid**—Returns the e-mail address of the user currently logged into the app. For public apps, this value is null.

- **zoho.adminuser**—Returns the username of the admin of the app.
- **zoho.adminuserid**—Returns the e-mail address of the admin of the app.
- **zoho.appname**—Returns the name of the current application, e.g. *careers* (for the *Careers* app).
- **zoho.appuri**:—Returns the URI (Unique Resource Identifier) of the current app, e.g. */zohoeducation/careers/*.
- **zoho.ipaddress**—Returns the IP address of the current user.

Reference Get a complete list of Deluge systems variables from the official documentation: `https://www.zoho.com/creator/help/script/deluge-system-variables.html`.

Operators

Operators are a foundational part of any programming language, including Deluge. Borrowed mostly from math, operators perform operations that output values based on input of one or more other values.

For instance, an *addition* operation adds two values together and outputs the sum of the two. In math and in programming languages, this operation is shown as $c = a + b$, where c is the result of summation of a and b.

Table 6-1 explains the basic Deluge operators.

Table 6-1. *Deluge Operators*

Type	Symbol	Details
Arithmetic	+, -, *, /	Basic arithmetic operators for addition, subtraction, multiplication and division
Arithmetic	%	Remainder of a division
Relational	> < >= <= == !=	Greater than Less than Greater than or equal Less than or equal Equal Not equal
Logical (Conditional)	&& || !	Logical AND Logical OR Logical NOT

Here are a few examples of operators in action:

```
Discount_Amount = input.Total_Amount * input.Discount_Amount / 100;
Discount_Allowed = (Discount_Amount <= Max_Discount) && Preferred_Client;
Age = ((zoho.currentdate - input.DOB) / (1000 * 3600 * 24 * 365)).
round(2);
```

■ **Reference** Read more about Deluge operators in the official documentation at: `https://www.zoho.com/creator/help/script/operators.html`.

Comments

As you go forward with programming, you will witness that your code grows from a few simple lines to hundreds and then thousands of lines of code. The longer the code, the harder it is to remember what a specific piece of code does. This is even more severe if you come back after a few months to edit the code (to fix an issue or improve it) and find yourself lost in the maze of all that code.

A best practice in programming is to add comments to your code as you go forward. Comments are blocks of text added to the body of the code that the program doesn't see or use. Comments are read by humans only so they can understand the code that they, or someone else, wrote.

In Deluge, because of the nature of Zoho Creator and its minimalist coding, your code will not grow that much. However, it is still a good idea to add comments to your code and explain your rationale.

To write comments in Deluge, you can simply add a // and write a line of explanation. If you want to write multiple lines, you can add // to each line, or group them all in a /* */.

Here is how a single line comment looks like:

```
// This is a comment
show is_PMP;  //show PMP checkbox.
```

Here is a multiline comment block:

```
/* This is a multiline comment
Here is another line. You can write as long as you want.
*/
```

Here is another, more realistic, example:

```
//This code hides unnecessary fields on load.
//They will be shown based on the user's choice of job vacancy.
hide is_PMP;
hide knows_Adobe;
hide Your_toolbox;
```

I recommend you make it a habit and write descriptive comments; however, don't get carried away. Here are five best practices for commenting your code: `https://improvingsoftware.com/2011/06/27/5-best-practices-for-commenting-your-code/`.

Control Statements

When you need to perform a set of tasks only when specific conditions are met, you can use control statements.

For example, in a product inquiry form, you want to alert the sales manager if a user wants to buy a product within a set time. To translate that into Deluge, you can write:

```
if (input.Purchase_Decision == "Within 1 month")
{
        sendmail
        [
                to: input.Email_Address
                subject: "Purchasing within a month"
                message: input.First_Name + " is interested in purchasing
                within a month. Follow up more aggressively."
        ]
}
```

Notice the special structure of a control statement. It starts with an *if* followed by the condition statement in parentheses. The condition statement must evaluate to *True* for the *if* statement to run the code enclosed in braces *{ }*.

You can make more complex *if* statements adding *else* and *else if*.

Here is a simple example:

```
if (input.Age_Range == "18 - 24")
{
        hide input.K12_Results;
        show input.High_Scool_Results;
        hide input.University_Results;
}
else if (input.Age_Range == "25 - 34")
{
        hide input.K12_Results;
        hide input.High_Scool_Results;
        show input.University_Results;
}}
```

```
else if (input.Age_Range == "35 - 54")
{
        hide input.K12_Results;
        hide input.High_Scool_Results;
        hide input.University_Results;
}
else
{
        hide input.K12_Results;
        hide input.High_Scool_Results;
        hide input.University_Results;
        show input.Senior;
}
```

As you can see in the code, you can chain multiple *else if* statements to get more specific with the conditions. Logically, there is only one *else* statement allowed at the end, for all scenarios that don't fall under either of the previous conditions.

■ **Reference** Read more about control statements in the official documentation at: `https://www.zoho.com/creator/help/script/control-statements.html`.

Alerting Users

Sometimes you need to display information related to the state of an app, which may not be related to data per se, but is important for users to be informed about them.

For instance, a user should be alerted about the successful or unsuccessful submission of a form and be given clear indication of why this happened, if necessary.

Deluge has a command, aptly named *alert*, which simply shows an alert box with a custom message (passed as a string value) and an *OK* button to continue.

Suppose in the Careers app that you want to alert the visitors when a job posting is no longer available, when they select an opening that is just been filled (Figure 6-10). You would write something along the lines of this:

```
if (Applying_For == "Project Manager")
{
        alert "Sorry! This job posting is no longer available";
}
```

Figure 6-10. *Alerting the user*

Debugging Apps

When writing code, you need to regularly check the value of different variables and outcome of certain statements to make sure that the program behaves as intended. Apps, especially when they get complex, may behave undesirably and introduce bugs into the code. The more complex an app gets, the harder it becomes to catch and fix these bugs (a process called *debugging*).

You can use an *alert* to display values while developing the app and remove them as you go forward; however, this is clunky and not recommended. There is a better way to show internal data while in development mode, and that's by using Deluge's *info* command.

The *info* command will let you output internal values and monitor the flow of the program. For instance, if you add the following lines where user input is monitored for the *Applying_For* field, you can check if values are captured properly:

```
info Applying_For;
info "is_PMP: " + is_PMP + " knows_Adobe: " + knows_Adobe;
```

When you run the app, a link will appear on the form, called *View Log Details*, which is only visible to you (the app developer). Clicking on this link will open a dialog box and the output of all *info* commands will be shown in order (Figure 6-11).

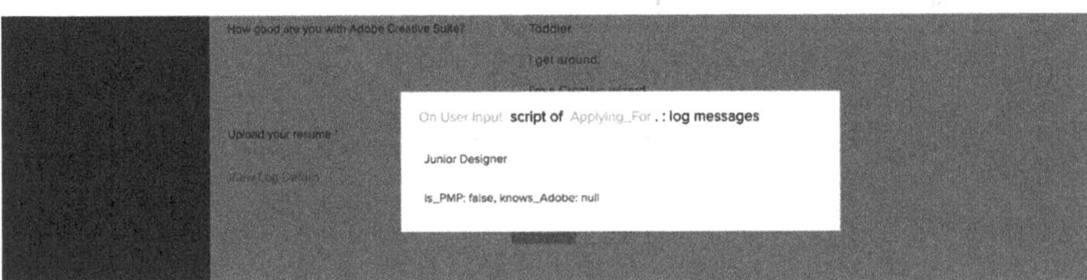

Figure 6-11. *Info dialog box*

Once you are done debugging, you can keep the `info` commands in your code or remove them. You can also comment them out, so they are not executed, but you have them handy when you need to come back and investigate your code again.

■ **Reference** While on the topic of debugging, read about handling exceptions in the official documentation at: `https://www.zoho.com/creator/help/script/try-catch.html`. Using exception handling properly will help you create more robust apps.

Data Access

Creator is all about storing and managing data and naturally Deluge comes with a number of functions and ways to access the data stored in an app. Using data access functions, you can perform the following:

- **Add, update, and delete records**—To create new records and update or delete existing ones in code without the interference of the user.
- **Fetch records**—To find specific records in a form (dataset) based on a given criteria.
- **Aggregate records**—To perform calculations, such as counting the number of records or calculating sum or average of specific fields in a list of records.
- **Iterate through records**—To go through a set of records one by one and interact with each one.

Manipulating data via code is an advanced topic and we will not get into more details in here. You can read more about each of these functionalities in the documentation; however, be extra careful when working with accessing data programmatically. You may perform tasks or introduce bugs that compromise or destroy data.

■ **Reference** To learn more about the data access functionalities of Deluge, refer to the official documentation at: `https://www.zoho.com/creator/help/script/data-access.html`.

Functions

Functions are sets of code that collectively perform specific tasks. Most function accept parameters, i.e. values, that will be passed to the function to go through the function logic.

So far, you have used a number of Deluge functions, maybe without realizing it. Methods such as *get()* in lists and maps are actually functions.

By packing logic in functions, code can be reused and programs look cleaner and more manageable.

Suppose you need to calculate taxes for a number of variables throughout the program. One way is to repeat the formula every time the calculation is needed, or put the formula in a function and call the function every time the calculation is needed. This way, you avoid code repetition, which is a programming best practice. Also, if the formula changes in the future, all you need to change is the function and all calculations throughout your code will be updated without having to change every single one.

■ **Reference** You can learn more about functions in the official documentation at: `https://www.zoho.com/creator/help/script/functions.html`.

Creating Functions

To see how functions look in Deluge, let's create one. You will learn how to create a function called *bc_tax()* that takes an amount as a parameter (argument) and calculates the total sales tax for the item, which is the sum of provincial (PST, 7%) and governmental sales taxes (GST, 5%) for the province of British Columbia in Canada.

Follow these steps to create a new function in Creator:

1. In Edit mode, open the *Workflow* page. Then click on the Functions tab.
2. If your app has no functions defined you will see an empty page with a *Create Function* button (Figure 6-12). Click on the button to proceed.

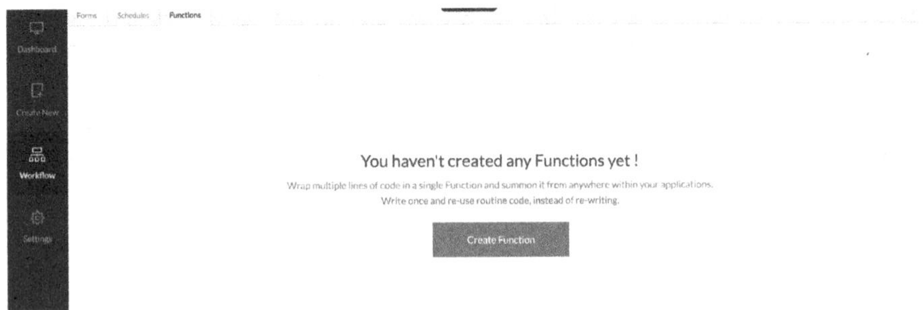

Figure 6-12. *Functions page for the first time*

3. On the next screen (Figure 6-13), enter *bc_tax* for the *function name* and *finance* for the *Namespace* (an identifier to group similar functions in one category). Then select *float* in the *Return Type*.

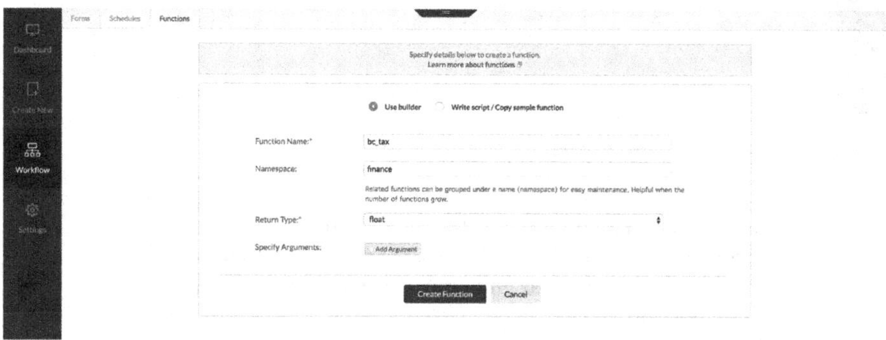

Figure 6-13. *Creating a new function*

4. Click on the *Add Argument* button. Then enter *Amount* and select *float* for the first argument (Figure 6-14).

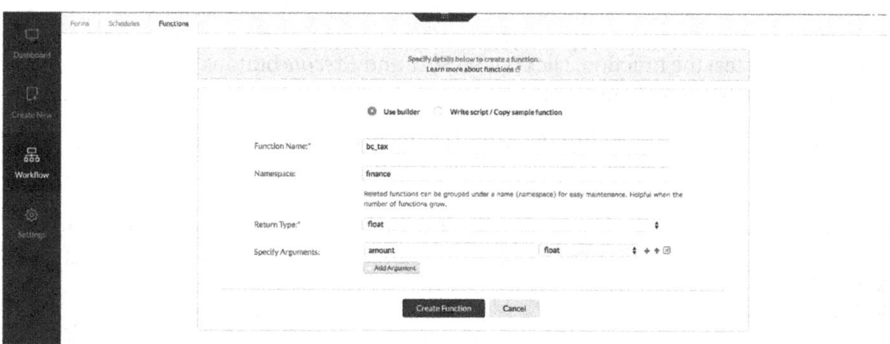

Figure 6-14. *Adding a new function*

5. Click *Create Function* to continue. An empty function with the specifications set in the previous section will be created. It's ready for you to create the logic for it (Figure 6-15).

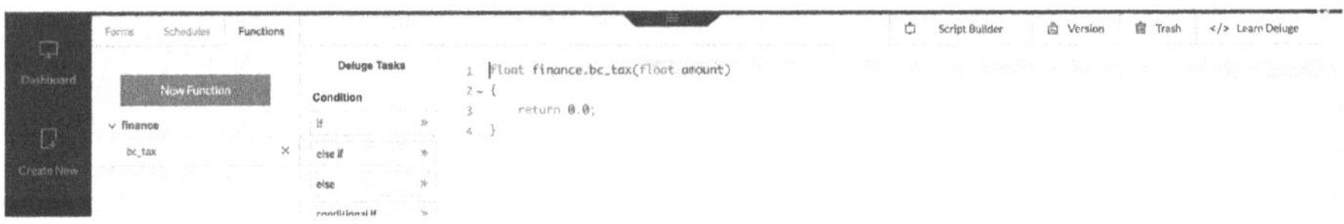

Figure 6-15. *New function skeleton*

6. In the function body (Figure 6-16), between the curly braces, type `return amount * 0.05 + amount * 0.07;`. This line will calculate the sales tax and return the results as the output of the function.

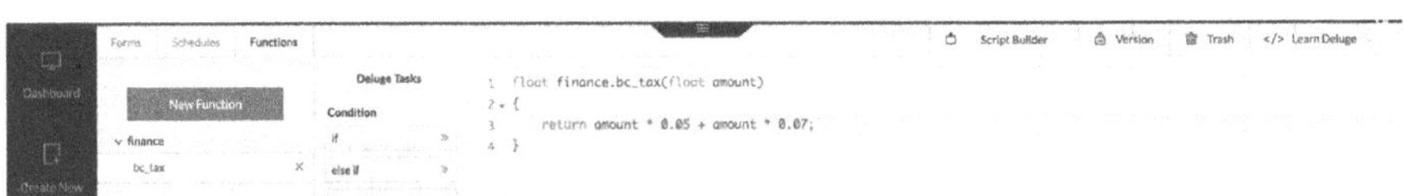

Figure 6-16. *Entering the function's code*

7. To test the function, click on the *Save* and *Execute* buttons at the bottom of the page.

8. In the *Execute Script* dialog box (Figure 6-17) enter an amount and click *Submit.*

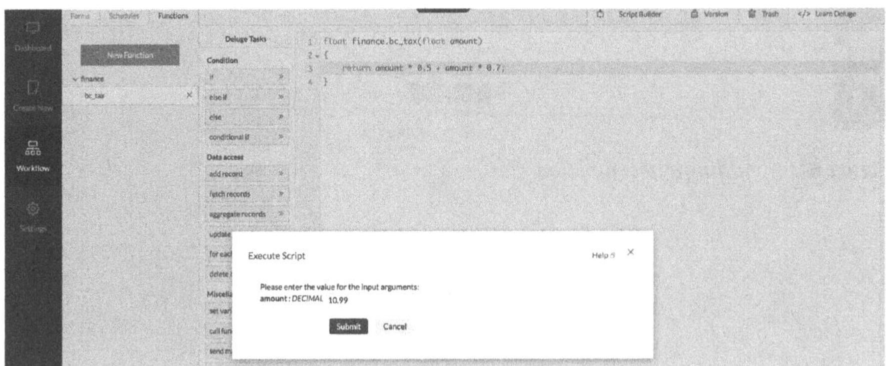

Figure 6-17. *Testing the function*

9. The result of the script will appear in the dialog box (Figure 6-18). The 5% + 7% sales tax is calculated and returned as the result. Click *Execute* to test the function with more numbers and click *Close* when you are done.

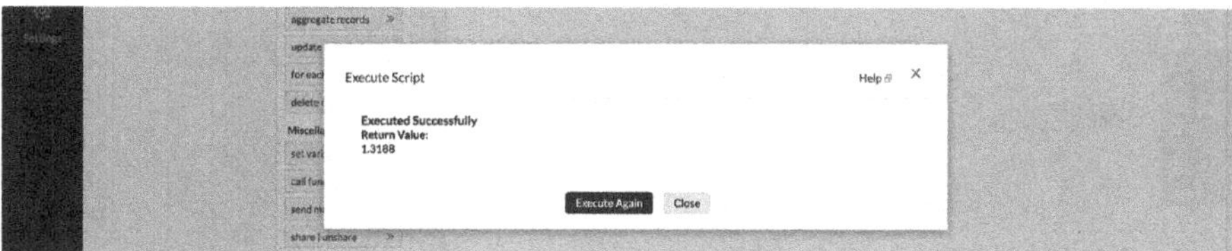

Figure 6-18. *Function test results*

Modifying Functions

This little function is quite handy and you can call it whenever you need to calculate sales tax for an amount anywhere in the application. However, it could use some improvement.

In the province of British Columbia, there are goods and services that are exempt from the provincial tax for a number of reasons. Let's add the option of including or excluding the PST in the *bc_tax()* function as well.

You will find yourself improving functions and updating their code often. This is one of the great benefits of using functions. You change the code once and the logic gets updated across the app.

To add the tax exemption item to the *bc_tax()* function, follow these steps:

1. Open the function code by choosing *Workflow* ➤ *Functions* ➤ *finance* ➤ *bc_tax*.

2. Add a second argument called *PST_Exemption* of type *Boolean*. This argument will tell the function whether to include PST in the calculation.

3. Add a new line before the *return* statement:

```
PST = IF(PST_Exemption, 0, amount * 0.07);
```

   This is a conditional `IF` statement, and it allows you to skip the longer `if () {}` statement and include the condition and action on one line.

   This line simply means that the value of variable *PST* will equal *0* if the value of *PST_Exemption* is *true*, or will equal 7% of the amount if *PST_Exemption* is *false*.

4. To include the PST value, change the `return` statement to:

```
return amount * 0.05 + PST;
```

The result should look like Figure 6-19.

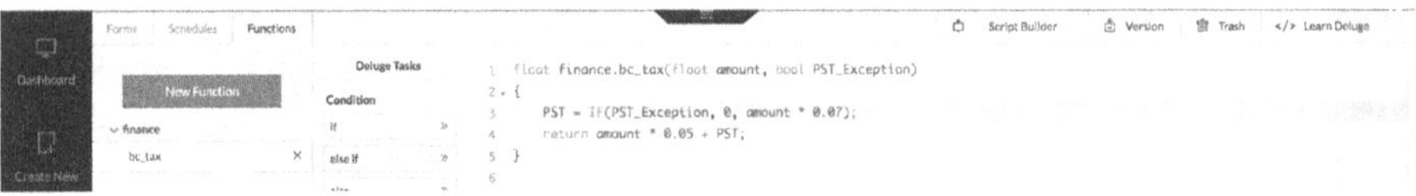

Figure 6-19. *Updated function code*

5. Click *Save* and the *Execute* buttons to test the code. This time, the second *PST_Exemption* argument will show up alongside the *amount*.

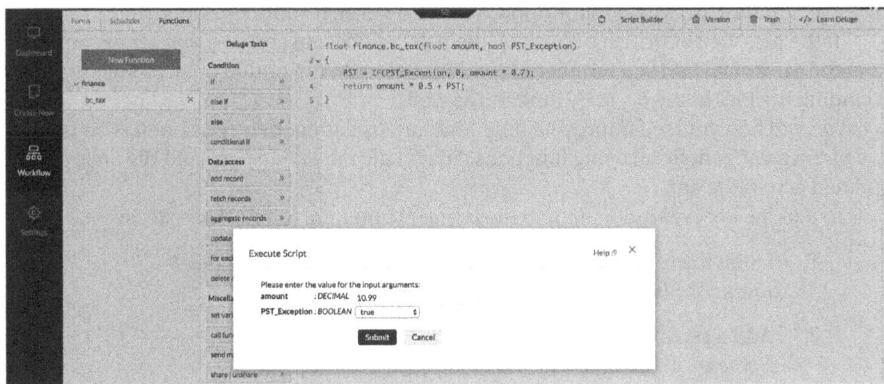

Figure 6-20. *Testing the updated function*

6. Click *Submit* to see the results with *PST_Exemption* set to *true* and *false*. Click *Close* when you are done (Figure 6-21).

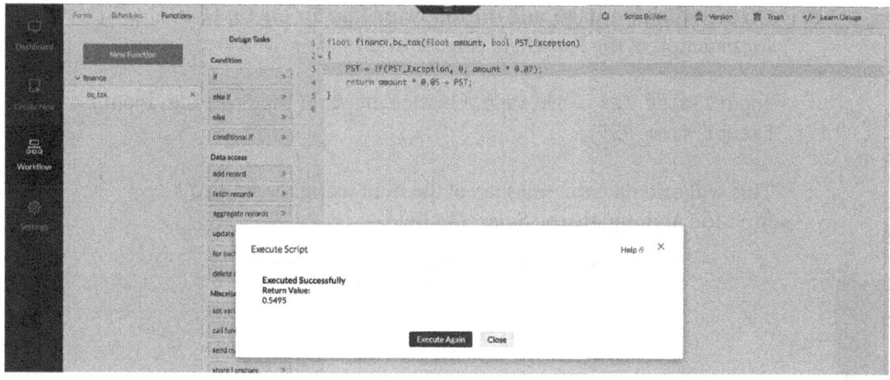

Figure 6-21. Function test results

Calling Functions

Now that this little *bc_tax()* function has passed the test with flying colors, let's use it in a real app. For this, create a new app that accepts goods items and prices as input:

1. Create a new *Creator* app and call it *Products.*
2. Add the following fields to the main form. The result should look like Figure 6-22.
    a. *Item Name*: *Single line* text
    b. *Price*: *Currency*
    c. *Sales Tax*: Currency
    d. *Total Price*: *Formula* (*Price* + *Sales_Tax*)

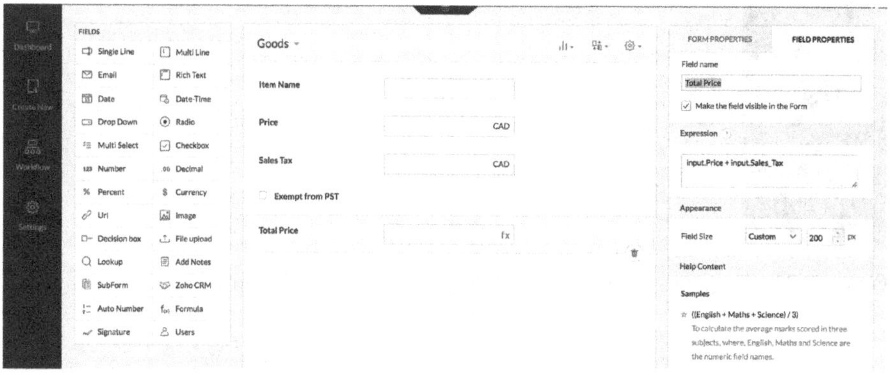

Figure 6-22. A new form to test the function

3. On the *Workflow* page, add the following line for *the On User Input* action of the *Price* field (Figure 6-23):

```
input.Sales_Tax = thisapp.finance.bc_tax(input.Price,input.
Exempt_from_PST);
```

This will calculate the sales tax of the item using the *bc_tax()* function and update the *Sales_Tax* field.

Figure 6-23. *Auto-calculating sales tax for the Price field*

4. Add the same line of code to the *On User Input* action of the *Exemption_from_PST* field.

5. Run the app to see the formula in action (Figure 6-24).
As soon as you change the value in the *Price* field, the amount of the *Sales Tax* changes too. Checking or unchecking *Exempt from PST* will change the amount of the sales tax as well as indicate whether to include or exclude the 7% PST.

Figure 6-24. *The goods form in action benefiting from bc_tax() function*

Built-in Functions

Deluge offers a host of built-in functions to help you write better programs and staying productive.

Here is a quick overview of these functions with two examples per category:

- String functions, such as:
    - *length()*—Returns the length of a string.
    - *toUpperCase()*—Converts the string to all caps.
- Math and trigonometry functions, such as:
    - *round(number)*—Returns the rounded copy of a float number.
    - *min(number1, number 2)*—Return the larger number of the passed arguments.
- Date-time functions, such as:
    - *toDate()*—Returns the date value of a string.
    - *today*—Returns today's date.
- Logical functions, such as:
    - *isNull(field)*—Returns *true* if the value of the *field* is null.
    - *isBlank(field)*—Returns *true* if the value of the *field* is empty.
- List functions, such as:
    - *get(index)*—Returns an element at a given index (starting from 0).
    - *sort()*—Returns a sorted copy of a list.
- Map functions, such as:
    - *keys()*—Returns a list of map keys.
    - *size()*—Returns the number of pairs of key/value in a map.
- XML functions, such as:
    - *toXml()*—Returns the XML of a string.
    - *executeXpath()*—Returns a formatted string from an XPath and XML.

- URL functions, such as:
    - *getUrl()*—Submits an HTTP GET request and returns a response in a string.
    - *postUrl()*—Submits an HTTP POST request and returns a response in a string.
- Form data functions, such as:
    - *getFieldNames()*—Returns a list with all the fields in a form.
    - *getFieldValue()*—Returns the value of a given field.
- Common functions, such as:
    - *getJSON()*—Returns JSON data by sending an HTTP GET request.
    - *toString()*—Converts a value to a string.
- Encryption functions, such as:
    - *urlEncode()*—Performs HTML encoding on a given URL.
    - *urlDecode()*—Performs HTML decoding on a given URL.

Reference Make sure you review the built-in functions in the documentation at: `https://www.zoho.com/creator/help/script/built-in-functions/built-in-functions.html`, especially before creating new functions. There is no point in reinventing the wheel when there are ready-made functions available.

Summary

This chapter delved a bit deeper into the basics of scripting in Deluge. You learned about tools provided by Creator to help you write code more efficiently. Then you moved on to learn about some of the most commonly used elements of the language.

In the interest of time (and paper), I covered only the essentials here. To go forward in your journey with Zoho Creator, the official documentation and the Creator forums will help you down the road.

Learning syntax and functionalities of a language is necessary, but that's not enough to become a good programmer. One key point to remember is that writing good code, even as lightweight as a few lines in Deluge (or any other language), is not just about knowing all the elements of the language by heart.

Programming is a way of thinking, with its own paradigms and best practices. It is important to think like a programmer. There are a number of books on the topic (e.g., *Think Like a Programmer,* `https://www.nostarch.com/thinklikeaprogrammer`). To put it simply, if you want to be a good programmer (in any language), adopt these practices:

- Put your problem-solving hat on
- Embrace trial and error
- Always document your code
- Write clean and readable code
- Never hesitate to ask the online community for help

■ **Reference** To learn more about Deluge, refer to official documentation at: `https://www.zoho.com/creator/help/script/`. If you get stuck anywhere, post your question on the Creator forum at: `https://forums.zoho.com/zoho-creator`. A generous community of professionals is there to help. And of course, you can reach out to me. I will be glad to help as well. ☺

CHAPTER 7

Building a Complete Real Estate Management System

By now you have a good grasp of the essential concepts of building apps in Zoho Creator. In this chapter, you are going to put it altogether and build a lightweight real estate management application while learning a few new concepts and practices too.

The proposed Real Estate Management System (REMS) will manage four essential elements of a typical real estate business:

- Listings
- Employees
- Clients
- Bookings

The chapter is divided into five sections that resemble the main phases of creating a software solution. Try to follow the same phases, even if briefly, whenever you build apps that will be rolled out to other users to improve the chances of success for the solution (app) dramatically.

Note To create business apps ready for prime-time, upgrading to the *Standard* edition of Zoho Creator is a bare minimum. Also, two of the topics discussed in this chapter (*Roles* and *Profiles*) require features that are only available in the *Enterprise* edition of Creator. Depending on your (or your client's) current plan, you may need to upgrade to a higher (and costlier) edition. To make the best decision or recommendation, make sure you review the complete comparison chart of features and limits per edition at: `https://www.zoho.com/creator/pricing-comparison-2016.html`.

A. Shabdar, *Mastering Zoho Creator*, DOI 10.1007/978-1-4842-2907-1_7

Gathering Requirements

This is where the fun begins. You or someone in your organization, or your client, identifies a challenge and need for an information solution of sorts to address these challenges.

A Crash Course on Gathering Requirements

According to an article in *Code Magazine,* "Studies indicate that between 40% and 60% of all defects found in software projects can be traced back to errors made while gathering requirements" (`http://www.codemag.com/Article/0102061`).

This is bad news and good news. The good news is that by gathering requirements properly, you can increase the chances of success for your business application considerably.

In general, gathering requirements is about documenting all the problems the software will solve from all stakeholders involved in the project, from the decision-maker to the end user.

This is often the job of the business analyst; however, it is common for developers to wear a business analyst's hat. You will need to interview all stakeholders, document all the requirements, review the current business processes, and obtain a sign-off from stakeholders and project owners. Getting approvals and sign-off at every stage is key to protecting everyone involved in the project, especially you.

It is interesting to see that sometimes different stakeholders have different views of what the software has to do, or the requirements don't fully match the current business process.

Requirements are often divided into two categories:

- **Functional**—What the application does and how it does it
- **Non-functional**—The user experience (including the look and feel) and usability of the application

---

■ **Reference** Learn more about requirement gathering from these sources: Introduction to Gathering Requirements and Creating Use Cases (`http://www.codemag.com/Article/0102061`) Process Approach To Requirements Gathering (`https://www.batimes.com/articles/process-approach-to-requirements-gathering.html`) Techniques Used in Business Requirements Gathering (`http://www.brighthubpm.com/project-planning/60264-techniques-used-in-business-requirements-gathering/`)

An outcome of this phase would be use cases, which are different scenarios in which the application will be used and how users and the application will interact. An example is adding a new listing item to the system.

Another outcome of requirements gathering are user personas, which are representations of users and how they will use the application. For example, a 25-year-old sales executive who is using the system on her mobile device.

■ **Reference** Read more about use cases and personas on `Usability.gov` at `https://www.usability.gov/how-to-and-tools/methods/use-cases.html` and `https://www.usability.gov/how-to-and-tools/methods/personas.html`.

REMS Requirements

Back story: The client is a reputable real estate company with a team of 40 people, 30 of which are sales executives active in residential and commercial real estate since 1999. They approached us for a new development of a real east management system (REMS) as their old system is slow and missed some key features.

After agreeing on the project basics, we went on a full-on requirement gathering spree and ended up with these high-level findings (I skip through some of the details in the interest of time and beautiful trees):

The REMS must be able to perform the following:

- Store all data on the cloud securely and be accessible to all users at all times without the need for a local server
- Provide secure access to various users in different ways:
    - Salespeople can only add clients and bookings and search in all listings and their own clients and bookings
    - Managers need full access except deletion of the records
    - Admin must have full access
- Manage adding, updating, and deleting listing items, employees, clients, and bookings
- Provide powerful and easy-to-use search mechanisms
- Generate reports of the following:
    - Master list (property listings)
    - Current bookings and the pipeline
    - Monthly and quarterly employee performance
    - Top 10 clients in a year
    - Year on year sales performance
- Provide a mobile app for salespeople on the go so they can easily access information

Based on this information, we can design use cases personas, such as salespeople and mangers, and determine how each one interacts with different parts of the system.

At the end, you must make sure that you have all the documentation in one package and have obtained the sign-off of all the stakeholders.

Design

Based on the requirements gathered in the previous section, we must first identify the best platform to create the solution with optimum efficiency and performance. It should also be future-proof.

We could design the application from scratch using a combination of leading web technologies (e.g., a combination of Node.js, Angular JS, and Ionic) to provide maximum flexibility and performance in the implementation. But it would take months to develop such system and thousands of lines of code. The client is (not surprisingly) in a rush.

Fortunately, you know a platform that can deliver above and beyond what the client wants: Zoho Creator. You can fulfill all the requirements of the REMS while providing the developer with a rapid development platform. Creator will also offer the flexibility and ease of development for future iterations of the REM.

Now that we have our platform selected, you can start designing the app.

Data Model Design

There is an ongoing debate in the software development community (oh, the never-ending debates) as to where to start designing software—from the frontend (the UI design and its logic) or the backend (the database design and business logic). A quick Google search of "frontend or backend first" or similar will prove my point.

In the modern UI-heavy apps, and rightfully so for consumer-oriented apps, UX (user experience) is often at the center of software design. You start with creating an appealing and intuitive look and feel and then work on the logic and data accordingly.

Zoho Creator takes this to the next level. You start by designing a UI, albeit within the constraints of the Creator, and it creates the underlying database for you automatically. In fact, in Creator, each form represents a data table that can optionally connect to other forms (i.e., a table).

After creating forms (and consequently the underlying tables), all you need to do is add business logic and automation, and you will have a functional piece of software.

However, this shouldn't stop you from thinking objectively about designing an optimal data model. You should know exactly what data needs to be stored in the app, what the data field types are, and how the data is related.

Reference Read more on data modeling on Agile Data (`http://www.agiledata.org/essays/dataModeling101.html`) and Talend (`https://www.talend.com/blog/2017/05/05/data-model-design-best-practices-part-1/`).

A Visual Representation of Data

Figure 7-1 is a simplified data diagram that shows data entities (tables, or forms in Creator) and their relationships in the REMS application.

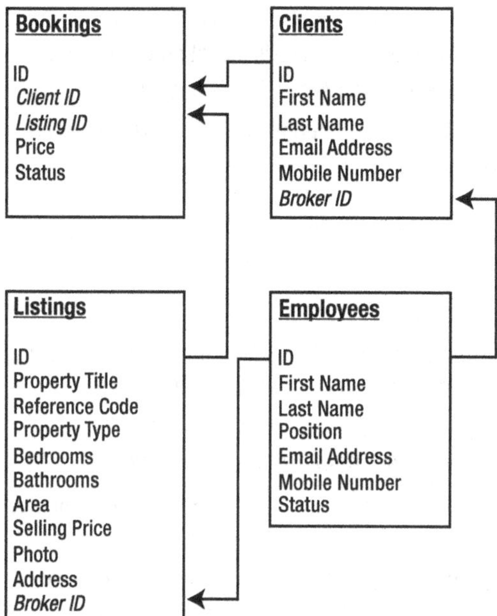

Figure 7-1. *REMS app simplified data model*

■ **Note** I made the diagram in Figure 7-1 in Lucidchart (`https://www.lucidchart.com/`), which is a powerful cloud-based diagraming tool. I am not affiliated with them in any way. I just enjoy their product and recommend you giving it a try too.

There are four data entities in the REMS, which will turn into Creator forms:

- Employees
- Listings
- Clients
- Bookings

Each one of these entities will store its corresponding records. Each record will have the fields shown in Figure 7-1.

You can see that there are relationships connecting entities to each other. For example, a Client record can have a related Employee record. This is a direct translation from how a real estate business operates, meaning that leads and contacts (clients) each belong to an employee to make sure clients are taken care of and commissions are paid out fairly.

The reason that we don't put employee information in the same place as the clients is that if, for example, one employee has multiple clients (which is usually the case), we won't need to repeat all the employee information (ID, First Name, Last Name, etc.) for each client record over and over again.

■ **Reference** Separating the data model into different entities is a best practice in data design and is called *normalization*. The topic is beyond the scope of this book; however, you can read about the concept in many resources, including Agile Data at: `http://www.agiledata.org/essays/relationalDatabases.html` and `http://agiledata.org/essays/dataNormalization.html`.

User Interface Design

This is where the fun begins. You get to design the look and feel of your masterpiece and make it as engaging and pleasant as possible for the users to interact with your app.

> *"A happy customer tells a friend; an unhappy customer tells the world."*
>
> —Source Unknown

I can't emphasize enough that the user is royalty and should be treated as such. So, it is paramount that every element of the UI be designed with the user in mind.

UI design is not easy. In fact, I would argue that it is harder than designing databases and writing code. The reason is that the UI is the part of the software that the user can see and use, so it's vulnerable to misuse and critique.

Although in Creator you are limited by its design elements and there is not wiggle room (thankfully, sometimes), there are still points that you need to keep in mind, such as:

- Choosing the right labels for fields
- Placing fields on forms in the optimum and logical order
- Enabling the right data validation and formatting mechanisms
- Designing reports that are easy to understand
- Displaying messages that provide users with easy-to-follow instructions

---

■ **Reference** There are virtually endless resources for learning UX and UI design. A good place to start are the courses offered by Coursera at: `https://www.coursera.org/courses?_facet_changed_=true&domains=computer-science&languages=en&query=ux`.

UI Mockups

You might remember from Chapter 4 that we used Mockflow to design the UI schematic. Having mockups prepared before the implementation phase and obtaining sign-off will make the lives of everyone on the project (including you) easier.

Figure 7-2 shows a mockup design of the Employees form.

Inquiry Form

First Name

Last Name

Position — Sales Director

Email

Mobile Number

Work Status — Active

Submit — Reset

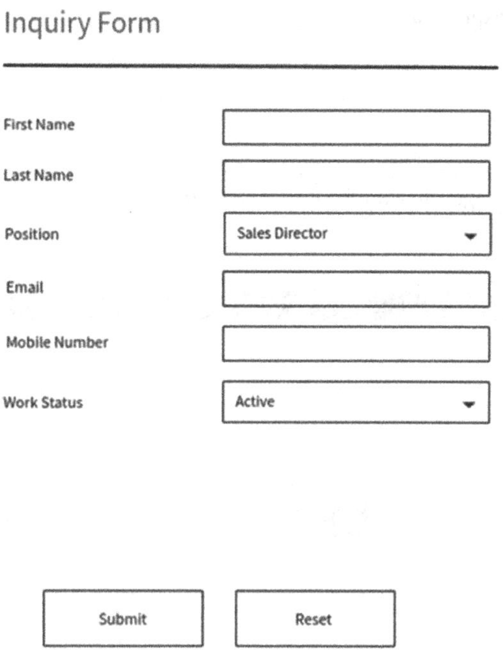

Figure 7-2. *A mockup design of the Employees form*

MORE MOCKUPS

Design three more mockups for the other forms:

- Listings
- Clients
- Bookings

You can also create mockups for the reports.

Implementation

Now that you have designed the data model and the UI, you can start building. Let's start with creating the app itself and all the forms and data relationships.

Then you will make it easier for your users to access the app elements by rearranging the sidebar. After that, you'll see how to configure sharing and data access levels. You will continue customizing existing reports and adding new ones. Finally, you will tap into the power of pages and add create a listing exposé (a factsheet).

Creating the App

As a refresher, to create the REMS, follow these steps:

1. On the Zoho Creator home page, click on the *New Application* button (Figure 7-3).

Figure 7-3. *Zoho Creator home page (logged in)*

2. Enter *REMS* in the *Application Name* dialog box (Figure 7-4) and click Create.

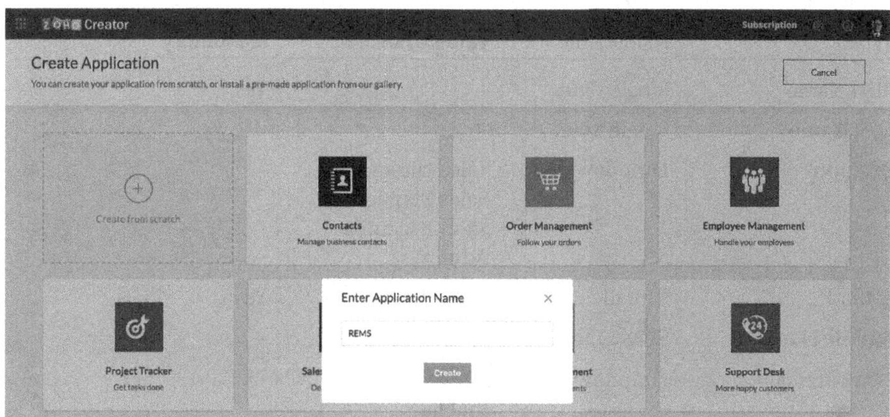

Figure 7-4. *Creating a new app*

Creating Forms

You will be creating four forms for the REMS app:

- Employees
- Listings
- Clients
- Bookings

By now, you are well versed in creating forms, so this section doesn't get into much detail. However, I review each form and make sure all the elements are added as mentioned here.

Employees Form

The REMS app opens in Edit mode with a default form named *Untitled* ready to be modified.

Rename the form *Employees* and add the fields listed in Table 7-1 to it.

Table 7-1. *Fields of the Employees Form*

Type	Name/Title	Value/Choices	Mandatory
First Name	Single Line	--	Yes
Last Name	Single Line	--	--
Position	Dropdown	Sales Director Sales Manager Sales Executive Admin	--
E-mail	E-mail	Table Text	Yes
Mobile Number	Single Line	--	--
Work Status	Dropdown	Active Inactive	--

The resulting form should look like Figure 7-5.

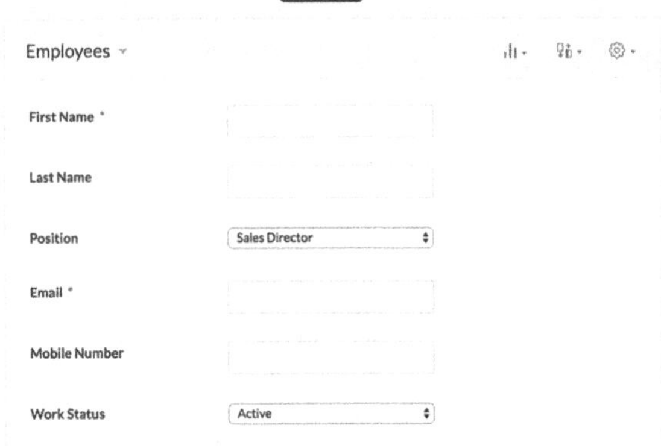

Figure 7-5. *Employees form is complete*

It is recommended that you run the app often, especially after adding a form or other elements. This will help you make sure the app is being built as per the envisioned design and all pieces work as intended.

Figure 7-6 shows the *Employees* form in action.

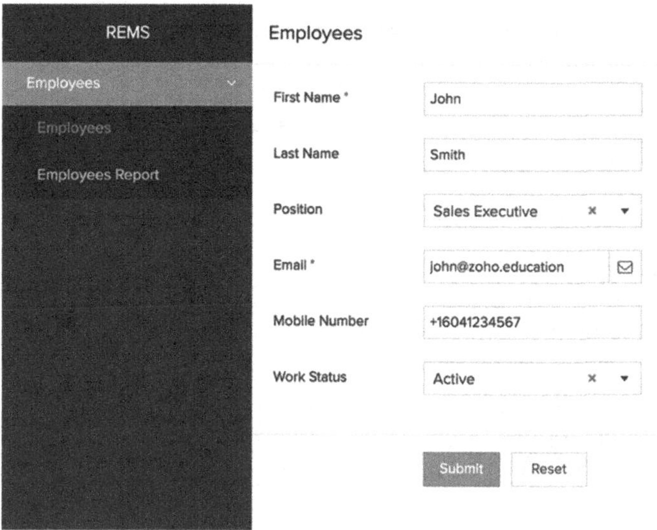

Figure 7-6. *Employees form populated in the runtime*

You can add records and check the data entered through the form in the automatically created *employees report* (Figure 7-7).

Figure 7-7. *Default employees report*

You will learn how to customize reports and add new one later in this chapter. You can now go back to Edit mode and continue adding the remaining forms.

Clients Form

Similar to the *Employees* form, you need to create a new form for the clients:

1. Click on the *Create* button on the left sidebar and choose *Form* from the context menu.
2. Populate the *New Form* dialog as shown in Figure 7-8 and then click *Create* to proceed.

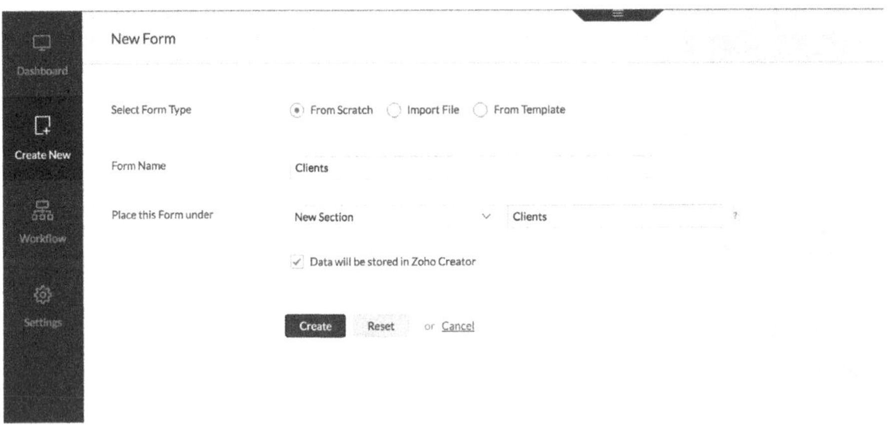

Figure 7-8. *Creating a new form called Clients*

3. On the *Clients* form, add the fields listed in Table 7-2.

Table 7-2. *Fields of the Clients Form*

Type	Name/Title	Value/Choices	Mandatory
First Name	Single Line	--	Yes
Last Name	Single Line	--	--
E-mail	E-mail	Table Text	Yes
Mobile Number	Single Line	--	--
Broker ID	Lookup	*(From Employees; see below)*	--

4. For the *Broker ID* field, you need to load the names of the employees from the *Employees* form. Drag a Lookup field on to the form. The *Create Lookup Relation* dialog box will open.

5. Select *REMS* in the *Applications* column, *Employees* in the *Forms* column, and *First Name* in the *Fields* column, as shown in Figure 7-9.

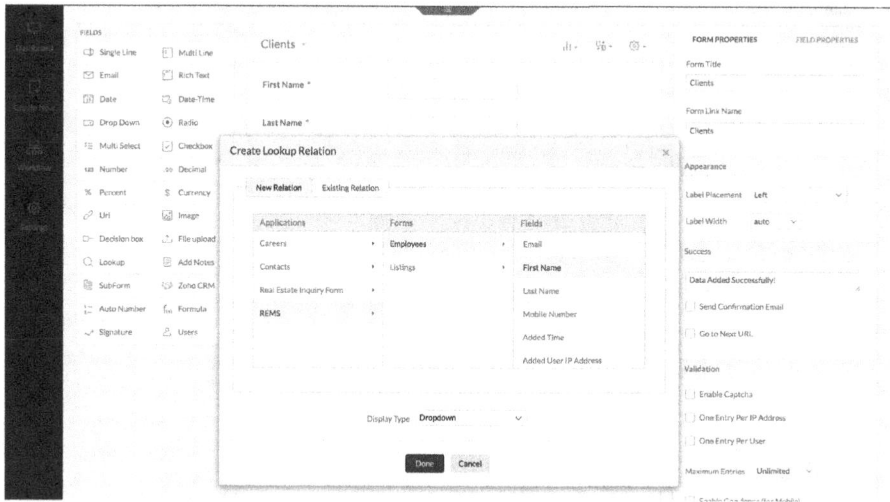

Figure 7-9. *Creating an Employees lookup field for the Clients form*

6. With the *Broker ID* field selected, add *Last Name* under *Display Fields* in the *Field Properties* sidebar.

7. Type a single space " " as a separator between the two fields (Figure 7-10).

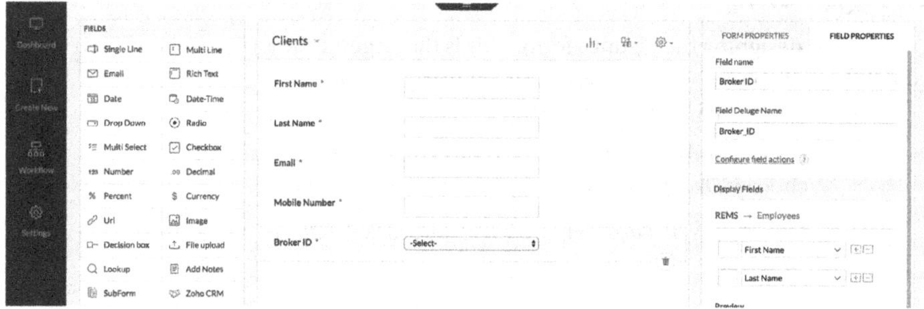

Figure 7-10. *Updating the display fields for Broker ID*

The *Clients* form is complete. The result should look like Figure 7-11.

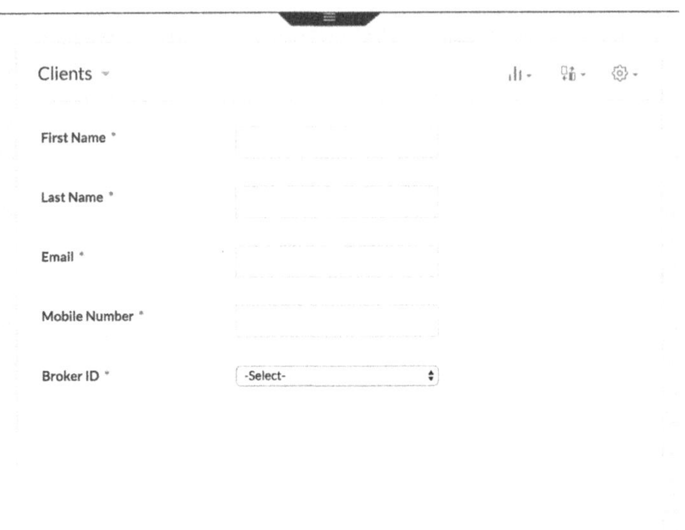

Figure 7-11. *Clients form is complete*

Run the app and test the *Clients* form. Add a few clients and make sure the form works as intended. See how you can add a *Broker* (employee) to a new client.

After testing the form, go back to Edit mode.

Listings Form

Continue by designing the Listings form. This is the largest form in the app and has (almost) all the information necessary for a property listing.

Follow these steps to create the Listings form:

1. In Edit mode, click the *Create* button on the left sidebar and choose *Form* from the context menu.
2. Fill in the *New Form* (Figure 7-12) and click *Create* to continue.

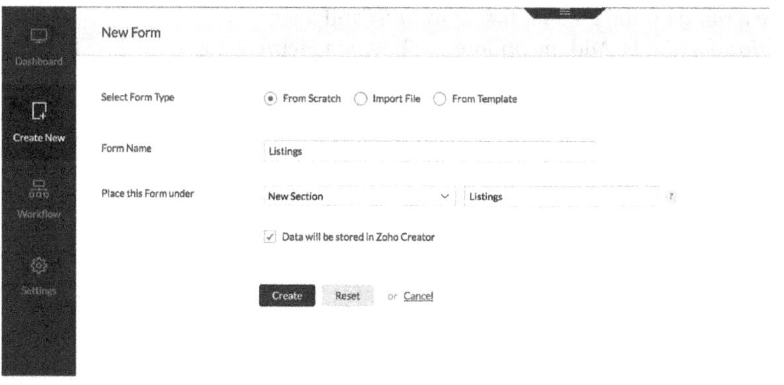

***Figure 7-12.** Creating a new form called Listings*

3. On the *Listings* form, add the fields listed in Table 7-3.

***Table 7-3.** Fields of the Listings Form*

Type	Name/Title	Value/Choices	Mandatory
Property Title	Single Line	--	Yes
Reference Code	Single Line	--	Yes
Property type	Dropdown	Apartment Villa Land	Yes
Bedrooms	Radio	Studio 0, 1, 2, 3, 4, 5	--
Bathrooms	Radio	1, 2, 3	--
Area (m2)	Decimal	--	--
Selling Price	Currency	--	--
Photo	Image	--	--
Address	Multi Line	--	Yes
Broker	Lookup	*(From Employees)*	

4. Use a *radio* button field for the *Bedrooms* (and later, *Bathroom*) fields. Add the options as shown in Figure 7-13.

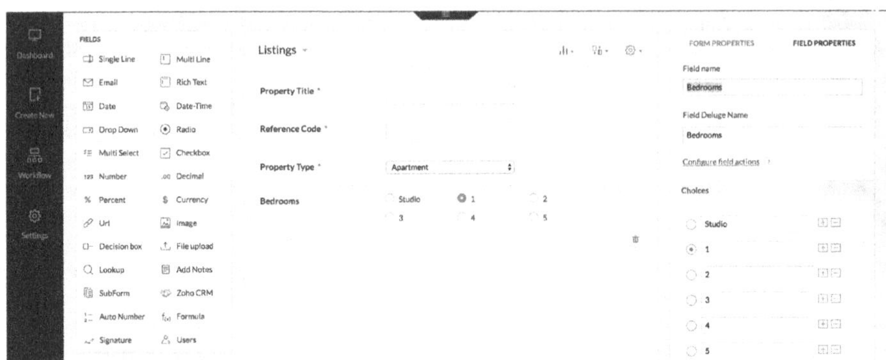

Figure 7-13. *Adding the Bedrooms field*

5. Finish by adding a *Broker* field similar to the *Clients* form. The resulting form should look like Figure 7-14.

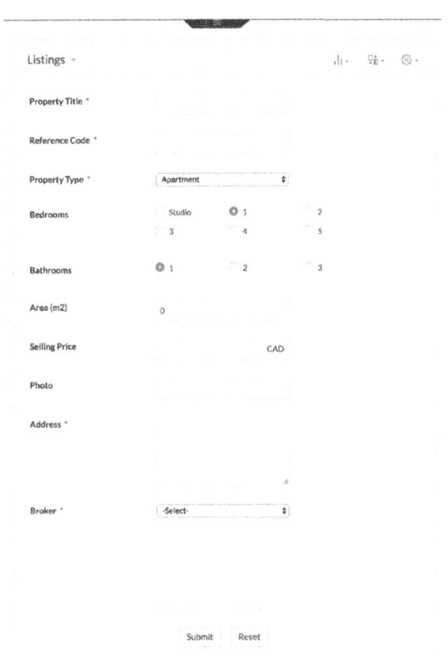

Figure 7-14. *Listings form is complete*

Bookings Form

There is one more form to create, called Bookings. The Bookings form is used when a property (listing) is booked by a client. It should collect the information of three different entities:

- The subject property, coming from the Listings form
- The seller, coming from the Clients form
- The buyer, coming from the Clients form

To create the Bookings form, follow these steps:

1. In Edit mode, click the *Create* button on the left sidebar and choose *Form* from the context menu.
2. Fill in the *New Form* (Figure 7-15) and click *Create* to continue.

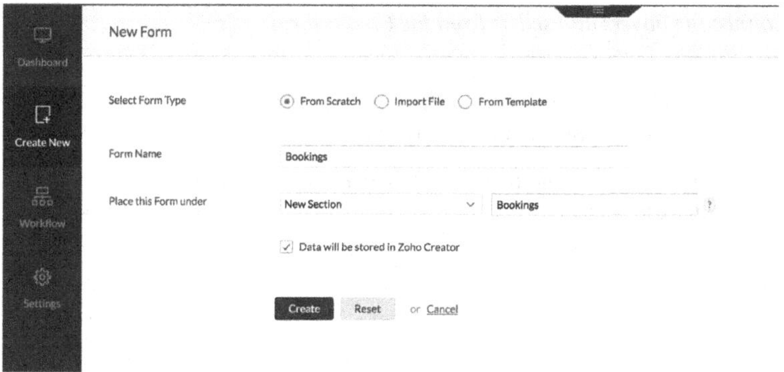

Figure 7-15. *Creating a new form called Bookings*

3. On the *Bookings* form, add the fields listed in Table 7-4.

Table 7-4. *Fields of the Listings Form*

Type	Name/Title	Value/Choices	Mandatory
Buyer's Name	Lookup	*(From Clients)*	Yes
Seller's Name	Lookup	*(From Clients)*	Yes
Subject Property	Lookup	*(From Listings)*	Yes
Offer Price	Currency	--	Yes
Deal Status	Dropdown	Offer Counter Offer Accepted Rejected	--

4. For the *Buyer's Name* and *Seller's Name* fields, add *Lookup* fields that load information from the *Clients* form (Figure 7-16).

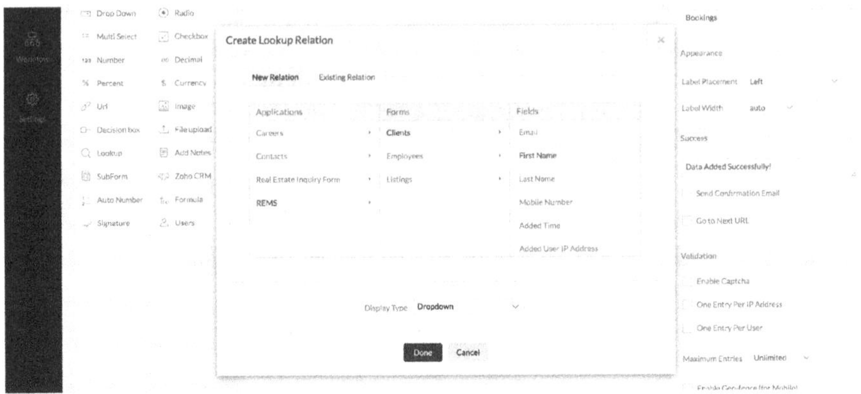

Figure 7-16. *Connecting buyers and sellers from the Clients form*

5. Configure *Display Properties* for both of these fields, so they show the first name and last name in order.

6. For the *Subject Property* field, add a *Lookup* field connected to the *Listings* form (Figure 7-17).

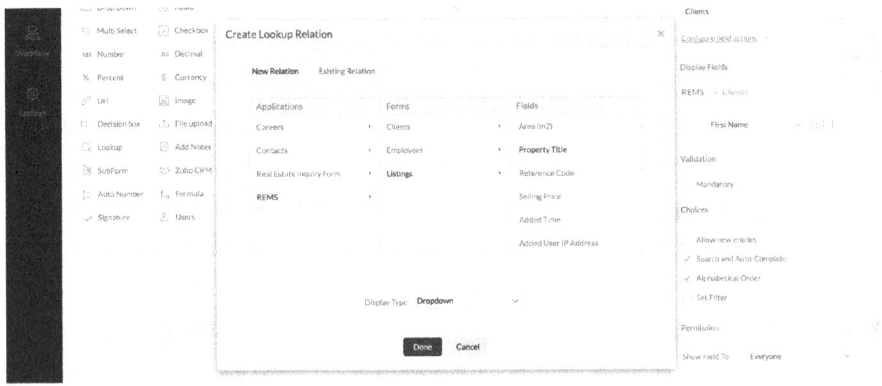

Figure 7-17. *Adding the Subject Property field*

7. Update the *Display Fields* for the *Subject Property* to show both *Property Title* and *Reference Code* separated by - .

The resulting form should look like Figure 7-18.

Figure 7-18. *The Bookings form is complete*

All the forms are created. Run the app and test the fields, lookups, and other elements. Then pour yourself cup of coffee (or your favorite beverage) and return to Edit mode to work on the app. You still have a lot to do.

Rearranging the Sidebar

While running Creator apps, you might have noticed that in the navigation sidebar forms, their corresponding reports are grouped together in separate sections for each form/report pair.

This is not optimal for all scenarios and can get confusing when mixing forms and reports together. You can change this and rearrange the sidebar in a way that is suitable for your users.

For the REMS app, you'll put all the reports in a separate section. Also, as you will see later in this chapter, you can limit access to the Employees form and report, so only the admin users can access them. You will put these two under a separate section too.

Let's get started:

1. In Edit mode, click *Settings* on the sidebar. Then click *Sections* on the left tab bar. The current sections will be shown (Figure 7-19).

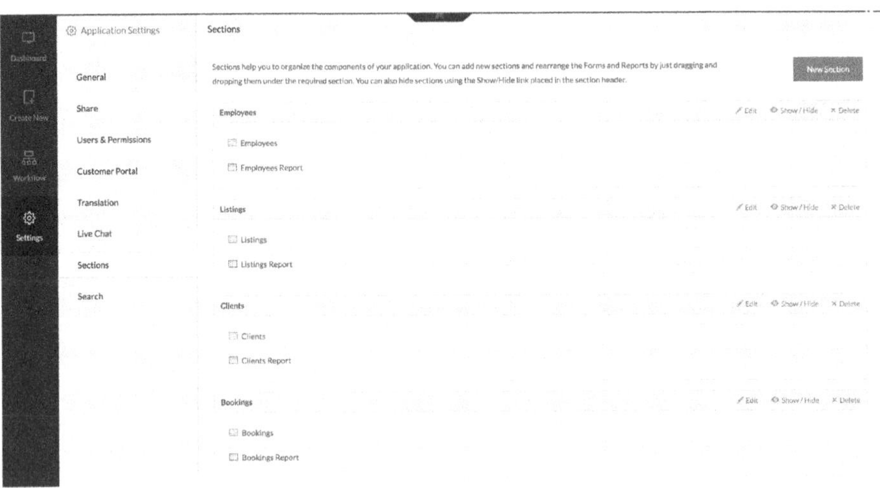

Figure 7-19. *App navigation sections and items*

2. Click the *New Section* button on the top-right side of the page and type *Reports* in the dialog box (Figure 7-20).

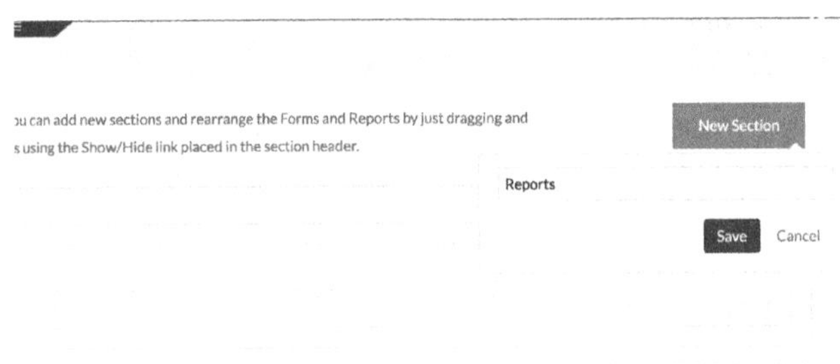

Figure 7-20. *Adding a new section*

3. Click *Save* to add the new section. It will appear at the bottom of the page (Figure 7-21).

Figure 7-21. *Newly created Reports section*

4. Drag and drop all the reports from other sections to the Reports section. You can order them in the section.

5. You can add another section and call it *Admin* to put the *Employee* form and *Report* link there. There is an easier way though—simply click on the little *Edit* icon on the *Employees* section and rename the *Section Name* and the *Section Link Name* to *Admin*.

The result should look like Figure 7-22.

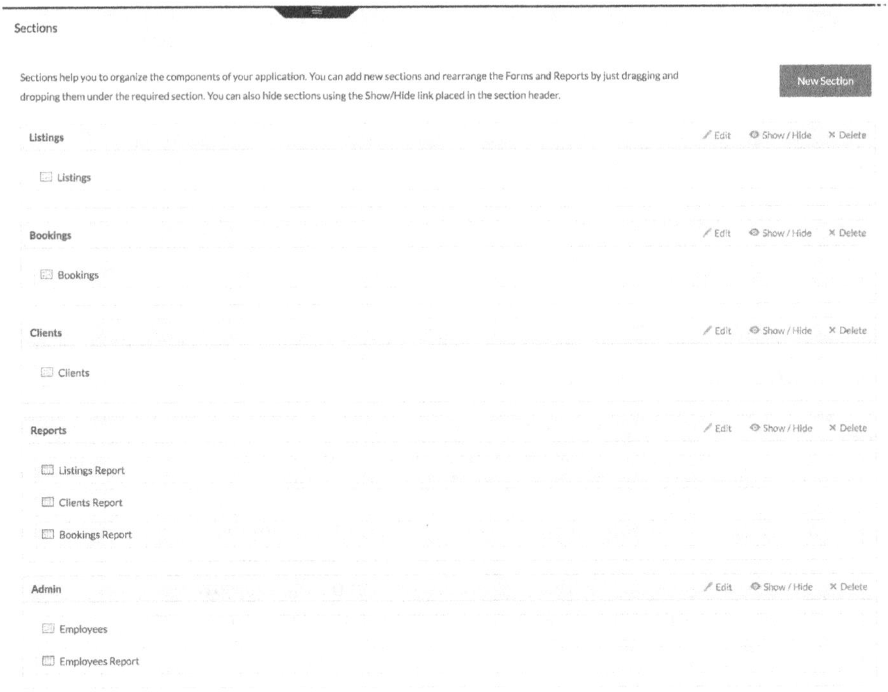

Figure 7-22. *Rearranged sections*

Now if you run the app, you will see the links rearranged nicely on the sidebar.

Reports

There are four reports generated automatically, one for each form in the app:

- Employees report
- Clients report
- Listings report
- Booking report

Each of these is simply a list of all the records available in each form. As you saw in previous chapters, Creator reports offer a host of features, such as filters, sorting, and search. Users can also export and print reports if they have enough permissions.

There are editing and addition features available by default—again, they are visible depending on the permission level of the users.

You can customize pretty much everything about a report. You can:

- Add, remove, and reorder columns
- Narrow down the results based on set criteria
- Limit access to information using permissions
- Change the report format to list, sheet, summary, or chart

For this REMS app, you need two new reports—a list of properties grouped by property type and a visualization of the listings based on a number of fields.

Creating a List Report

To create a new report showing all the listings grouped by property type, follow these steps:

1. In Edit mode, click on *Create New* in the sidebar and then select *Report* from the context menu.
2. Fill in the *New Report* page, as shown in Figure 7-23. Then click *Create and Customize* to continue.

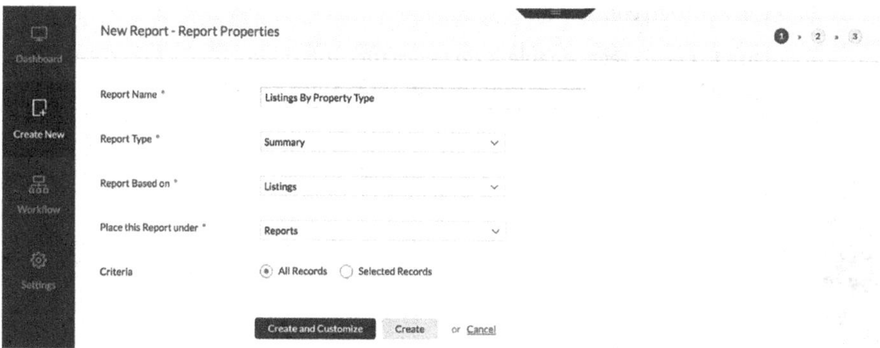

Figure 7-23. *Creating a new report*

3. On the *Grouping and Sorting* tab of the *Report Settings* page, drag the *Property Type* field from the field list on the left and drop it into *Grouping* on the right.

4. Then drag and drop the *Bedrooms* and *Bathrooms* fields to *Sorting*. The result should look like Figure 7-24.

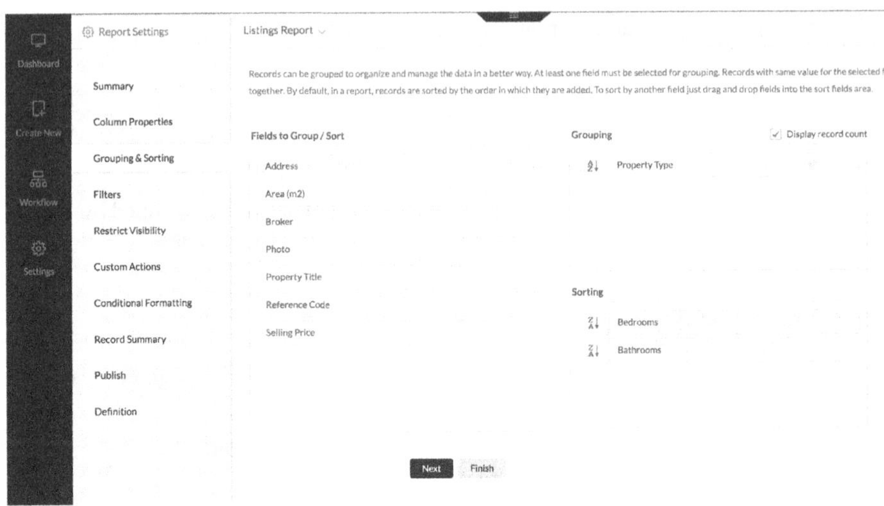

***Figure 7-24.** Customizing the grouping and sorting of the new report*

5. Click *Next* to continue.

6. On the next screen, enable *Auto Filters* for *Bathrooms, Bedrooms,* and *Property Type* (Figure 7-25). Click *Finish* to complete the process.

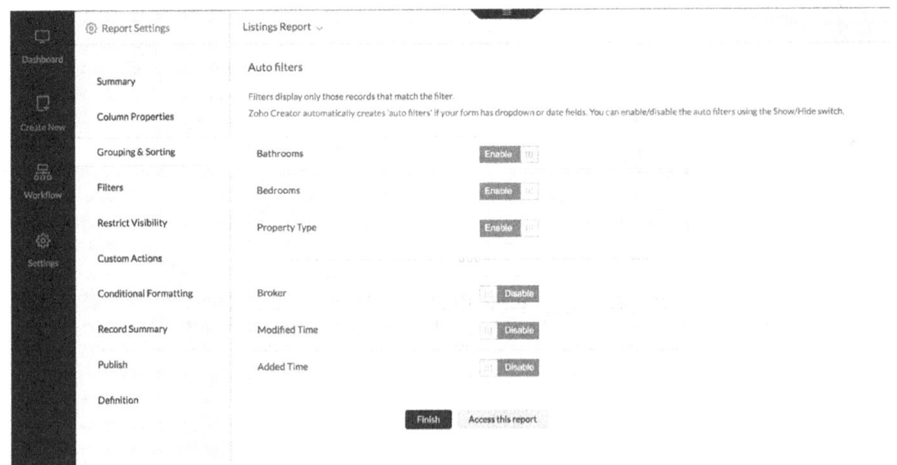

***Figure 7-25.** Enabling Auto Filters for three fields*

7. Run the app and check the newly created *Listing By Property Type* report (Figure 7-26). The entire listing is divided into groups based on the *Property Type* field.

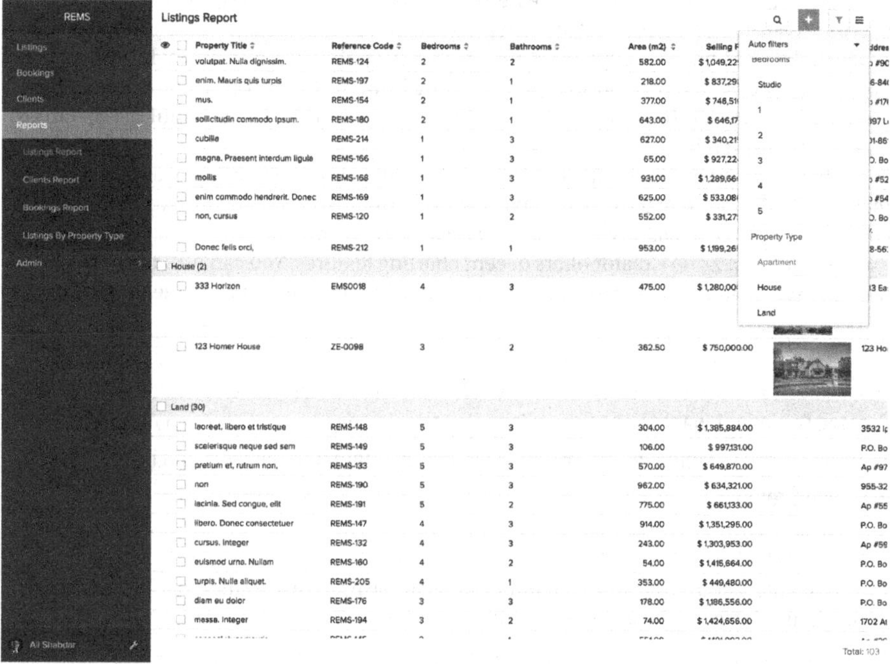

__Figure 7-26.__ The newly created Listing By Property Type report

8. Click on the *Filter* (funnel icon) button on the top-right of the screen. Notice the fields with auto filter enabled are listed for quick selection.

■ **Tip** The listing data shown in Figure 7-26 is created via a useful online tool, `generatedata.com`, and then imported into the REMS app. You can create virtually any kind of dummy datasets for testing purposes.

Visualizing Data

Data visualization is one of the top trends of the past couple of years. We live in an era in which information is a ubiquitous and inseparable part of human civilization.

Terabytes of information are created by humans and machines every single day (`https://analyticsweek.com/content/big-data-facts/`) and the ability to make sense of data has become a must for any organization that wants to stay relevant. Possessing the right information and generating human-digestible business intelligence are the biggest assets (or weapons) at the disposal of winners. At least until the machines take over completely.

This little app can generate important information. For instance, you as a decision maker of a successful real estate company want to understand market trends and stay competitive. You can easily visualize otherwise dizzying rows of data.

Fortunately, Zoho Creator offers decent charting features. You can turn textual and numeric values into useful charts and share them with internal users and the outside world.

■ **Note** If your data analysis and reporting requirements exceed the limits of Zoho Creator, you might want to check out Zoho Reports (`https://www.zoho.com/reports/features.html`). It offers a host of advanced features for large datasets and is integrated well with Creator.

To create a chart that shows market trends in terms of distribution of different types of properties based on size and price, follow these steps:

1. Create a new report for the Listings form with the information shown in Figure 7-27. Choose *Pivot Chart* as the *report type*.

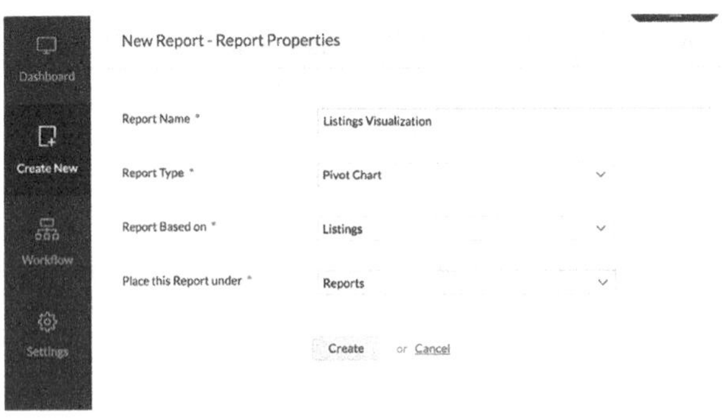

Figure 7-27. *Creating a chart report*

2. Familiarize yourself with the chart designer (Figure 7-28). On the left is the list of available fields. In the middle, you can set graph axes and other elements. On the top, you can choose from different types of charts.

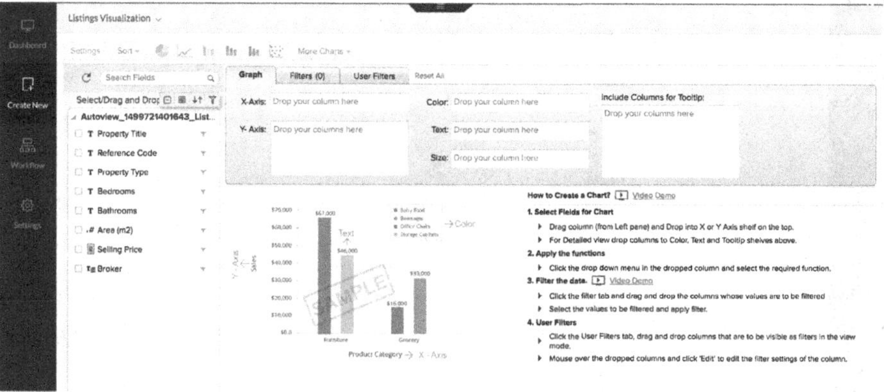

Figure 7-28. *Chart designer*

3. Referring to Figure 7-29, add four fields to the chart:

    a. Drag the *Area* field and drop it into the *X-Axis* box. Select *Actual(M)* in the field option dropdown.

    b. Drag the *Selling Price* field and drop it into the *Y-Axis* box. Select *Sum* in the field option dropdown.

    c. Drag *Property Type* and drop it into the *Color* box. Select *Actual* in the field option dropdown.

    d. Drag *Bedrooms* and drop it into the Text box. Select *Actual* in the field option dropdown.

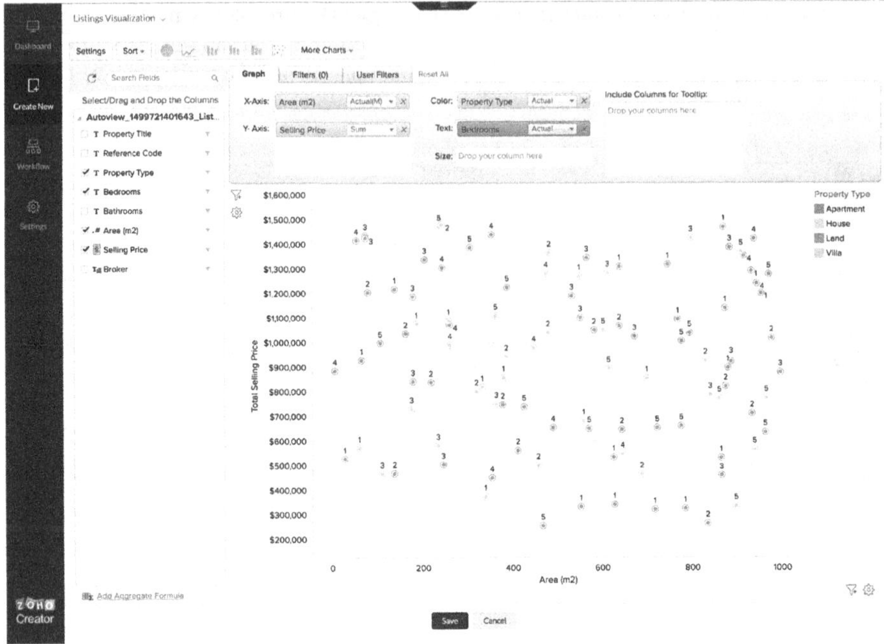

Figure 7-29. *Constructing the chart*

4. Experiment by moving fields around and changing the field options. Check the results in the chart preview.

5. Click the *Filters* tab and drag and drop Broker to the *Filters* box. Then select one or more brokers and see how the results on the chart change based on your selections (Figure 7-30).

***Figure 7-30.** Adding filters to the chart*

6. Click *Save* to finish creating the chart and run the app to see the chart in action (Figure 7-31).

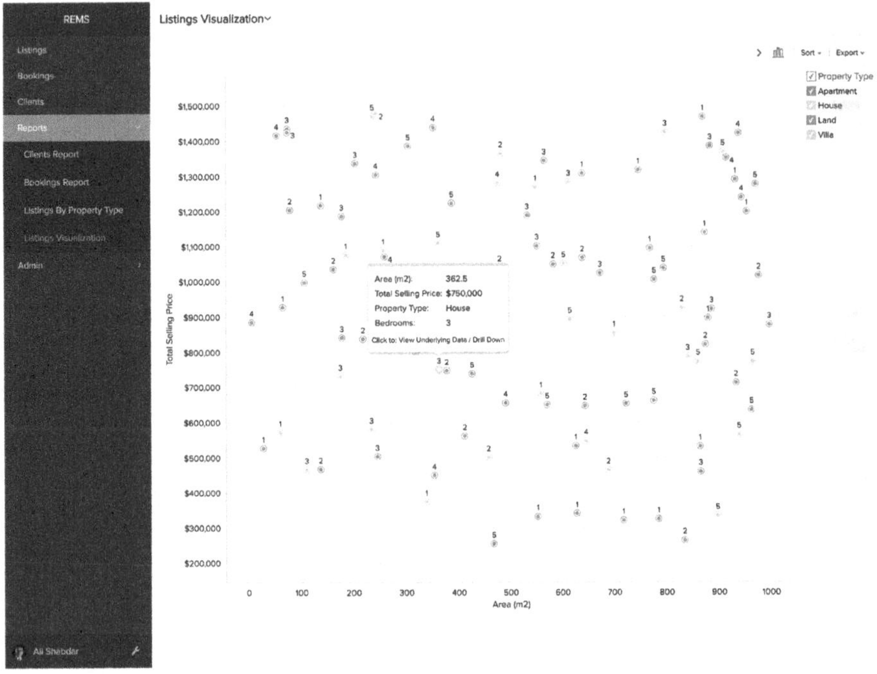

Figure 7-31. *The Listing Visualization chart in action*

Publishing Charts

The result of the *Listings Visualization* chart (report) is quite informative and is not giving away trade secrets. It would be a good idea to share this with the world and attract potential customers.

To publish a chart, open it in Edit mode and click the *Publish* button. Then confirm the procedure. You will be given two options to share the chart (Figure 7-32):

- A *Publish URL*, which just opens the chart in a standalone web page
- An HTML (IFRAME) snippet to embed in any web page

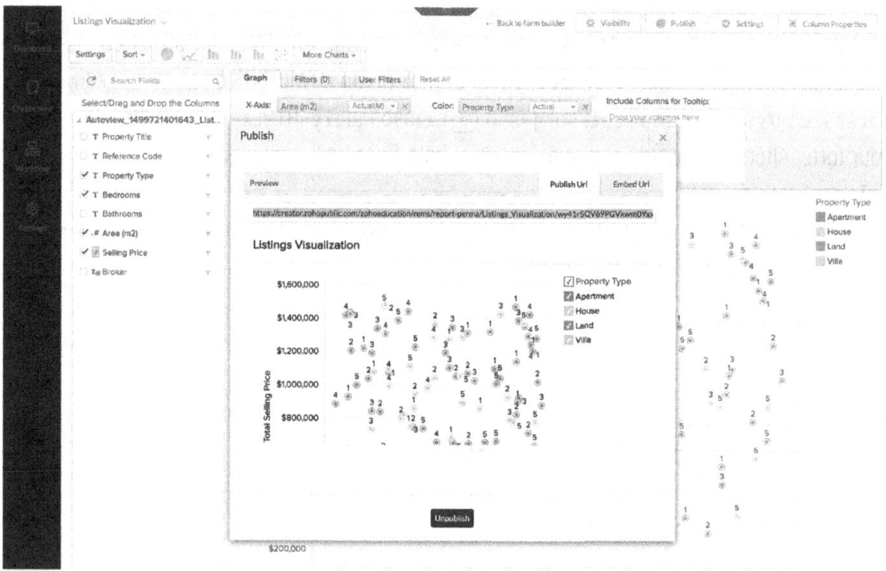

Figure 7-32. Publishing the Listings Visualization chart

EXPLORE REPORTS

There is more to reports. Change the report and chart types and see which one fits the requirements of the application better.

Also, open Visibility and Settings using the corresponding button on top of the page and customize the reports even further.

Pages

One of the more powerful features of Creator is the Pages feature, which allows you to create complex interfaces for your app beyond forms and reports.

Pages are essentially HTML pages with the capability of showing dynamic content directly from the data stored in Creator. They give you a great level of flexibility in what can go on a page.

You can mix elements from forms, reports, and other internal and external web pages, creating dashboards, invoices, and other elements.

Creating an Exposé Page

One of the common documents used in a real estate company is an exposé or factsheet of listing items. Realtors share these documents with potential customers to provide them with a summary of key information.

Although the REMS app has a number of reports, none of them is suitable as an exposé. You can use the Pages feature of Creator to generate them for each listing item.

■ **Note** Creating pages requires intermediate knowledge of HTML and CSS. Head to W3 Schools (`https://www.w3schools.com`) or pick up an HTML/CSS book (`http://www.apress.com/gp/search?facet-subj=subj__i29050&query=HTML%2FCSS`) if these are not your forte. Alternatively, you can seek external help from web designers.

Figure 7-33 shows a wireframe of how the exposé should look. We will try to create a page as close as possible to this wireframe.

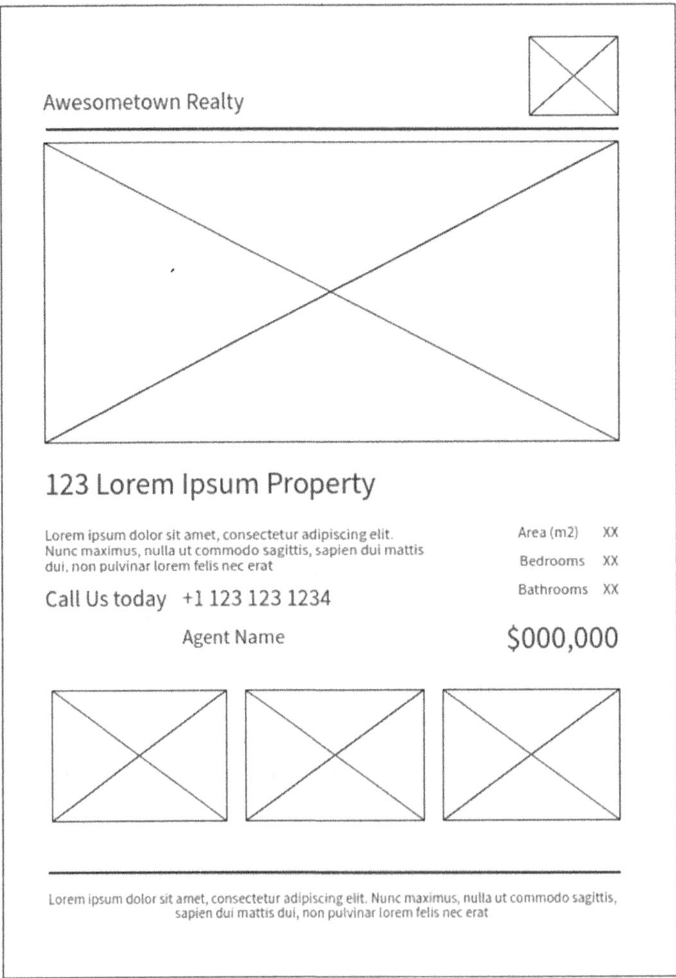

Figure 7-33. *The conceptual design of the exposé*

You'll now create your first Creator page:

1. In Edit mode, click *Create New* on the sidebar and then select Page from the context menu.
2. Name the new page **Expose** and place it under the *Reports* section (Figure 7-34).

Figure 7-34. *Creating a new page*

3. Click *Create* to proceed. The new page will open for editing in the Script Builder (Figure 7-35).

Figure 7-35. *Newly created page opens in Script Builder*

4. Click the *Click to Add New Parameters* link on top-left side of the page. Then type *listing_id* and click *Done* in the *Add Parameters* dialog box (Figure 7-36). You will use this URL parameter later to tell the page which listing item to use to show information.

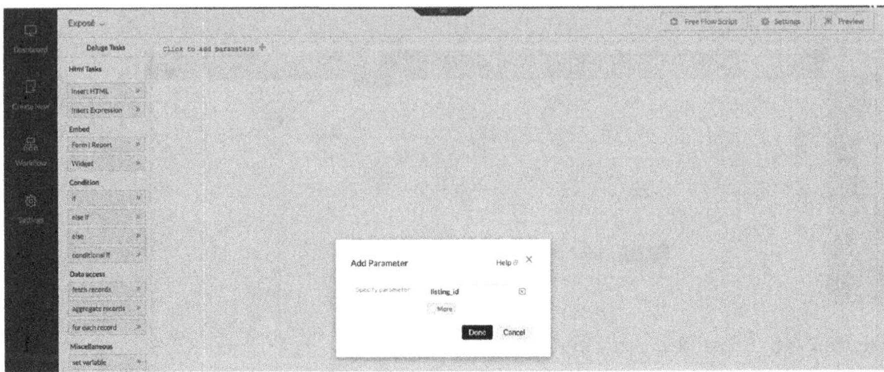

Figure 7-36. *Adding an URL parameter*

5. Switch to Free Flow Script. The underlying code will be shown (Figure 7-37). Between the curly brackets in Lines 4 and 6, you will write all the code.

Figure 7-37. *The skeleton (Deluge) code of the new page*

6. First, you need to load the data to be displayed on the page, i.e. a listing item. Add this line of code right after the opening curly bracket:

   ```
   listing = Listings[Reference_Code == listing_id];
   ```

   This line loads the record with *Reference_Code* indicated in the URL parameter, *listing_id*, and stores it in the *listing* variable.

7. With the data loaded and available, it is time to display the data. Add the following lines after the previous line:

   ```
   <%= listing.Property_Title %>
   <%= listing.Reference_Code %>
   <%= listing.Property_Type %>
   <%= listing.Area_m2 %>
   <%= listing.Bedrooms %>
   <%= listing.Bathrooms %>
   <%= listing.Address %>
   <%= listing.Offer_Price; %>
   ```

■ **Note** Notice the peculiar tag `<%= %>`. This tag is used to embed dynamic results generated by code directly into the body of a page. For example, the line `listing.Property_Title` gets the property title of a listing record. Putting it into the `<%= %>` tags simply places the value wherever in the page the tags are placed. The `<% %>`, on the other hand, just encloses code that doesn't have output to the page.

---

8. To test the code, click on the Preview button on the top-right of the page.

9. A dialog box will appear asking you to enter a value for the `listing_id` URL parameter. Enter a reference code from an existing record in the Listings and click Submit.

10. The page will open in preview mode and you can see the results of the code you just entered (Figure 7-38). You can see that the field values are displayed, but it lacks context and needs major formatting. HTML and CSS to the rescue.

REMS-219 nonummy Villa 964.00 5 3 847-9618 Purus Road 772684.00

Figure 7-38. *Results of the first code are not impressive*

11. Type in the code in Listing 7-1. This code adds the basic HTML skeleton as well as some static sample content. It also places the field values (indicated in bold) in the right places, so the page looks formatted and is usable.

Listing 7-1. Creating the HTML Skeleton Page

```
htmlpage Expose(listing_id)
displayname = "Exposé"
content
<%{
  listing = Listings[Reference_Code == listing_id];
  %>
<table style="border:solid 1px #d1e0e0; margin:30px; padding:20px">
    <tr id="header">
      <td style="border-bottom: 3px solid #d1e0e0;">
        <img style="width:200px" src="http://zoho.education/books/images/
        awesometownlogo.png">
      <h2>Awesometown Realty</h2>
      <p>123 Sunshine St. | www.awesometown.realty | @awesometownrealty</p>
      </td>
    </tr>
    <tr id="title">
      <td>
      <h1><%=listing.Property_Title%> (<%=listing.Reference_Code%>)</h1>
      </td>
    </tr>
<tr>
  <td>
  <table>
    <tr id="body" style="vertical-align: text-top;">
      <td>
        <p>This amazing <%=listing.Property_Type%> is located in the prime
        location in the city.
          Don't miss this opportunity. Contact us for a viewing today</p>
      <% broker = Employees[ID == listing.Broker]; %>
      <h3>Call Us Today: <%=broker.Mobile_Number%> (<%=broker.First_Name + "
      " + broker.Last_Name%>)</h3>
      </td>
    <td>
        <ul>
          <li> Area (m2): <br><strong><%=listing.Area_m2%> </strong></li>
          <li> Bedrooms:   <br><strong><%=listing.Bedrooms%> </strong></li>
          <li> Bathroom:   <br><strong><%=listing.Bathrooms%> </strong></li>
          <li> Address:   <br><strong><%=listing.Address%> </strong></li>
        <h2> $<%=listing.Selling_Price%> ASKING PRICE</h2>
        </ul>
    </td>
```

```
      </tr>
    </table>
    </td>
    </tr>
      <tr id="footer">
      <td style="border-top: 3px solid #d1e0e0; text-align: center;">
        <p>Lorem ipsum dolor sit amet, consectetur adipiscing elit, sed do
        eiusmod tempor incididunt ut labore et dolore magna aliqua.</p>
        </td>
      </tr>
</table>
<%}%>
```

You could design this page any way you like or use different techniques, such as `<div></div>` instead of `<table></table>`. The important point here to see how this page template works and how it mixes HTML, CSS, and Deluge.

12. Preview the page again. Oh, the difference (Figure 7-39). Although not a show stopper, the page looks more appealing and the information is properly placed.

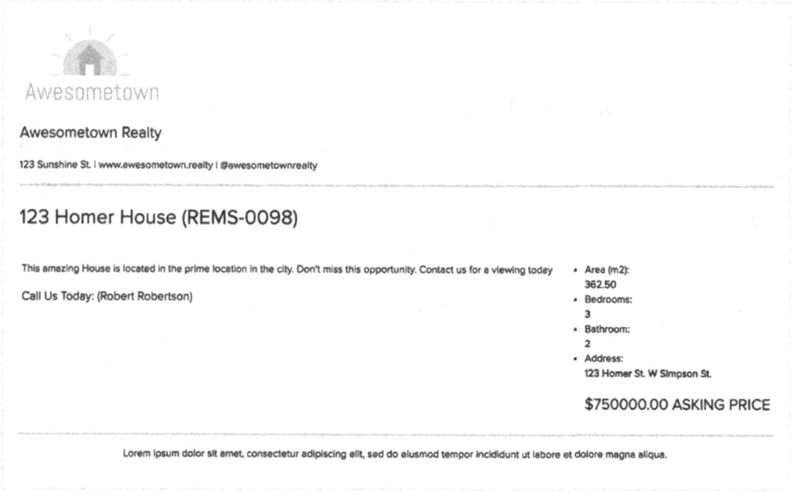

Figure 7-39. *Thanks to a dash of HTML and CSS, the page looks much better now*

13. The next step is to add a feature image (or more) to the page. Go back and add the following code (Listing 7-2) after the closing `</tr>` in Line 21.

Listing 7-2. Adding a Feature Image to the Page

```
<tr id="feature_image">
  <td>
    <%
      img = listing.Photo;
      img = img.replaceFirst("/sharedBy/appLinkName/", zoho.appuri);
      img = img.replaceFirst("appLinkName", "rems");
      img = img.replaceFirst("viewLinkName", "Listings_By_Property_Type");
      img = img.replaceFirst("sharedBy", "zohoeducation");
      img = img.replaceFirst("sharedBy", "zohoeducation");
      img = img.replaceFirst("fieldName", listing.ID + "Photo");
      img = img.replaceFirst("image", "image-download");
      img = img.replaceFirst(">", "style='width:100%'");
    %>
    <%=img%>
  </td>
</tr>
```

■ **Note** You might be as puzzled as I am about the code in Listing 7-2, but you can't simply show `listing.Photo`. Creator, for reasons unknown to me, stores the whole `<img>` tag instead of a simple URI to the image file. To make it worse, the URI is wrong and needs to be reconstructed correctly. This tiny hack may not work in the future if Zoho opts to take a less annoying route to store images. So, be on the lookout and fix your code accordingly.

---

14. Save and preview the page. The feature image will be displayed on the page (Figure 7-40).

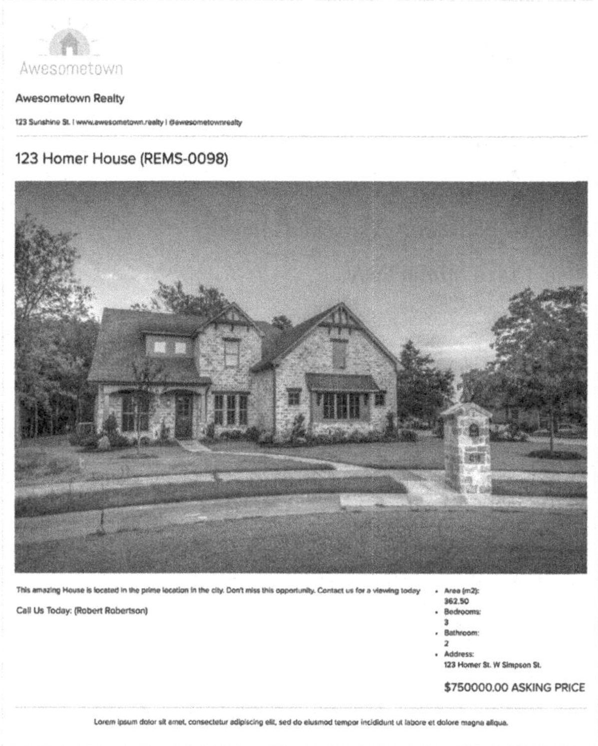

Figure 7-40. *The formatted exposé with a featured image*

Using the Page

If you run the app and click on *Exposé* on the *Reports* sidebar, you will receive an error in executing the page: "*Value is empty and 'replaceFirst' function cannot be applied Line:(24)*".

This is simply because merely opening the page will not pass the required *listing_id* parameter to the code, resulting in the error.

You need to add the following bit to the *Exposé* page URL and pass a reference code along with it to:

```
?listing_id=<Reference_Code>
```

One way is to add an *URL* field to the *Listings* form that stores the link to the Exposé page matching the listing and then show that *URL* field in the reports, so users can open it with a simple click.

Let's see how to do this:

1. Open the *Listings* form in Edit mode.
2. In the Listings form (Figure 7-41):
    a. Add an URL field to the form.
    b. Rename it *Expose Link*.
    c. Under URL Options, enable *Link Name* and *Title*.
    d. Change *Show Field To* to *Admin Only*.

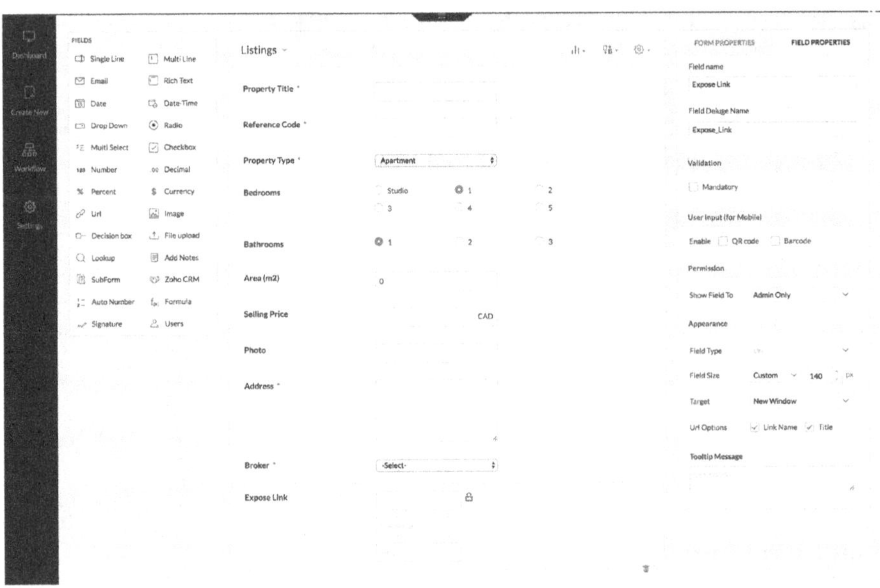

***Figure 7-41.** Adding an URL field to the Listings form*

3. Open the workflow area and add the following code to the *On User Input* action of the *Reference Code* field (Figure 7-42):

```
link = trim(input.Reference_Code); //ensures no white
space around the code
input.Expose_Link = "<a target='_blank'
href='https://app.zohocreator.com/zohoeducation/
rems/#Page:Expose?listing_id=" + link + "'>" + link +
"</a>";
```

This way, whenever a user changes the reference code, the corresponding URL to the *Exposé* page will be updated too.

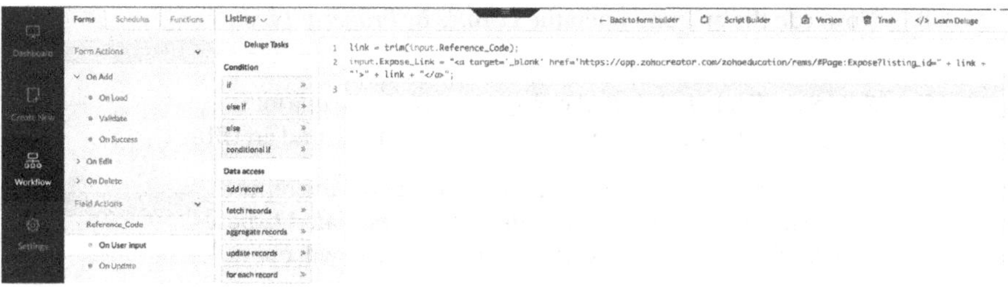

***Figure 7-42.** Dynamically constructing an URL for listing as a link to their respective Exposé page*

4. Click *Save* and then move to the *Listing By Property Type* report.

5. In the Column tab, add an *Expose Link* field to the report as the last column. This will enable the view to show the URL title link to the URL, which opens the exposé for a specific record.

6. Move to the *Settings* page. In the *Sections* tab, add a new section called Hidden.

7. Move the *Exposé* item to the *Hidden* section. Then click on the *Show/Hide* link to hide the *Hidden* section from the users in the runtime (Figure 7-43). This is because you don't want the users to open the *Exposé* page directly and cause an error.

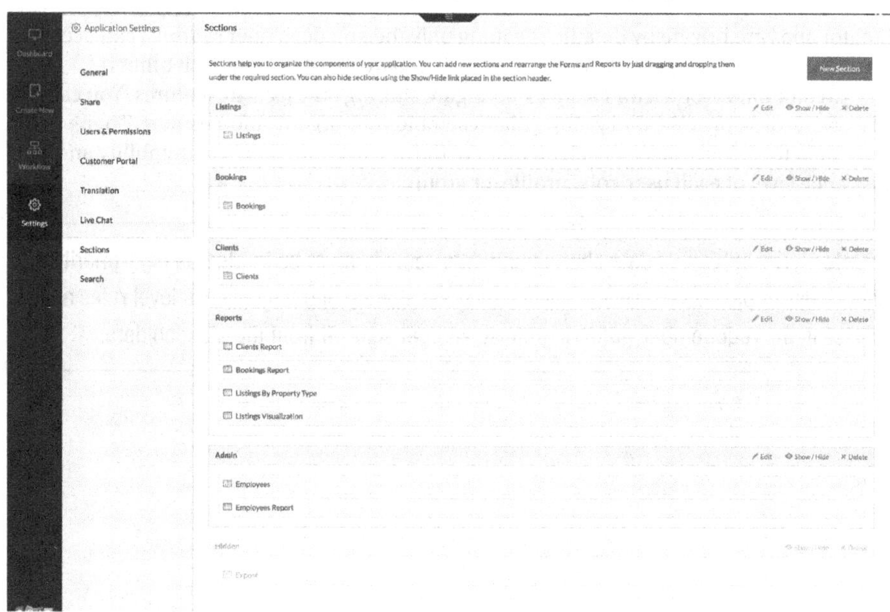

***Figure 7-43.** Adding a new hidden section to hide the direct link to the Exposé page*

8. Now, run the app and open the *Listings By Property Type* report.

9. Edit one of the records and change the *reference code* for it. The *Expose Link* column will populate with a title and an URL.

10. Save the changes. You will be redirected back to the report. Notice the updated *reference code* and the populated *Expose Link* fields (Figure 7-44). Clicking on these links will open their *Exposé* pages.

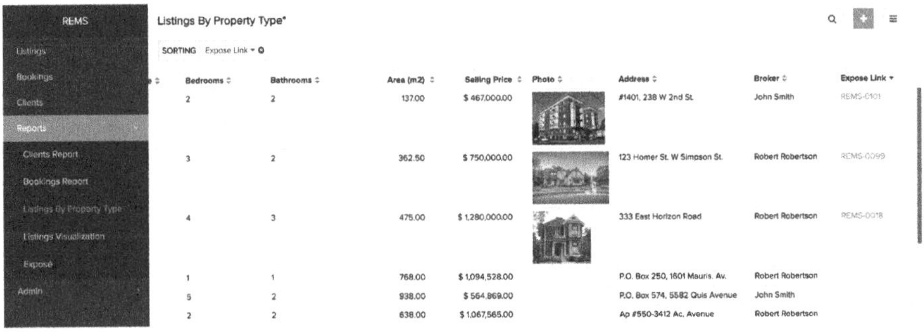

Figure 7-44. *The Expose link added to the report linking to the corresponding Exposé page*

Security and Access Management

Creator apps are private by default, meaning only the app developer (admin) can access them. But what is the point of an app if you can't share the goodness with others?

Creator offers robust and easy-to-configure sharing and security features. You can add users, roles, profiles, and groups that resemble your organizational chart. Then you can define who accesses each element of the app according to accountability and clearance level of each user, role, profile, or group.

■ **Note** The subject of data sharing and data security must be treated as high-priority in all business apps. Make sure you collect accurate sharing and data access level rules and policies in the requirement-gathering phase and get sign-off from the stakeholders.

Creating Roles

Each Creator user must belong to a role and a profile. By default, there are three roles defined in the system:

- *CEO*
- *Manager*
- *Employee*

Roles are arranged in a hierarchy to resemble the organizational chart of a company. This helps with reporting and data sharing mechanisms.

There are also two default profiles:

- *Administrator*
- *User*

The first user (you) is set automatically by Creator to *CEO* and *Administrator* for highest permission levels.

For the REMS app, you need one more role for the sales director, called Director.

Follow these steps to create the Director role:

1. In Edit mode, open the *Settings* page and select the *Users & Permissions* tab.
2. Click on the *Roles* tab (top). Then click on the *New Role* button.
3. In the New *Role* dialog box (Figure 7-45), enter *Director* in the *Role Name* field and *CEO* in the *Reports To* field. Click *Save* to continue.

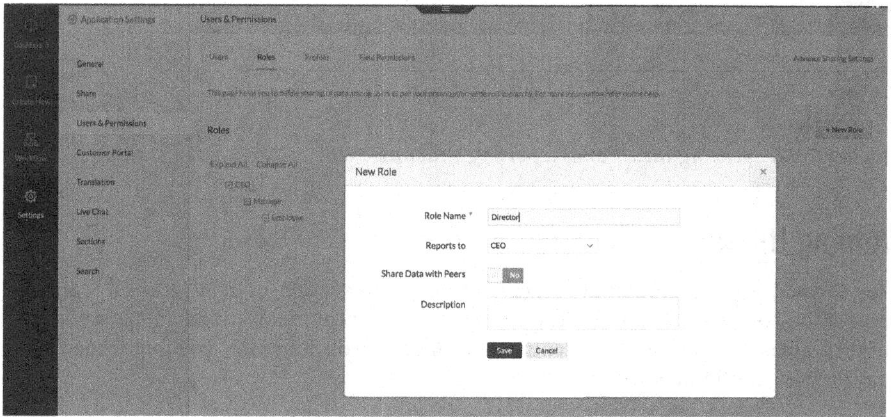

***Figure 7-45.** Adding a new role*

4. With a new director in town, the existing *Manager* role should report directly to the director. In the *Roles* page, click on *Manager* to open the *Edit Role* form (Figure 7-46). Then change *Reports* To to *Director*.

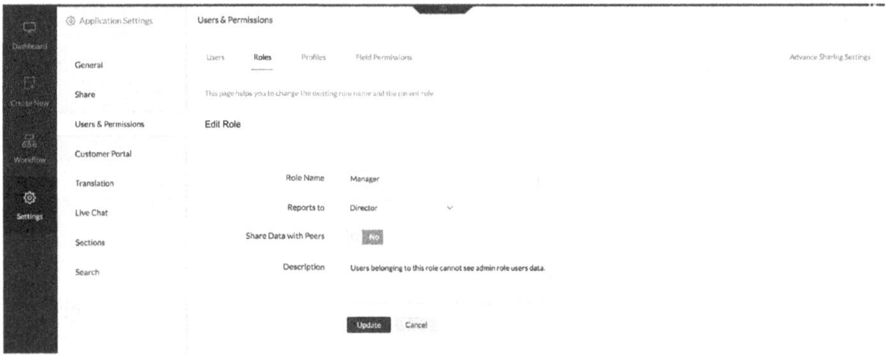

Figure 7-46. *Changing the reporting structure for the Manager role*

5. Click *Save* to apply the changes. The new reporting structure is shown in Figure 7-47.

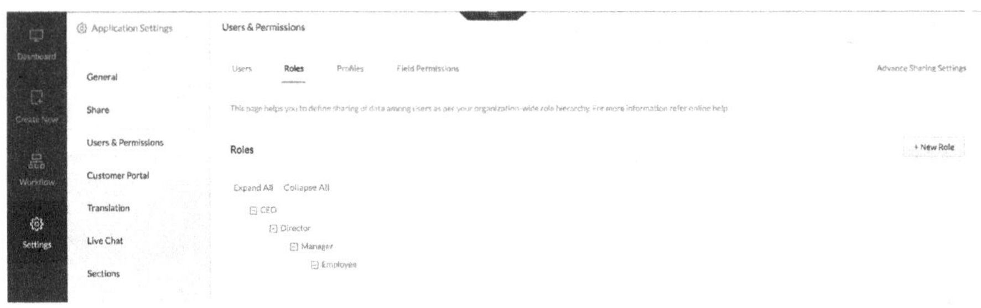

Figure 7-47. *New organizational reporting structure*

Adding Users

You can add, edit, and remove users either from within an app, or in the general *Setup* area of the Zoho Creator. In both cases, these users will count toward the total number of users available to your Creator account. So, depending on your plan, you might need to pay for every additional user.

To add new users to the app, follow these steps:

1. In Edit mode, click on the *Settings* button on the sidebar. Then click *Users & Permissions* in the *Applications Settings* tab bar. Alternatively, you can click the *Home* button in the top menu bar, then the *Settings* button. Then click *Users* under *User Management* (Figure 7-48).

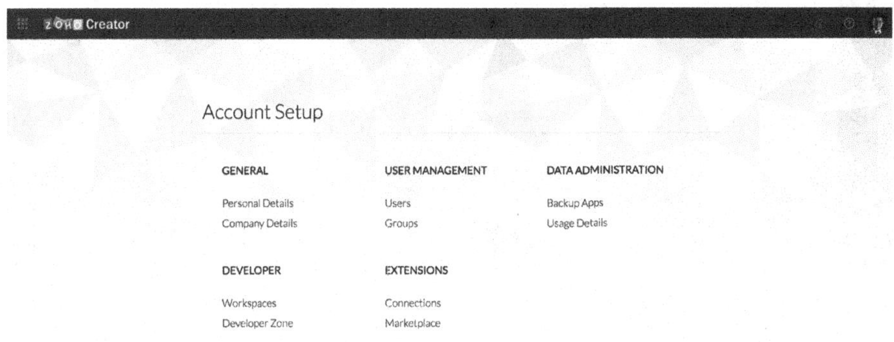

Figure 7-48. *Creator Setup page*

2. On the Users page (Figure 7-49), click *Add Users*.

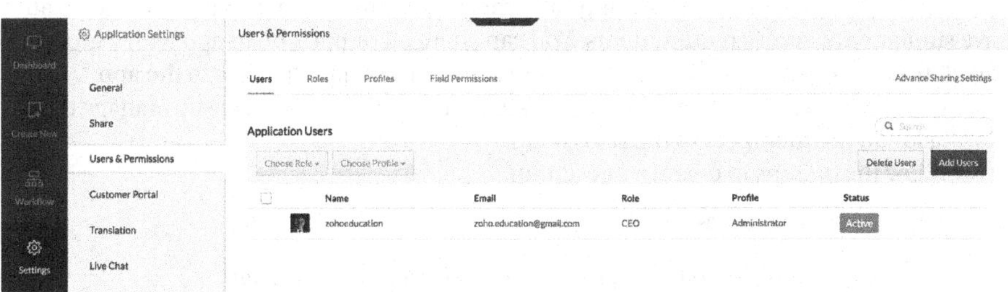

Figure 7-49. *Users page*

3. On the *Add Users* dialog box (Figure 7-50), enter the e-mail addresses of the users you want to add, separated by commas. Choose the right role and profile for the users.

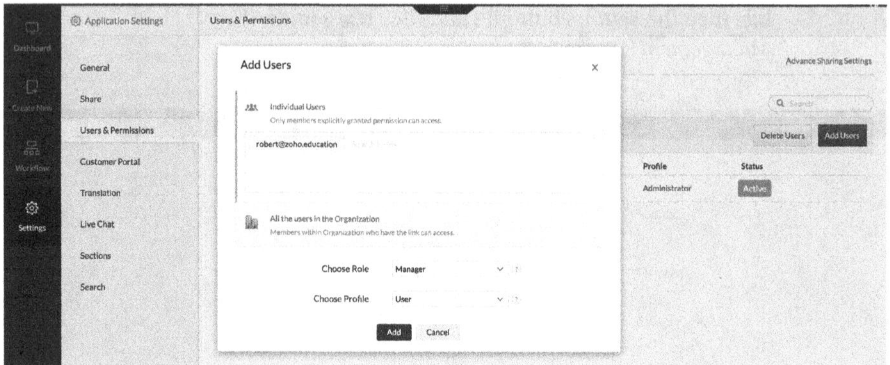

Figure 7-50. *Adding new users*

4. Click *Add* to add users to Creator.

Creating a Group

Groups will make it easier to share apps and their elements with a group of users who all have similar data access requirements. You can share all or parts of an app with a group and all the existing and future users in that group will gain equal access to the app.

For the REMS app, you need a Sales Team group so that you can easily manage data sharing for all the members of the sales team.

Follow these steps to create a new group:

1. *Choose Home ➤ Setup ➤ Groups.*

2. On the *Groups* page (Figure 7-51), click on the *Create New Group* button.

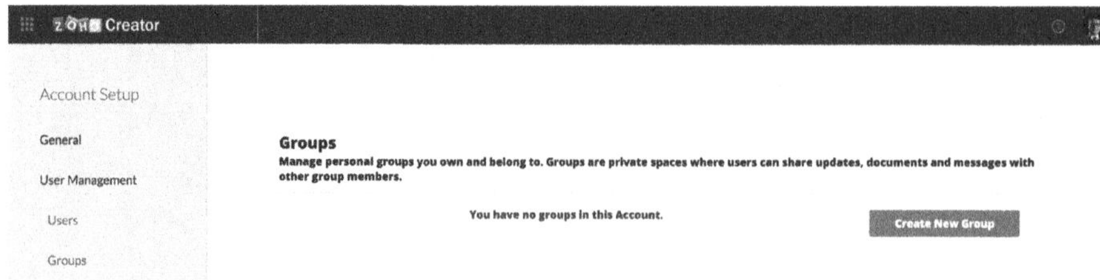

Figure 7-51. *Creating a new group*

3. Enter the group information shown in Figure 7-52. Then click *Create.*

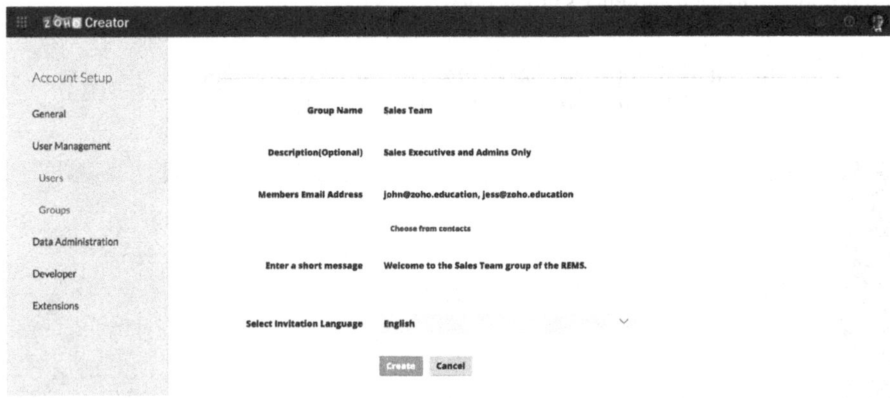

Figure 7-52. *Entering group information*

The new (*Sales Team*) group is created and listed on the *Groups* page (Figure 7-53). You can add and remove members to/from the group by clicking on the small *Members* button.

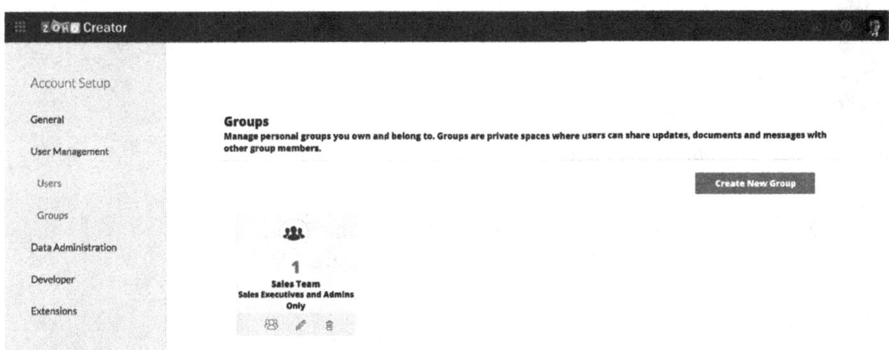

Figure 7-53. *Newly created group listed on the Groups page*

Sharing the App

Now that you have all the necessary users, roles, and groups in place, you can give access as appropriate to each audience's provisioned access level.

Follow these steps to share the REMS app with the users:

1. In Edit mode, open *Setting* ➤ *Share*. All forms, reports, and pages will be grouped into sections (Figure 7-54).

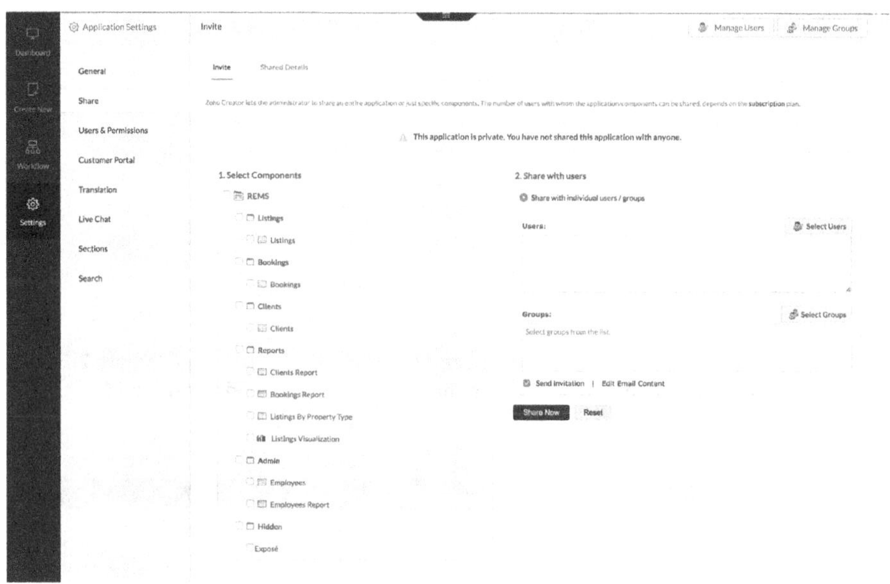

Figure 7-54. *The app Share page*

2. Click on the *Select Groups* button. Then in the *Select Users* dialog box, select the *Sales Team* group (Figure 7-55).

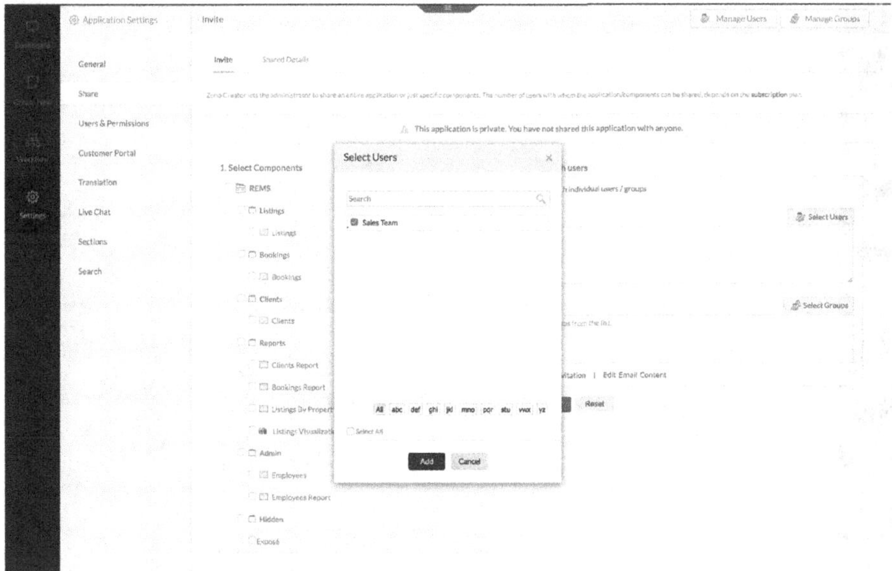

Figure 7-55. *Adding the Sales Team group to the Share page*

3. Click *Add* to continue. The *Sales Team* group will be added to the *Groups* box on the bottom-right side of the screen.

4. Select the components you want to share with the *Sales Team* group, as shown in Figure 7-56. Based on these requirements, the *Sales Team* can access all components, except the ones under the *Admin* and *Hidden* sections.

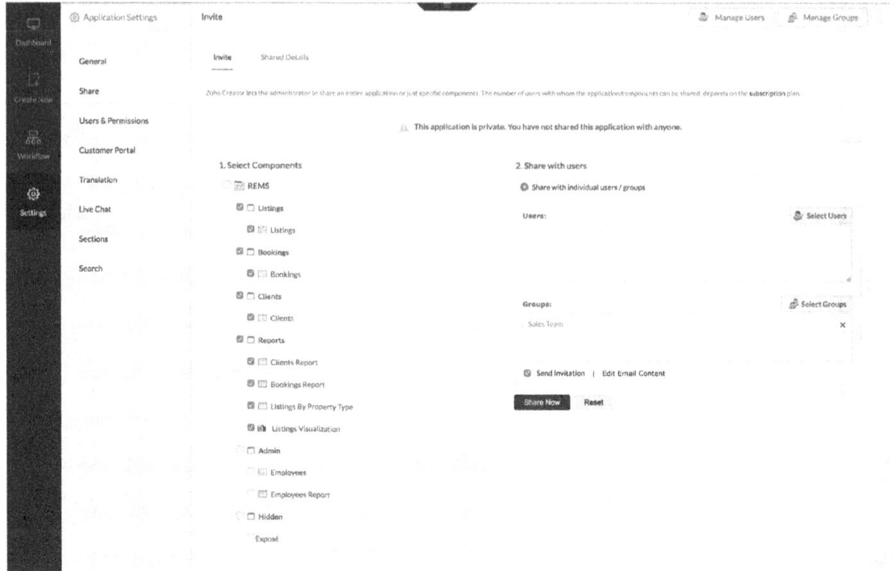

Figure 7-56. Selecting which components to share with the Sales Team

5. Click the *Share Now* button to apply the changes. The view will switch to *Shared Details*, showing which components are shared (Figure 7-57).

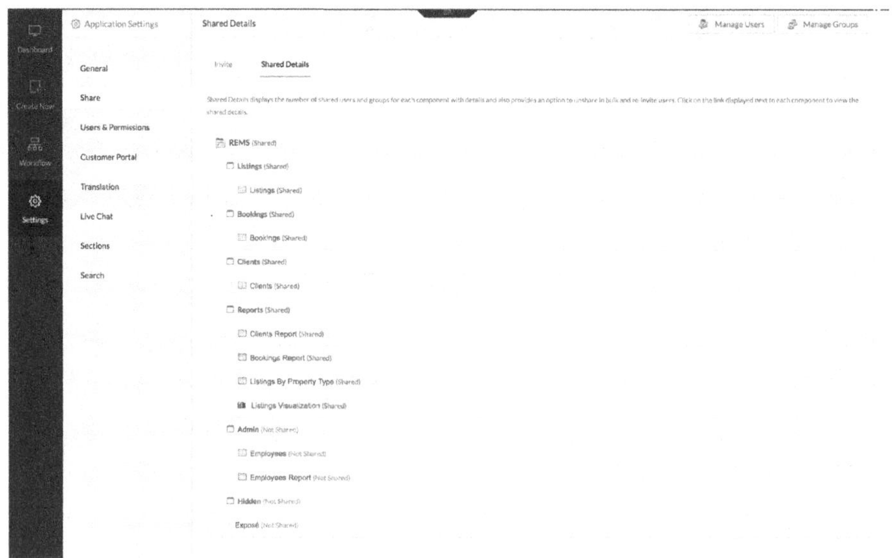

Figure 7-57. List of the components shared with the Sales Team

Going forward, you can click on each component on the Shared Details page to see and modify its share details (Figure 7-58).

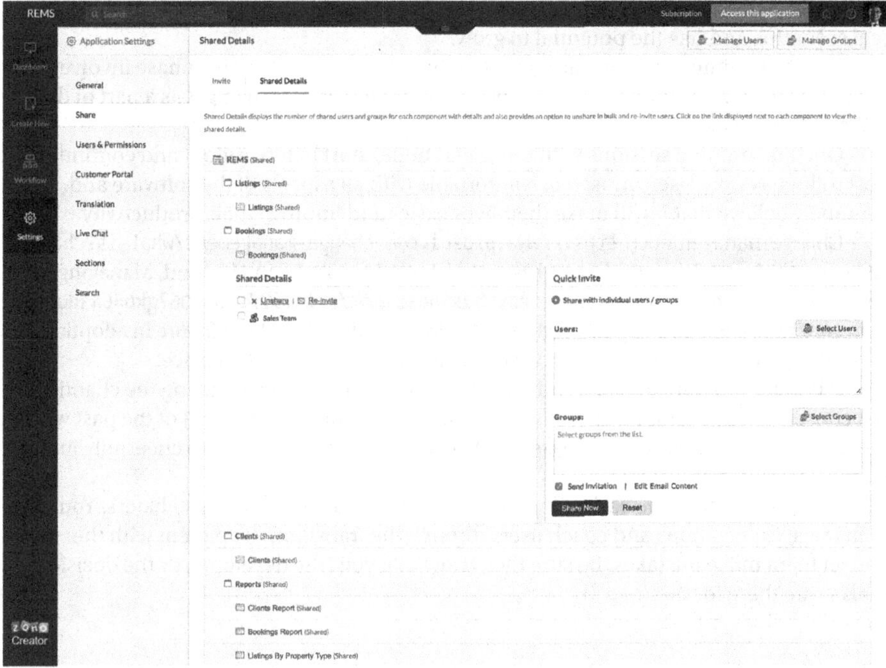

Figure 7-58. *Changing the share detail of various components*

Testing

You have been testing the REMS app here and there to see how it runs. However, a big part of the testing happens in the field with actual users.

It is in the testing phase that the hidden bugs and quirks surface, as the field experts (i.e. users) use and abuse the software, pushing it to its limits.

I don't want to get into testing methodology here. Zoho Creator apps don't need to be tested the way other software does. However, I encourage you to learn about beta testing, as well as functional and non-functional testing, at `https://en.wikipedia.org/wiki/Software_testing#Functional_vs_non-functional_testing`.

A well-tested application will cause you less headaches once it's rolled out.

Rollout

Congratulations! The hard part is over. You have designed, implemented, and even rigorously tested the REMS app. It has turned out to be a decent app that's usable for real scenarios and has the potential to grow.

Now is the time to do the harder part of the work, the rollout! This phase involves releasing the app fully or partially to users, so that they can start using it as a part of their day-to-day business.

Ongoing training sessions with the users should start before rollout and continue post rollout as well. Users must feel comfortable with all aspects of the software and genuinely believe that it will make their lives easier and improve their productivity.

Change management (`https://www.prosci.com/change-management/what-is-change-management`) is another foundational aspect of the rollout phase and beyond. Managing change properly (`https://www.strategy-business.com/article/rr00006?gko=643d0`) can help your new system succeed and grow. Ignoring it could bring about failure in adoption and will impact the initial intention of creating a new system in the first place.

It is human nature to resist and often fear change. If you are replacing the chaotic but convenient and familiar spreadsheet-based real estate management of the past with modern feature-rich and cloud-based REMS, don't expect your users to cheerfully jump on the new software wagon.

There are going to be early adopters, skeptics, complainers, and also haters. You have to manage expectations and coach users through the transition. Be patient with them and let them make mistakes. Be sure they know that you (the developer, or the decision maker) are there for them.

Summary

This is arguably the most important chapter in the book. It summed up the knowledge from the previous chapters and took you through all the steps of creating functional and successful business software.

You have (I hope) learned more than just dragging and dropping components and building an app. This chapter, although lightly, touched on some of the best practices of building good information solutions and succeeding in implementing and rolling them out.

There are endless resources to learn about concepts, methodologies, and best practices mentioned in this chapter. The key is to learn as much as you need and practice as much as possible.

The REMS is in a good shape to be developed more and become a real app you can use in a small- to medium-sized real estate operation. I will leave that to your imagination, skills, and requirements.

In the next chapter, you look at how to connect Creator apps to the outside world and extend their capabilities even further.

CHAPTER 8

Connecting Your Apps to the World

You have come a long way since you started reading this book. You learned how to create business applications that solve real-life problems, without spending an arm and a leg developing them.

But there is still much more you can with Zoho Creator. You can extend Creator's capabilities by connecting it to other apps and services. In the cloud, integration and interoperability with other apps and services are essential for any decent platform. Creator offers both.

There is a host of all the apps and services that Zoho Creator can integrate with. You should familiarize yourself with these, so you can utilize them as needed, instead of replicating their features in Creator.

For example, if you want to add invoicing features to your app, you will be happy to know that Zoho Creator and Zoho Invoice can connect and take care of your invoicing requirements for you. Incorporating external tools could dramatically reduce the resources needed to implement information systems for your organization.

Reference This chapter looks at some of integrations available to Zoho Creator. You can read about all of them on the Zoho web site and delve deeper in each one as per your business requirements: `https://www.zoho.com/creator/integration.html`.

Connecting to Zoho Apps

One of the USPs (unique selling propositions) of the Zoho Suite is that you have a choice of more than 30 business apps to work with a single Zoho account (i.e., single sign-on). Of course, you may need to pay for each app separately. However, the convenience of single sign-on and the smoother learning curve due to the familiar look and feel makes a strong case for Zoho apps.

A. Shabdar, *Mastering Zoho Creator*, DOI 10.1007/978-1-4842-2907-1_8

Another key factor in choosing Zoho apps over the competition is that almost all of them integrate out-of-the-box. Some integrations are as easy as drag and drop and others need a bit of work on the API (application programming interface) side.

Creator integrates with these Zoho apps:

- **Zoho CRM**—From Creator, you can manage CRM records (find, add, edit, delete, and attach files) as well as show CRM data in a Creator app. This allows you to create Creator apps that extend the features of the CRM or apps that consume data stored in the CRM.
- **Zoho Invoice**—From Creator, you can manage invoices (find, add, and edit) and rely on its advanced invoicing capabilities in Creator apps.
- **Zoho Books**—Creator can manage records in Books (find, add, and edit) and provide advanced accounting in one package.
- **Zoho Calendar**—From Creator, you can create calendar events from and automate event booking for your business.
- **Zoho Reports**—From Creator, you can manage records (add, edit, and delete) in tables in Reports. By manipulating the Reports data, your app can have access to complex reporting and data analysis features.
- **Zoho Recruit**—From Creator, you can manage records in Recruit (find, add, edit, and upload files) and extend the capabilities of HR related apps.
- **Zoho Desk**—Creator can manage records in Desk (find, add, and edit) and add user support to the apps.
- **Subscriptions**—You can manage records in Subscriptions (find, add, and edit) and add subscription features to your apps.

■ **Reference** You can learn about Zoho's integration with these apps in the official documentation at: `https://www.zoho.com/creator/help/script/integration-with-other-zoho-products.html`.

Connecting to G Suite

Zoho Creator for G Suite (`https://gsuite.google.com/together/`) (formerly known as Google Apps) enables G Suite users to have easy access to Zoho Creator applications. If your organization is using G Suite, you can install the Zoho Creator service on your organization's G Suite account and extend G Suite with the power of Zoho Creator.

■ **Note** Before connecting Creator and G Suite, make sure you are fully aware of the ramifications of sharing vital information between the two platforms. You will need to check with the administrators of both G Suite and Creator to determine what information can be shared and what level of access G Suite users can have to the information stored in Creator apps (and vice versa).

Using G Suite integration, you can perform a number of tasks:

- Convert Google Sheets spreadsheets to Zoho Creator apps in a couple of easy steps (`https://www.zoho.com/creator/google-sheet-to-app.html?src=gsuite`), which among other benefits, will help you:
  - Transition from managing large and error-prone spreadsheets to nicely designed database apps.
  - Add business logic and workflow automation.
  - Control data access and manage the safety of information in a much more controlled way.
- Import G Suite users to Creator and allow them to connect with their G Suite credentials. This helps G Suite admins maintain control in a more managed and central manner, while extending the capabilities of G Suite with Creator.
- Share apps fully or partially with Google Groups and manage data access levels more efficiently.
- Access Google Calendar and create events directly from Creator.
- Access Google Drive and upload documents to Google Docs from Creator.

■ **Reference** Learn more about Zoho Creator integration with G Suite from the official documentation at: `https://www.zoho.com/creator/help/gapps/zoho-creator-for-google-apps.html`.

Other Integrations

Integration with Zoho Apps and G Suite gives you an edge. To make Creator even more powerful, you can integrate it with eternal services, such as SMS providers, accounting software, payment gateways, third-party CRMs, and others.

Some of these integrations are available from within Creator, and this chapter touches on those in a bit. Some need more work from your side.

■ **Reference** Check out Zapier at https://zapier.com/zapbook/zoho-creator/ for various integrations. Check out Creator Scripts for useful posts on Zoho integrations at https://www.creatorscripts.com/blogs/.

SMS

You might wonder how SMS (Short Message Service) is still a thing in the age of social messaging (WhatsApp, Facebook Messenger, etc.); however, 25 years later (https://en.wikipedia.org/wiki/SMS#History), SMS is still alive and kicking especially in marketing and sales.

If you are not convinced yet, read about some of the use cases of text messages on Twilio's web site (https://www.twilio.com/use-cases).

Zoho Creator offers a useful SMS gateway to send SMS from within apps to automate dynamic messaging to prospects, clients, and users alike. As of this writing, Creator supports five major SMS providers: Twilio, Clickatell, Screen Magic, ClockWorkSMS, and Hoiio.

The usage is fairly simple. All you need to do is call the sms.send() method for the specific provider in your code. For example, to send a SMS using Twilio, you can simply write:

```
SMS_Response = twilio.sms.send("<sms notification name>","<to>","<message>");
```

- If the SMS is sent successfully, the value of the *SMS_Response* variable is set to {"status":"success"}. Otherwise, it will be {"message":"<Reason for failure>","status":"failure"}.
- *<to>* is the mobile number of the recipient.
- *<message>* is the text message to be sent to the recipient.
- *<sms notification name>* differs for each provider.

To set up *<sms notification name>* for Twilio, follow these steps:

1. While you're logged in, open the Zoho Creator home page.
2. Click the *Setup* icon (it's shaped like a gear) on the top bar.

3. On the *Account Setup* page (Figure 8-1), under Extensions, click *Connections.*

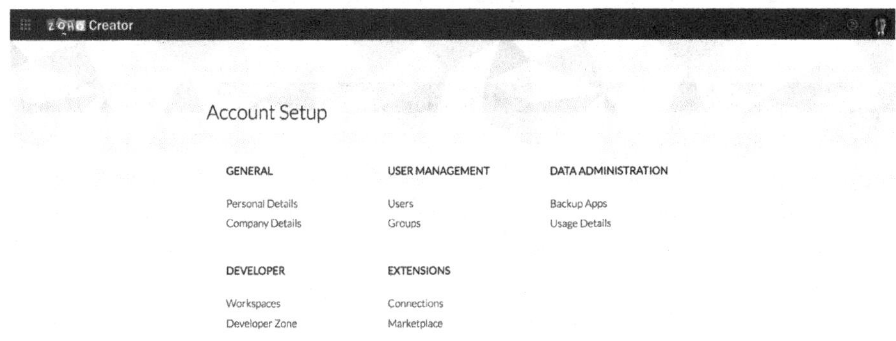

Figure 8-1. *Zoho Creator Setup page*

4. On the *Connections* page, click *Add Connection.* Then under *SMS,* click on *Twilio* (Figure 8-2).

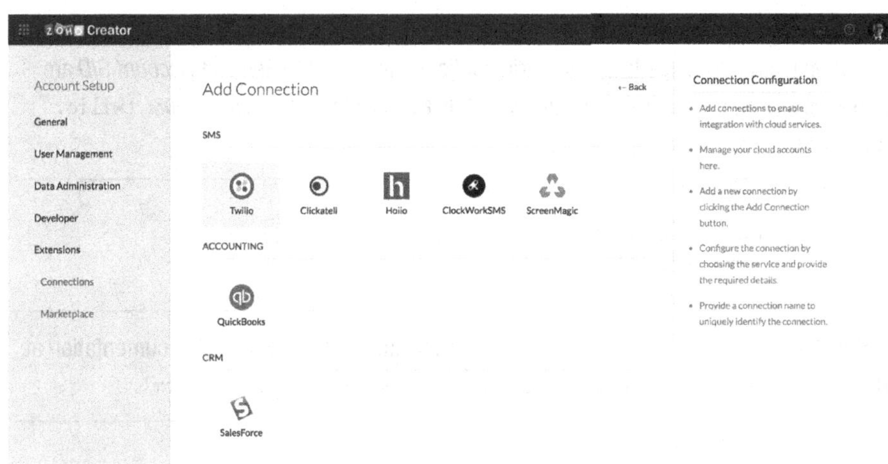

Figure 8-2. *Choose the Twilio SMS option*

5. On the *Add Connection* page, enter a *Connection Name*.
6. Enter the *Auth Token* and *Account SID* from your Twilio account. Then enter the Twilio number in the *From* field (Figure 8-3).

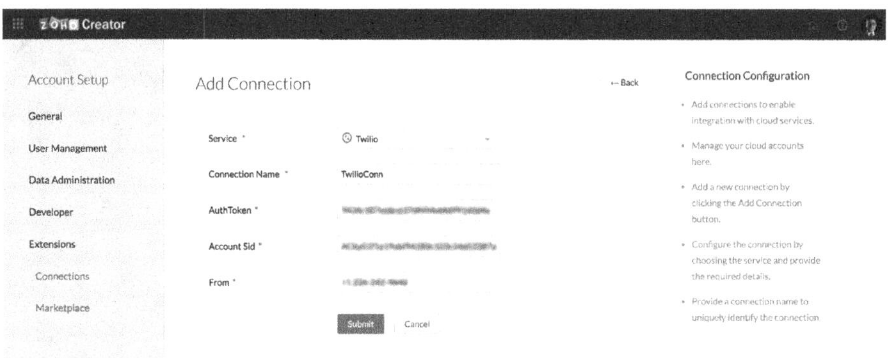

Figure 8-3. *Adding a new Twilio connection*

■ **Note** If you don't have a Twilio account, head to `https://www.twilio.com/` and create one. Then follow the steps to set up a trial Twilio number. *Auth Token* and *Account SID* are both available on the Twilio Dashboard, which is accessible from `https://www.twilio.com/console`.

---

7. Finish by clicking *Submit*. The new connection will be listed on the Connections page.

■ **Reference** You can learn about other SMS providers from the official documentation at: `https://www.zoho.com/creator/help/script/add-sms-with-script.html`.

QuickBooks

When it comes to SME accounting software, Intuit® QuickBooks is a household name. It is smart that Zoho Creator connects to QuickBooks, as many companies already use it for all their accounting needs.

Creator connects directly to any QuickBooks account (from the Connections page, as you saw in the previous section) and allows you to access supported modules and perform the following tasks in QuickBooks in your Creator apps:

- Create new records in QuickBooks in any module listed here
- Get a number of records from QuickBooks into Creator based on specific criteria
- Get a single record from QuickBooks based on a record ID
- Search in QuickBooks with a SQL (Structured Query Language) query string
- Update records in QuickBooks using their record IDs

  These QuickBooks modules are supported in Creator:

  - Customer
  - Vendor
  - Item
  - Invoice
  - Account
  - Employee
  - Department

■ **Reference** Learn more about Zoho Creator integration with QuickBooks from the official documentation at: `https://www.zoho.com/creator/help/script/integration-with-quickbooks.html`.

You might want to also check out the *QuickBooks API Guide* at: `https://developer.intuit.com/docs/api/accounting`.

PayPal

We live in the age of ecommerce. Amazon just swallowed Whole Foods, Etsy is booming, and everyone is selling something online.

Since the early days of ecommerce, PayPal (and a number of others) became the de facto payment gateway when working with bureaucratic and clunky online gateways offered by the big banks weren't worth the effort. Today, PayPal is more relevant than ever and if they start accepting Cryptocurrencies, it is safe to say that will stay to see the next century.

The good news for us humble users and developers of Zoho Creator is that it integrates well with PayPal and allows Creator apps to accept recurring and non-recurring payments via PayPal.

All you need is a PayPal business account (`https://www.paypal.com/buinsess`) and some configuration in Creator.

■ **Reference** Learn more about accepting payments via PayPal from the official documentation at: `https://www.zoho.com/creator/help/forms/accept-payments-through-forms.html`.

Salesforce

Salesforce is the poster child of modern CRMs. It is a behemoth of a platform with endless features and great flexibility to be customized and programmed. It is impressive how it actually ignited a movement and contributed greatly to the success of SaaS (Software as a Service).

Zoho offers its own CRM, which is a powerful, robust, and flexible solution delivering on its promise. As mentioned previously in this chapter, Zoho CRM integrates perfectly with Creator; however, Creator keeps an open mind and works with Salesforce too.

Creator integration with Salesforce allows you to do the following in any of the supported modules:

- Create new records in Salesforce
- Get a number of records based on specific criteria from Salesforce into Creator
- Get single records by record ID
- Search for records in Salesforce by sending a SQL query

These are the Salesforce modules supported in Zoho Creator:

- Lead
- Contact
- Account
- Case
- Solution
- Product
- Campaign

■ **Reference** Learn more about accessing Salesforce in Creator from the official documentation at: `https://www.zoho.com/creator/help/script/integration-with-salesforce.html`

REST API

So far this chapter has covered how Zoho Creator can access and consume data from other apps and platforms, but Creator also generously allows external apps to access its data as well.

Zoho Creator offers a set of REST (Representational State Transfer) and RPC (Remote Procedure Calls) APIs to share data with the outside world.

You can use these APIs and write code in any of your favorite programming languages to connect to Creator.

This section focuses on REST API simply because Creator offers more flexibility with REST. I also find REST to be more common when it comes to connecting to other apps and services.

■ **Reference** Learn more about REST from `http://www.restapitutorial.com/lessons/whatisrest.html`.
Also, if you like to join the debate of REST vs. RPC, you are more than welcome to indulge yourself in a Google search: `https://www.google.ae/search?q=rpc+vs+rest`.

Using Creator REST API

To use the Zoho Creator API, you need an authentication token (auth token) unique to your Creator account. This key is for security measures and allows Creator to recognize third-party apps as friendly.

There are two ways to generate an auth token in Creator:

- Using the API mode, where you call the link in your app and receive the auth token in response: *`https://accounts.zoho.com/apiauthtoken/nb/create?SCOPE=ZohoCreator/creatorapi&EMAIL_ID=`Zoho CREATOR Username or Email ID&PASSWORD=Zoho CREATOR Password.*

- Using Browser mode by opening this link in your browser while logged in to Creator: *`https://accounts.zoho.com/apiauthtoken/create?SCOPE`*.

The auth token is a 32-letter code (e.g., `01db6dfc41cd6edef8496b8b53f14254`). You use it in your external programs to connect to Creator.

REST API Capabilities

A REST call in Creator is basically a URL formatted in a certain way so that it gets called from an external program via `GET` or `POST`.

For example, to add a new record to a Creator app, you would use:

```
https://creator.zoho.com/api/<ownername>/<format>/<applicationName>/
form/<formName>/record/add
```

- `<ownername>` is the app owner name, i.e. `admin username`
- `<format>` is JSON or XML and will determine in which format the response will be generated
- `<applicationName>` and `<formName>` are self-explanatory

If you are sending this request using a `GET` method, you must include the auth token in the URL too:

```
https://creator.zoho.com/api/<ownername>/<format>/<applicationName>/
form/<formName>/record/add?authtoken=<AuthToken>
```

For a `POST`request, for example from an HTML form, you can add a *hidden* `authtoken` field and pass along the auth token as a *value*.

Using the Creator API, you can perform the following:

- Add new records to Creator forms
- Edit existing records to Creator forms
- Delete existing records
- View records in Creator reports
- Get a list of
  - Form fields in a given form
  - Applications in an account
  - Forms and reports in an application

Reference To learn more API methods in Creator, refer to the official documentation at: `https://www.zoho.com/creator/help/api/`.

What's Next?

I am sure that you already have a few cool app ideas that you want to implement in Creator or you have already started with one or two.

As you go forward and become better at Creator, you can call yourself a Zoho Creator developer and get that well-deserved promotion or attract more customers and charge them for your hard-earned skills.

At this stage, you may want to join the budding Zoho Creator Developer community and take your work to the next level.

Simply log on to the Developers' page and check out what is available to developers: `https://www.zoho.com/creator/developers/`.

If you haven't yet, sign up for the Develop Edition of Zoho Creator at: `https://www.zoho.com/creator/developers/signup.html`. The Developer Edition is a special edition that allows Creator developers to use the full version only for app development and testing at no cost.

Moreover, to show the world your expertise, you can apply for the Zoho Creator Certification Program and become a Zoho Creator Certified Developer or a Zoho Creator Certified Solution Provider at: `https://www.zoho.com/creator/developers/certification.html`

You can also check out the App Gallery to download or buy the useful apps that other members of the community have built (see `https://www.zoho.com/creator/apps/`). It is a good idea to check out the App Gallery before you start developing a new app.

Last, but not least, the Marketplace is where you can look for apps, ask others to build you a custom app, and sell your own apps to others (see `https://marketplace.zoho.com/creator`).

Summary

In this chapter, you got a bird's eye view of Zoho Creator integrations with the outside world, within the Zoho ecosystem, and beyond.

It touched on some of the most important integrations and left the rest for you to discover.

This book has provided you with all the necessary knowledge to get up and running with Zoho Creator and start building useful business applications for yourself, your organization, and your clients.

However, there is still much to learn. I strongly recommend you study the underlying concepts, such as user experience design and usability as well as process mapping and flowcharting. The more you learn about the foundations of building good software and understanding users and business requirements, the better your apps will be for the world to use and appreciate.

Do not stop at mastering Deluge. Pick up a book or take some online courses about JavaScript or Python. Learn more about HTML and CSS and expand the breadth and depth of your knowledge about cloud-based programming. This will help you make better Creator apps that you can extend through APIs and that are not bound to Creator's limits.

Zoho is actively developing Creator as a viable app development platform. Make sure you keep an eye on the news at: `https://www.zoho.com/creator/whatsnew/` and `https://www.zoho.com/creator/blog`.

Rely on the official documentation and, when in doubt, look into the forums at: `https://forums.zoho.com/zoho-creator`.

Welcome to the joyful and rewarding world of building software. Congratulations for taking on this journey.

Good luck.

Index

A. Shabdar, *Mastering Zoho Creator*, DOI 10.1007/978-1-4842-2907-1

S, T

U, V, W, X, Y

Z

Printed in the United States
By Bookmasters